The American Biographical Novel

The American Biographical Novel

Michael Lackey

Bloomsbury Academic
An imprint of Bloomsbury Publishing Inc

B L O O M S B U R Y
NEW YORK · LONDON · OXFORD · NEW DELHI · SYDNEY

Bloomsbury Academic

An imprint of Bloomsbury Publishing Inc

1385 Broadway
New York
NY 10018
USA

50 Bedford Square
London
WC1B 3DP
UK

www.bloomsbury.com

BLOOMSBURY and the Diana logo are trademarks of Bloomsbury Publishing Plc

First published 2016

Library of Congress Cataloging-in-Publication Data
Names: Lackey, Michael, author.
Title: The American biographical novel / Michael Lackey.
Description: New York: Bloomsbury Academic, 2016. | Includes bibliographical references and index.
Identifiers: LCCN 2015038230| ISBN 9781628926347 (hardback) | ISBN 9781628926330 (paperback)
Subjects: LCSH: Biographical fiction, American–History and criticism. | Historical fiction, American–History and criticism. | Truth in literature. | History in literature. | Politics in literature. | Literature and history–United States–History–20th century. | Literature and society–United States–History–20th century. | BISAC: LITERARY CRITICISM / American / General.
Classification: LCC PS374.B56 L32 2016 | DDC 813/.08209–dc23
LC record available at http://lccn.loc.gov/2015038230

ISBN: HB: 978-1-6289-2634-7
PB: 978-1-6289-2633-0
ePDF: 978-1-6289-2636-1
ePub: 978-1-6289-2635-4

Typeset by Deanta Global Publishing Services, Chennai, India
Printed and bound in the United States of America

For my daughters,
Anya and Katya,
who make life magical

CONTENTS

ACKNOWLEDGMENTS

Four years ago, my wife recommended that I read Jay Parini's *Benjamin's Crossing*, a biographical novel about the literary critic Walter Benjamin. That was the beginning of this project, so my biggest debt is to my wife, Julie Eckerle. Shortly after reading *Benjamin's Crossing*, I contacted Jay to see if he would be willing to lecture at my university and participate in a round-table forum at the University of Minnesota's Institute for Advanced Study. Bruce Duffy and Lance Olsen also participated in the round-table forum, and I am still in the process of reflecting on, absorbing, and registering all that I learned from that experience. Jay, Bruce, and Lance have done more to help me get a better grasp of biofiction than anyone else.

In 2014, Bloomsbury published my book *Truthful Fictions*, which consists of my interviews with prominent American biographical novelists such as Joyce Carol Oates, Russell Banks, Michael Cunningham, Julia Alvarez, Joanna Scott, Edmund White, Madison Smartt Bell, Jay Parini, Bruce Duffy, Lance Olsen, Anita Diamant, Ron Hansen, M. Allen Cunningham, Kate Moses, Rebecca Kanner, and Sherry Jones. Those interviews have done much to further my understanding of the biographical novel. But it was my conversations both before and after the interviews that have been so incredibly useful. It is not possible to adequately express my gratitude to these writers for their generosity in sharing their thoughts and time with me.

Scholars and friends who have assisted me by patiently attending to me ramble on about the biographical novel and then helping me refine my ideas about it include Ludwig Pfeiffer, James L. W. West, Dan Ross, Baron Reed, Carlos Prado, Sylke Boyd, Brad Deane, Brook Miller, Pieranna Garavaso, David Ebershoff, David Berman, Genevieve West, Max Saunders, Catherine Belling, Julia Novak, David Stern, Dana Nelson, John Ernest, Chris Douglas,

Ricia A. Chansky Sancinito, Nathaniel Cadle, Pamela L. Caughie, Anna Poletti, and Friedrich Stadler.

There are those rare students who enable professors to see things in a new way. As I have been working on and teaching the biographical novel, three students have been particularly astute in their analysis of the form and of particular works. To Kelsey Butler, Tyler Winstead, and Pengxeu Thao I owe a special debt.

The University of Minnesota—Morris, the University of Minnesota, and the University of Minnesota's Institute for Advanced Study have generously contributed to this project. Without the necessary research money and leave time, this book could not have been written. Our university at Morris in particular is lucky to have Roger Wareham, who aggressively secures funding for faculty members.

I would also like to thank my editor, Haaris Naqvi, who always gives me excellent feedback and direction. He has helped me turn a monograph idea into a multi-book project. Haaris is one of those rare editors who gives excellent advice about an individual project but also has an overarching vision that extends far beyond a single work.

Finally, I would like to thank my daughters, Anya and Katya. To complete this project, I had to visit many archives and sites in Europe and the United States. Their patience with and support of me during these long research trips has been truly remarkable. But I am most grateful to them for bringing so much magic and joy into my life.

1

The rise and legitimization of the American biographical novel

The biographical novel's complicated journey to legitimization began in the 1930s, which is when the aesthetic form had—paradoxically—become popular and was roundly condemned.[1] In 1937, Georg Lukács acknowledged "the popularity of the biographical form in the present-day historical novel."[2] Works from the decade that immediately come to mind include Leonard Ehrlich's *God's Angry Man* (1932), Lion Feuchtwanger's Josephus Flavius novels (the first of which was published in 1932), Thomas Mann's Joseph novels (the first of which was published in 1933), Robert Graves' Claudius novels (the first of which was published in 1934), Irving Stone's *Lust for Life* (1934), Bruno Frank's *A Man Called Cervantes* (1934), Heinrich Mann's King Henry IV novels (the first of which was published in 1935), Arna Bontemps' *Black Thunder* (1936), Graves' *Count Belisarius* (1938), Stone's

---

[1]There were a few notable biographical novels before the 1930s, but these were so scattered and anomalous that they could not be characterized as part of a movement. For instance, Herman Melville published in 1854 *Israel Potter: His Fifty Years of Exile*, and the Russian writer Dmitri Merezhkovsky authored a number of biographical novels in the late nineteenth and early twentieth centuries. From 1906 through 1908, Ford Madox Ford published *The Fifth Queen* trilogy, which examines the life of King Henry VIII's fifth wife. In 1929, C. Lenanton authored *Miss Barrett's Elopement*, the first of many biographical novels about Elizabeth Barrett Browning.
[2]Lukács (1983), *The Historical Novel*. Translated by Hannah and Stanley Mitchell. Lincoln and London: University of Nebraska Press, 300.

Jack London, Sailor on Horseback (1938), Zora Neale Hurston's *Moses, Man of the Mountain* (1939), and Thomas Mann's *Lotte in Weimar* (1939). Based on this list, which consists of some notable works, it might seem that the biographical novel would have been officially recognized as a legitimate aesthetic form by the late thirties. But such is not the case.

In fact, Lukács devotes an entire section of *The Historical Novel* to a critical analysis clarifying precisely why the biographical novel is necessarily doomed to aesthetic failure. Lukács' critique is multifarious and intricate, so much so that I will return to it throughout this book. But for now, let me detail one of his most searing criticisms. For Lukács, the effective historical novel pictures the social, political, economic, and intellectual forces that created the great collisions of a particular age. Since the biographical novel centers the narrative in the life story of a single heroic figure, it necessarily distorts and misrepresents the historical reality, because "the character is inevitably exaggerated, made to stand on tiptoe, his historical calling unduly emphasized while the real objective causes and factors of the historical mission are inevitably omitted."[3] This is not something that has just randomly happened within particular biographical novels. It is the inevitable consequence of the aesthetic form. Thus, Lukács concludes:

> We may generalize this weakness of the biographical form of the novel by saying that the personal, the purely psychological and biographical acquire a disproportionate breadth, a false preponderance. As a result the great driving forces of history are neglected. They are presented in all too summary a fashion and relate only biographically to the person at the centre. And because of this false distribution of weights what should be the real centre of these novels—the given historical transformation—cannot make itself felt sufficiently strongly.[4]

According to Lukács, there is something intrinsic to the literary form of the biographical novel that necessarily leads it to distort and misrepresent the historical and the political. Therefore, it is an irredeemable aesthetic form.

---

[3]Lukács (1983), 314.
[4]Lukács (1983), 321.

Lukács' critique is the most focused and direct of the time, but there were other notable ones that led many to conclude that the biographical novel is either an impossible or illegitimate aesthetic form. For instance, without directly mentioning the biographical novel, Virginia Woolf, at roughly the same time (1939) as the publication of Lukács' book, makes it clear in her essay "The Art of Biography" why such an aesthetic form could not work, though her critique focuses less on history than on the impossibility of combining the actions distinctive to the creative writer and the traditional biographer. Lytton Strachey and the new biographers of the early twentieth century revolutionized the biography by making liberal use of the creative imagination and fictional techniques in depicting a person's life, thus giving the artist/biographer the "freedom to invent" something new, "a book that was not only a biography but also a work of art."[5] But ultimately, Woolf concludes, this "combination proved unworkable," because "fact and fiction refused to mix."[6] As Woolf claims, the "novelist is free" to create, while "the biographer is tied"[7] to facts. It should seem odd that Woolf would reject the biographical novel, because she published in 1928 the novel *Orlando: A Biography*. This work is important, because it challenged conventional genre distinctions. Critics have noted and Woolf has acknowledged that the novel is very loosely based on the life of Vita Sackville-West, and since the work is subtitled a biography, it has sometimes been characterized as an experimental biography that captures the spirit of her friend.[8] But

---

[5]Woolf (1942), "The Art of Biography," in *The Death of the Moth and Other Essays*. London: The Hogarth Press, 123.
[6]Ibid. For useful discussions of Woolf's complicated approach to biography, see Ray Monk's "This Fictitious Life: Virginia Woolf on Biography and Reality" and Mark Hussey's "Woolf: After Lives."
[7]Woolf (1942), 120.
[8]Elizabeth Cooley has written a very insightful essay that examines Woolf's engagement with and contribution to the innovative developments in biography of the 1920s and 1930s. However, her essay underscores the problem of an undefined terminology. The title of her essay is "Revolutionizing Biography: *Orlando, Roger Fry*, and the Tradition," which suggests that *Orlando* is a biography. Cooley creates additional confusion, because she refers to *Orlando* as a "biography" (71), "a novel" (75), and a "quasi-biographical novel" (71). But ultimately, she analyzes and assesses the work as a biography, which seeks to capture the "reality" of "Vita-Sackville West" (71). My claim is that *Orlando* is not an experimental biography that seeks to capture the reality of her friend. Rather, it is a novel that uses and radically alters the

calling it a biography is problematic for two separate reasons. First and foremost, Woolf did not name the protagonist Vita. Second, the work is less focused on picturing accurately the life of the biographical subject, which would make it a biography, than on creating a story and character in order to project Woolf's vision, which makes it a novel. After all, instead of clarifying how the work strategically and accurately represents the life and person of Sackville-West, scholars tend to use *Orlando* to define Woolf's view of the fragmented or multiple self, the construction of gender and sex identity, the role of language in producing a subject, alternative conceptions of female subjectivity, an insightful critique of traditional biography, and pernicious forms of heteronormative coercion. So *Orlando* is a novel, because it gives readers Woolf's vision of life and the world rather than accurately representing a biographical subject, but it is not a biographical novel, because it does not name its protagonist after an actual historical person.

Flush is another work that scholars could wrongly consider a biographical novel.[9] Published in 1933, this work is about Elizabeth Barrett Browning's dog, but there are two separate reasons why it

---

life of Sackville-West in order to examine the linguistic techniques of constructing character and structuring a life and to expose the limits and problems of biographical representation. The impulse and/or tendency to read *Orlando* alongside *Roger Fry* is a problem, because, as works belonging to separate and distinct genres, they seek to do incompatible things, which is something that Woolf acknowledges in a letter to Sackville-West. When discussing her work on the *Roger Fry* biography, Woolf says: "My God, how does one write Biography?" After confessing her puzzlement on this score, Woolf speculates if she should convert her book about Fry into fiction: "Or ought one, as I incline, to be purely fictitious?" (qtd. in Cooley, 79). For Woolf, there is an either/or choice. This is significant because, if she thought of *Orlando* as a biography, then she would know how to write one in 1939 when working on *Roger Fry*, since she would have already written one. Given that she admits that she does not know how to write a biography, it must be the case that she did not consider *Orlando* a biography. For Woolf, biography and fiction are separate and distinct, and as such, there need to be separate criteria for analyzing and assessing them.
[9]Marie-Luise Kohlke interprets Woolf's work as an "early comic biofiction," which re-focalizes "Barrett Browning's life through the eyes of her dog" (10). Julia Novak and Sandra Mayer have adopted this same approach in their essay "Disparate Images: Literary Heroism and the 'Work vs. Life' Topos in Biofictions about Victorian Authors." Both works use confusing terminology and fail to make a distinction between a historical and a biographical novel. If the book had been titled *Elizabeth Barrett Browning as seen through the Eyes of her Dog Flush*, then it would have been much closer to being a biographical novel. But given the work's focus on Flush as a historical-social type and Barrett Browning's subordinate

does not qualify as a biographical novel. First, biographical novels are based on the lives of actual historical figures. While it is true that Barrett Browning had a dog named Flush, Woolf acknowledges in a postscript that her story is an invention and not based on an actual life: "It must be admitted that there are very few authorities for the foregoing biography."[10] Given this fact, *Flush* actually fits more within the tradition of the historical rather than the biographical novel, because the effective historical novel foregrounds invented figures that embody "historical-social types."[11] For instance, Flush is an isolated dog who knows little about himself and other dogs. But after going for many walks, he discovers that there are various types of dogs and that he belongs to the canine aristocracy:

> Flush knew before the summer had passed that there is no equality among dogs: there are high dogs and low dogs. Which, then, was he? No sooner had Flush got home than he examined himself in the looking-glass. Heaven be praised, he was a dog of birth and breeding![12]

Creating the protagonist as a historical-social type enables Woolf to critique not the actual animal-figure or character Flush but the English aristocracy. On occasion, there are actual personages in historical novels, but these are peripheral figures that function to lend credibility to the portrait of the historical-social type and to place the created character within a specific spatial-temporal context. Barrett Browning is Woolf's actual personage, and she is certainly given a more prominent role than most actual figures within historical novels. But since the novel is titled *Flush: A Biography* and focuses mainly on its canine hero, it would be considered a comic and experimental variation of the historical novel rather than a legitimate biographical novel.

There is a clear reason why Woolf could not imagine her way to the biographical novel. In 1939, when Woolf published "The Art of Biography," she was writing a biography about her friend Roger Fry. Given all of her genre-bending and blending experiments, it

---

position within the work, it is a variation of the historical novel and not an example of a biographical novel.
[10]Woolf (1933), *Flush: A Biography*. New York: Harcourt, Brace, & World, Inc., 171.
[11]Lukács (1983), 35.
[12]Woolf (1933), 40.

would seem that she, more than anyone else, would have been able to use the occasion to author a biographical novel. But the strange fact is that Woolf could not imagine her way to the biographical novel, because she could not allow herself to take the liberty of altering facts about an actual person in order to convert him or her into a literary symbol. If she named her protagonist after an actual historical figure (Roger Fry), then she believed that she was bound to a specific truth contract, one that restricts the writer to the act of accurately representing the established facts. To be more specific, Woolf did not believe that she could make Fry into a woman midway through her biography in order to communicate something important about human subjectivity or sexual politics. Consciously and strategically inventing stories or altering established facts about the biographical subject in order to communicate a more substantive interior or cultural "truth" is not an option for Woolf in her biography of Fry. The only way she could justify doing so would be to change the biographical subject's name from, let us say, Roger to Orlando. Having changed the name, she could then take as many liberties as she wanted. To put the matter simply, for Woolf, writers have to choose between the art of representing a person's life accurately, which would lead them to produce a biography, or creating a living and breathing character, which would lead them to produce a work of fiction. Blending the two in the form of the biographical novel is not an option.

It would seem that the biographical novel achieved some formal academic acceptance in February 1955, because in that year the American literary and cultural critic Carl Bode wrote a groundbreaking essay ("The Buxom Biographies") about it. But there are two separate reasons why this is not the case. Bode opens the essay by claiming that "in the last ten years prominent people have been doing their best to make an honest woman out of the biographical novel." Based on this comment, it would seem that Bode intends to offer a spirited defense of the genre, but he actually goes on to argue that the aesthetic form has not yet reached maturity: "The biographical novel still goes its bosomy way, its flimsy clothing tattered and torn in exactly the wrong places." Consequently, Bode concludes that "the biographical novel deserves more to be pitied than censured."[13]

---

[13]Bode (1955), "The Buxom Biographies," *College English* 16(5): 265.

What makes Bode's article ultimately unfortunate is less his condemnation than his muddled understanding of the biographical novel. For Bode, if a biography is either bad or stylized, then it would qualify as a biographical novel. For instance, in charting what he considers the rise of the biographical novel, Bode does not begin with a discussion of books that strategically invent characters and scenes in relation to a factual historical figure. Rather, he begins with a brief analysis of Mason Weems's 1927 biography of George Washington. Here is his logic: because Weems took the liberty of including undocumented fables about Washington, his work is disqualified from being a biography and therefore becomes a novel. Bode's approach, however, is not always so negative. When discussing Carl Sandburg's biography of Abraham Lincoln, Bode suggests that Sandburg's "felicity of style" implicitly renders his "life of Lincoln" a biographical novel.[14] Implicit in Bode's article are the two following assumptions: First, the biography gives readers "unadorned truth."[15] Second, what qualifies a work as a novel is the introduction of an embellished truth or "an orderly, almost a symphonic, structure and a literary richness of style."[16] According to this logic, if a biography contains an undocumented "truth" or is well written, then it would become a de facto biographical novel.

Stone was one of the most important figures in this story, as he used the phrase biographical novel as a subtitle for many of his works: *Jack London, Sailor on Horseback: A Biographical Novel* (1938); *Immortal Wife: The Biographical Novel of Jessie Benton Fremont* (1944); *The Agony and the Ecstasy: A Biographical Novel of Michelangelo* (1961); *Those Who Love: A Biographical Novel of Abigail and John Adams* (1965); *The Greek Treasure: A Biographical Novel of Henry and Sophia Schliemann* (1975); *The Origin: A Biographical Novel of Charles Darwin* (1980); and *Depths of Glory: A Biographical Novel of Camille Pissarro* (1985). Despite Stone's considerable success, he expresses much frustration with academics for not recognizing the legitimacy and value of the biographical novel. In a 1957 lecture at the Library of Congress, Stone confirms that Bode's essay, which he discusses at some length, did not lead to the legitimization of the biographical novel. In a

---

[14]Bode (1955), 268.
[15]Bode (1955), 266.
[16]Ibid.

perceptive remark about the implicit prejudices against the aesthetic form, he queries: "I would like at this moment to interject, with less bitterness than puzzlement, I hope, the question of why the historical novel, with its accurate background but fictional characters, should have been more acceptable to the academicians than the biographical novel, which is accurate not only in background but in the people involved?"[17] The reading public may be excited about the biographical novel, but, as Stone rightly notes, academics continue to treat it as a "bastard form."[18]

One of the most important, contentious, and sophisticated debates about the biographical novel occurred in 1968, when the historian C. Vann Woodward moderated a forum with Robert Penn Warren, Ralph Ellison, and William Styron on the topic of "The Uses of History in Fiction." To start the debate, Woodward claims that there is a "distinction between the historian and the novelist."[19] Unlike the novelist, the historian cannot "invent characters, invent motives for his characters."[20] But Warren rejects this assumption because he holds that the past is always mediated through a specific consciousness, which means that historians, whether they realize it or not, use the creative imagination as much as novelists in order to construct their "historical characters."[21] Warren would clearly reject Bode's naïve belief in the existence of "unadorned truth." Though Warren claims that historians and novelists are the same in that they use imagination to access and construct their subjects, he does make a distinction between the two. The fiction writer "claims to know the inside of his characters, the undocumentable inside," while the historian "wants to find the facts *behind* the world."[22] Like Warren, Ellison rejects the idea that there is a distinction between "American historiography and American fiction," for "they're both artificial," which is why Ellison refers to historians as "responsible liars."[23]

---

[17]Stone (1957), "The Biographical Novel," in *Three Views of the Novel by Irving Stone, John O'Hara and MacKinlay Kanton.* Washington: The Library of Congress, 14.
[18]Stone (1957), 16.
[19]Ralph Ellison, William Styron, Robert Penn Warren, and C. Vann Woodward (Spring 1969), "The Uses of History in Fiction," *Southern Literary Journal* 1(2): 59.
[20]Ellison et al. (1969), 59.
[21]Ellison et al. (1969), 61.
[22]Ibid.
[23]Ellison et al. (1969), 62.

Since Ellison considers history fiction, it might seem that he would favor the biographical novel. But such is not the case. At one point during the discussion, Ellison praises Warren for engaging history correctly in *All the King's Men*:

> I think that Red Warren, who has always been concerned with history, has offered us an example of how to confront the problem of history as the novelist should. I think that when he wrote about a great American politician who governed his state and refused to intrude into the area of the historian, he refused because he was canny enough to realize that he could never get *that* particular man into fiction. And yet, I believe that he did use that man to bring into focus within his own mind many, many important facts about power, politics and class, and loyalty.[24]

Warren's decision not to name his character Huey Long was sound and astute, because he was able to articulate some crucial historical "truths" about the dynamics of power, the psychology of politics, and the structures of class. Had Warren ventured into the realm of the historian by specifically naming his character Huey Long, thus making *All the King's Men* a biographical novel, he would have failed to represent the complexity and details of the man and he would have made himself vulnerable to attack from historians.

While Ellison's comments are about Warren's work, they are also a not-so-subtle critique of Styron's 1967 biographical novel *The Confessions of Nat Turner*, which differs from *All the King's Men* because Styron named his character after the original historical figure. This novel caused considerable controversy for exactly the reasons Ellison mentions: people claimed that Styron misrepresented Nat Turner and made factual errors about him. For Ellison, when novelists encroach on the historians' intellectual terrain by writing a biographical novel, they make themselves vulnerable to critique: "The moment you put any known figures into the book, then somebody is going to say, 'But he didn't have that mole on that side of his face; it was on *that* side. You said that he had a wife; he didn't have a wife.'"[25] Therefore, instead of naming the main character

---

[24]Ellison et al. (1969), 64–5.
[25]Ellison et al. (1969), 74.

after the original, as Styron does, Ellison counsels writers to "lie and disguise a historical figure,"[26] as Warren does.

As it happens, Ellison failed to understand the trajectory of contemporary literature, for the American biographical novel has now become a dominant literary form. Gore Vidal's *Burr* and *Lincoln*, Bruce Duffy's *The World As I Found It* (Ludwig Wittgenstein), Michael Cunningham's *The Hours* (Virginia Woolf), Russell Banks' *Cloudsplitter* (Owen Brown), and Joyce Carol Oates' *Blonde* (Marilyn Monroe) are just a stellar few that have received considerable praise from respected scholars and general readers. But what intellectual and aesthetic developments made this valorization of the biographical novel possible? I will provide numerous answers to this question in the following pages, but for now, I want to focus on postmodernism, which radically compromised the traditional literary symbol and led general readers to give authors more creative license in their representation of historical figures.

To clarify the nature of these developments, it would be useful to examine specifically how the committee for the Pulitzer Prize in fiction struggled to understand and ultimately came to accept the biographical novel. The first biographical novel to pose a serious challenge for the Pulitzer committee was Styron's *The Confessions of Nat Turner*. Significant is the fact that the committee did not yet have a suitable vocabulary or conceptual framework for making systematic sense of the biographical novel, which in part explains its difficulty in assessing it. The 1968 report notes that "the Fiction Jury could not reach a unanimous opinion" about this novel, so it submitted a form with "a minority and a majority opinion and a possible compromise selection."[27] To come to terms with its own confusion, there is an extended discussion of Styron's novel. The report is six pages and consists of twenty-two paragraphs. Styron's novel is discussed in twelve of those paragraphs, and it is the exclusive subject of ten. The only other novel to come close is Isaac Bashevis Singer's *The Manor*, which is mentioned in six paragraphs and the primary subject of only two.

As important as the length and focus of the report are the comments about Styron's novel, which shed considerable light on

---

[26]Ibid.
[27]Fischer and Fischer (2007), *Chronicle of the Pulitzer Prizes for Fiction: Discussions, Decisions, Dissents*. München: K.G. Saur Verlag, 294.

the committee's assumptions and expectations regarding fiction. Even though Lukács would have characterized and faulted *The Confessions of Nat Turner* as a biographical novel, both Styron and the committee saw it as a historical novel. This is clear from the decision of John K. Hutchens, one of the committee members, to cite Styron, who says that *The Confessions* is "less an 'historical novel' than a meditation on history."[28] Lessening the degree to which *The Confessions* is a historical novel does not negate it as one. And it is worth noting that, when Styron defined and defended his novel during the forum with Ellison and Warren, he used Lukács' *The Historical Novel* to do so. What Hutchens admires so much about the work is Styron's ability to do two things simultaneously: to use rich, imaginative language in order to engage the reader and to represent the historical figure accurately. On the basis of these criteria, Hutchens concludes that Styron "has written what is, in my opinion, the finest American novel of 1967, and the one that promises to be most enduring as art and re-created history."[29]

Maxwell Geismar and Melvin Maddocks were the two other readers, and they disagreed with Hutchens on both accounts. Their comments are useful, because they indicate what the members consider the freedoms a writer is allowed and not allowed to take with the historical record. Geismar and Maddocks claim that *The Confessions* is a flawed novel because there are "serious defects in the use of its historical material" as well as the "prose style." It might seem that these two problems are separate and distinct, but for these readers they are actually inextricably linked. Maddocks claims that the novel's "writing" is "too smooth, too 'literary.'"[30] This is a problem because such literary language lacks verisimilitude. According to Geismar, instead of replicating the "early 19th century language" of Nat Turner or Thomas Gray, the lawyer who took the rebel slave's confession, "Styron has added a large percent of romantic Southern rhetoric to the point of making the novel's prose so fragrant, redolent, and prolix as to be overblown and luscious."[31] The literary expectation is this: for a historical novel to be effective and legitimate, the language must accurately reflect the way people

---

[28]Ibid.
[29]Fischer and Fischer (2007), 295.
[30]Ibid.
[31]Fischer and Fischer (2007), 297.

spoke from the represented period. And if the language fails to do this, then the author must have a faulty understanding of the historical period.

Most prominent biographical novelists reject the Geismar/ Maddocks view. In their effort to represent a structure of consciousness or a political ideology, biographical novelists frequently subordinate empirical facts to a symbolic truth. For instance, when discussing the construction of her fictional characters, Oates told me in an interview that her "characters are more interesting, elastic and subtle than the real people." Indeed, she goes on to say that the actual historical figures are "not nearly as nuanced or subtle as my fictitious characters."[32] This is the case because Oates uses her characters to access and represent a larger political, psychological, and/or cultural truth. In their assessment of a literary work's engagement with history, Geismar and Maddocks acknowledge that novelists can use fiction to illuminate the historical record, but they forbid tampering with the literal facts, which explains why they drew a damning conclusion about *The Confessions of Nat Turner*: "While William Styron may have the right to 'invent' historical incidents within the framework of recorded history, he has in this book taken some dubious liberties with history itself."[33] For Geismar and Maddocks, Styron has the right to invent scenes within the context of an established historical frame, but he does not have a right to alter history itself. For Oates, however, altering history is precisely what the biographical novelist does.

So contra Geismar and Maddocks, biographical novelists unapologetically take "liberties with history itself." But what enables them to justify this is not so much a cynical rejection of historical truth as a subordination of a particular narrative truth. To illustrate, let me supply an example from Julia Alvarez's *In the Time of the Butterflies*, which is about the lives of the Mirabal sisters in the Dominican Republic during the reign of the dictator Rafael Trujillo, who frequently used young girls for his own personal satisfaction. Trujillo took a particular interest in Minerva Mirabal, who was repulsed by the older man's advances. At a formal party, Trujillo

---

[32]Oates (2014), "Enhanced Symbolic Interiors in the Biographical Novel," in *Truthful Fictions: Conversations with American Biographical Novelists*. Editor and Interviewer Michael Lackey. London and New York: Bloomsbury, 188.
[33]Fischer and Fischer (2007), 296.

clearly made an indecent remark to Minerva, which prompted her, so the story goes, to slap him so hard that it left an imprint on his face. In my interview with Alvarez, she told me that the surviving Mirabal sister said that "there had been no slap."[34] It was just part of Dominican folklore. And yet, Alvarez decided to keep the slap in the novel. Why? Through the story of the Mirabal sisters, Alvarez could express some important political and psychological truths. Men in the late 1950s felt that they were entitled, that they could take all kinds of liberties with women. How could Alvarez best express the psychological rage that women felt about the political system that allowed men to violate women with psychological and legal impunity? The slap, while literally untrue, expresses a psychological truth that women experienced about the unjust political system in which they lived. Many biographical novelists agree on this principle: it is permissible to alter historical fact, so long as the writer remains faithful to more important symbolic truths. More specifically, a political truth about the psychic life of women in the 1950s is more important than a literal truth about a slap.

So let me generalize at this point. Biographical novelists privilege symbolic representation over historical or biographical fact, because they think that a symbolic reality will give readers something more substantial about the nature of a historical period. In other words, they are different from historians and biographers in that they seek to create symbolic figures, while historians and biographers seek to represent factual "reality." With regard to Styron's novel, all three Pulitzer committee members did not yet have an epistemological or aesthetic framework that would enable them to understand or appreciate the biographical novel. Geismar and Maddocks failed to see how Styron's subordination of certain historical facts enabled him to symbolically access and represent more substantive historical structures and truths (I will define these "structures" and "truths" in Chapter 5). As for Hutchens, while he praises *The Confessions*, it is clear that he considers it a historical rather than a biographical novel.

It might seem that 1980 marks the official arrival of the American biographical novel, for it was in this year that Norman Mailer

---

[34]Alvarez (2014), "Fixed Facts and Creative Freedom in the Biographical Novel," in *Truthful Fictions: Conversations with American Biographical Novelists*. Editor and Interviewer Michael Lackey. London and New York: Bloomsbury, 31.

received the Pulitzer Prize in fiction for *The Executioner's Song*, which chronicles the last nine months of Gary Mark Gilmore's life. But there are two separate reasons why this is not the case. First, by virtue of Mailer's own definition, *The Executioner's Song* would not qualify as a biographical novel. If, as Woolf claims, the art of representing a person accurately is the primary task of the biographer while the art of inventing scenes to create a living character is the primary task of the novelist, then Mailer's novel would qualify as a biography but not a novel. As Mailer claims in his a Afterword, *The Executioner's Song* is a "factual account," a "*true life story.*"[35] The "novel" makes use of "interviews, documents, [and] records of court proceedings" to give readers "a factual account of the activities of Gary Gilmore,"[36] and when Mailer gets conflicting evidence about Gilmore, he chooses "the version that seemed most likely."[37] Given the absence of overt creative invention, it is difficult to justify calling *The Executioner's Song* fiction.

An example from Bruce Duffy's work, which I will discuss in considerable detail in Chapter 2, will enable me to bring into sharp focus the distinction between *The Executioner's Song* and a biographical novel. Postmodernists argue that fictionalizing reality is inescapable because the art of framing a character or story necessitates a creative shaping of material. While most biographical novelists acknowledge the inevitable fictionalization inherent within all writing, they also do something more conscious and strategic. They invent stories that never occurred in order to answer perplexing questions, fill in cultural lacunae, signify human interiors, or picture cultural ideologies. For instance, Ludwig Wittgenstein had a conflicted sense of himself, for he was a Jew whose family became Catholic. In *The World As I Found It*, Duffy brilliantly dramatizes the famous biographical moment when Wittgenstein confesses to the philosopher G. E. Moore that he deceived him and others by concealing his Jewish heritage. Had Duffy only included scenes like Wittgenstein's confession, *The World As I Found It* would be an engaging biography and not a biographical novel. But to access and represent Wittgenstein's conflicted self, Duffy creates a scene much earlier in the novel with the Austrian philosopher in a Jewish

---

[35]Mailer (1998), *The Executioner's Song*. New York: Vintage Books, 1053.
[36]Mailer (1998), 1051.
[37]Ibid.

theater, which features a play about the Jewish monster figure Yosele Golem, who is described as "a kind of beast." So captivated by the performance is Wittgenstein that "for five hard minutes he *was* the play, Yosele Golem."[38] During my interview with Duffy, he said that his Wittgenstein was "so upset by a seemingly garish scene and simple-minded scene—and so unconscious of his deeper emotions—that he passes out." This is the case because he was forced to confront in the theater "his true past,"[39] specifically his Jewish heritage. However, as Duffy went on to say, this scene never actually occurred. This is the kind of scene that does not appear in *The Executioner's Song*, which is why 1980 cannot be considered the official arrival year of the American biographical novel.

This lack of strategic and overt invention explains the 1980 Pulitzer committee's conflicted response to *The Executioner's Song*. The committee obviously recognized that there was a problem giving Mailer's work an award for fiction, for it tries to make the case for it as a novel in the first sentence of the report: "*The Executioner's Song* is subtitled 'A True Life Novel.'"[40] Something is not entirely right about this work, which is why the committee members feel the need to justify that it is actually a novel. Indeed, in its six-sentence report, the members strategically and repeatedly emphasize the way the novel expands "our conceptions of the limits of history and fiction" and "challenges our notions of fiction."[41] The members obviously want to underscore how *The Executioner's Song* challenges our definitions of fiction so that they can justify their decision to give Mailer an award for fiction. This becomes most apparent when we look at the letter that the chairman of the committee, Frank McConnell, submitted to the advisory board. McConnell notes that one committee member, Anatole Broyard, "expressed some concern that Mailer's book may not really be a novel (whatever that means)."[42] McConnell obviously did not agree with that assessment, which is clear from his parenthetical

---

[38]Duffy (2010), *The World As I Found It*. New York: New York Review Books, 145.
[39]Duffy (2014), "In the Fog of the Biographical Novel's History," in *Truthful Fictions: Conversations with American Biographical Novelists*. Editor and Interviewer Michael Lackey. London and New York: Bloomsbury, 125.
[40]Fischer and Fischer (2007), 349.
[41]Ibid.
[42]Fischer and Fischer (2007), 348.

interjection. But Broyard was rightly "worried that giving the prize to" Mailer's book "may raise unpleasant controversy and embarrass the Pulitzer Committee,"[43] because, if it is correct to say that *The Executioner's Song* contains no overtly fictional characters or scenes, then it would be difficult to justify awarding it the Pulitzer Prize for fiction.

The second reason why 1980 does not mark the official arrival of the biographical novel is the committee's subtle bias against the genre. The report says: "And although the story told is about real people, and based upon a great mass of documentary material, *The Executioner's Song* is an extraordinarily ambitious and powerful narrative."[44] Note the hint of surprise ("although") that a "novel" about a "real" person that uses "documentary material" could be a "powerful narrative." These are clearly people who have not yet read J. M. Coetzee's *The Master of Petersburg*, Colum McCann's *Dancer*, Anne Enright's *The Pleasure of Eliza Lynch*, Hilary Mantel's *Wolf Hall*, and Laurent Binet's *HHhH*. At this point, the literary establishment still needs to undergo a few more transformations before it could understand or appreciate the biographical novel.

In 1982, Ina Schabert published a very important and useful essay titled "Fictional Biography, Factual Biography, and their Contamination," which advanced our attitude toward biographical fiction. In addition to identifying numerous biographical novels, Schabert provides some useful frameworks for understanding scholarly efforts to define the aesthetic form and for distinguishing the biographical novel from biography. However, there is good reason to have some serious reservations about Schabert's work and approach. Her essay was published in the journal *Biography*, and so she defines and assesses the biographical novel as biography rather than fiction. Paul Murray Kendall, whose work Schabert discusses at some length, was the first major scholar to approach biographical fiction in this manner. In his 1965 book *The Art of Biography*, he refers to "the radical left" invention of "the novel-as-biography," which, he contends, is "almost wholly imaginary."[45] For Kendall, the novel-as-biography is like the fictional biography in that it makes use of the "literary element" in the construction of

---

[43]Ibid.
[44]Fischer and Fischer (2007), 349.
[45]Kendall (1967), *The Art of Biography*. New York: The Norton Library, 126.

a life, but it is different from fictional biography because novels-as-biography "imaginatively take the place of biography where there can be no genuine biography for lack of materials."[46] Kendall's logic here is confusing. If novels-as-biography displace the biography, thus rendering them not biographies, then on what grounds can Kendall call them biographies (novels-as-biography) and critique them as a biography? The whole point is that they are not biographies. As such, standards for determining the quality of biography cannot and should not be applied to the biographical novel.

Kendall's work has had an extremely negative and lasting impact on scholarship about the biographical novel. There has been, fortunately, an explosion of interest in biography, autobiography, memoir, and life writing since the publication of Kendall's book. Unfortunately, this has led many scholars to define and assess biographical novels as biography. For instance, while Schabert references and has a positive approach to the "biographical novel," she interprets the genre through the lens of biography, which is obvious from the title of her 1990 book *In Quest of the Other Person: Fiction as Biography*. As Schabert claims, her project examines how fictional biographies and biographical fictions, terms that she unfortunately uses interchangeably, enable readers "to get knowledge of the real, other person."[47] Since the publication of Schabert's book, scholars have been analyzing, interpreting, and assessing biofiction primarily in relation to the methods and objectives of biography. Let me cite just a few important studies to illustrate this point.

In his 1991 essay "Biofictions," Alain Buisine clarifies how postmodernism contributed to the making of the biographical novel, because it underscores the degree to which fiction necessarily plays a role in the construction of a biographical subject and why, therefore, an accurate representation of the biographical subject is ultimately impossible. For Buisine, these intellectual developments led to the rise of biofiction, which is a postmodern form of biography that implicitly concedes through its dramatization that it cannot accurately signify or represent the biographical subject because the author's subjective orientation will always

---

[46]Kendall (1967), 127.
[47]Schabert (1990), *In Quest of the Other Person: Fiction as Biography*. Tubingen: Francke Verlag, 1.

inflect the representation.[48] John Keener follows suit in his 2001 book *Biography and the Postmodern Historical Novel*, which examines the continuum of what he calls "biographical narrative."[49] According to his model, "biographical fiction" is that which "applies 'novelistic' discourse to the representation of an historical life."[50] While Monica Latham tries in 2012 to show how biofiction straddles the two worlds of fiction and biography, she ultimately defines biofiction in terms of the biographer's attempt to represent with as much "verisimilitude" as possible the biographical subject's "life story."[51] Julia Novak and Sandra Mayer uncritically take this approach as a given when they claim in their recent article that biofiction is an effort to recover "the (historical) author's 'true' and 'authentic' self behind the mask of his/her renowned public persona."[52] All these scholars define biofiction primarily in relation to the goals and techniques of biography.

But foregrounding the biographical is problematic because most authors of biofiction explicitly claim that they are not doing biography. As Ehrlich claims in the author's note to *God's Angry Man*, which was initially published in 1932: "This work is a *novel*, not a biography or a history."[53] Subsequent biographical novelists make an almost exact claim. For instance, in the foreword to *Wife to Mr. Milton*, Robert Graves says that "this book is a novel, not a biography"[54]; in the note to *Death of the Fox*, George Garrett says that "this is a work of fiction," and he goes on to claim that "it is not supposed to be in any sense a biography of Sir Walter Ralegh"[55]; and in the afterword to *An Imaginary Life*, David Malouf states that what he "wanted to write was neither historical

[48]Buisine (1991), "Biofictions," *Revue des Sciences Humaines* 224: 7–13.
[49]Keener (2001), *Biography and the Postmodern Historical Novel*. Lewiston: The Edwin Mellen Press, 1.
[50]Keener (2001), 183.
[51]Latham (Winter 2012), "'Serv[ing] under two masters': Virginia Woolf's Afterlives in Contemporary Biofictions," *a/b: Auto/Biography Studies* 27(2): 355.
[52]Novak and Meyer (2014), "Disparate Images: Literary Heroism and the 'Work vs. Life' Topos in Contemporary Biofictions about Victorian Authors," *Neo-Victorian Studies* 7(1): 25.
[53]Ehrlich (1941), *God's Angry Man*. New York: The Press of the Readers Club, ix.
[54]Graves (1962), *Wife to Mr. Milton: The Story of Marie Powell*. New York: The Noonday Press, vii.
[55]Garrett (1971), *Death of the Fox*. New York: Doubleday & Company, Inc., 9.

novel nor biography, but a fiction"[56]—Schabert refers to these last three novels as fictional biographies in both her article and book, but these authors would clearly reject the idea that their works are biographies. More recent biographical novelists are just as adamant in stating that their works are fiction, not biography. As Duffy says in the preface to *The World As I Found It*: "This is a work of fiction: it is not history, philosophy or biography."[57] On the copyright page of *Blonde*, Oates tells her reader explicitly that "*Blonde* should be read solely as a work of fiction, not as a biography of Marilyn Monroe."[58] In an interview, Banks characterizes his biographical novel about Owen Brown (*Cloudsplitter*) as something other than a biography: "It seemed to me a given that I could write from inside a historical figure. I could write a 'life' of that figure, using that figure's life, but I would be writing a dramatic narrative, a work with a dramatic shape and intent, rather than a biography of that character."[59] The biographical novel is, first and foremost, fiction, which is why Parini insists in the acknowledgments of *The Passages of H.M.* (Herman Melville) that "this is a novel, not a literary biography."[60]

In the postscript to the biographical novel *In the Time of the Butterflies*, Alvarez clearly expresses why it is important to keep in mind that what she is writing is an experimental form of the novel and not an experimental form of the biography. For Alvarez, what readers get in her work "are not the Mirabal sisters of fact, or even the Mirabal sisters of legend." Alvarez makes this claim not because she wants to ward off criticism nor because she has a dismissive view of biography. Rather, she makes it because she wants to identify one of her limitations. As she says, she does not have "the talents and inclinations of a biographer to be able to adequately record"[61] the lives of the Mirabal sisters. The biographer

---

[56]Malouf (1978), *An Imaginary Life*. New York: George Braziller, 153.
[57]Duffy (2010), *The World As I Found It*. New York: The New York Review of Books, "Preface."
[58]Oates (2009), *Blonde*. New York: The Ontario Review.
[59]Banks (2014), "The Truth Contract in the Biographical Novel," in *Truthful Fictions: Conversations with American Biographical Novelists*. Editor and Interviewer Michael Lackey. London and New York: Bloomsbury, 43–4.
[60]Parini (2010), *The Passages of H.M.: A Novel of Herman Melville*. New York: Anchor Books, 453.
[61]Alvarez (2010), *In the Time of the Butterflies*. Chapel Hill: Algonquin Books of Chapel Hill, 324.

has talents, skills, and sensibilities that are different from those of a novelist. Alvarez is not a biographer, because she lacks those talents and sensibilities. Instead, she is a novelist, who uses fictional techniques to narrate a story, which just happens to be based on the lives of real people. Therefore, when people assess the quality of *In the Time of the Butterflies*, they should judge it as a novel and not a biography. Joanna Scott puts the matter best. Discussing her biographical novel *Arrogance*, which centers on the life of the Austrian artist Egon Schiele, Scott says: "I wasn't trying to pretend that my Schiele was the real Schiele. I just wanted him to be real."[62] In other words, Scott wants to be judged for doing what she does, which is to create a real and memorable character in a novel and not to accurately represent the life of a real person.

What we get in a biographical novel, then, is the novelist's vision of life and the world, and not an accurate representation of an actual person's life. Put differently, biographical novelists differ from biographers, because, while authors of traditional and fictional biographies seek to represent the life (or a dimension of a life) of an actual historical figure as clearly and accurately as possible, biographical novelists forgo the desire to get the biographical subject's life "right" and rather use the biographical subject in order to project their own vision of life and the world (I will develop this idea in much greater detail in Chapter 5). Given the nature and extent of the liberties these creative writers take with the biographical subject, we could say that Lukács was right to analyze the genre through the lens of fiction rather than biography. The unfortunate trend among many scholars of biofiction, however, is that, when they define the genre, they rarely, if ever, take into account the work of Lukács.

The years 1996 (*Benjamin's Crossing*) and 1997 ("Fact or Fiction: Writing Biographies Versus Writing Novels") are of crucial importance but in ways that are difficult to document adequately. Within an American context, Parini has probably done more to advance the contemporary biographical novel than any other scholar or writer.[63] Parini has published poetry, biographies,

[62]Scott (2016), "On Hoaxes, Humbugs, and Fictional Portraiture," *a/b: Auto/Biography Studies*, (forthcoming).
[63]For a more extensive discussion of Parini's important role in the making of the American biographical novel, see my "Introduction" to Jay Parini (2014),

novels, cultural criticism, scholarly essays, and, most importantly, biographical novels. As a friend of Warren, Parini learned much from the Southern writer, but he also had a very close friendship with Vidal, who authored notable biographical novels such as *Burr* and *Lincoln*.[64] In 1990, Parini published his first biographical novel *The Last Station*, which is about Leo Tolstoy, and he confesses that Vidal, who read early drafts of the work, gave him many useful suggestions for structuring the multi-perspective narrative. Like Warren, Parini foregrounds history in his novels, but he differs from Warren in that he, like Vidal, names his protagonists after the actual historical figure. In fact, in an interview, Parini claims that Warren's decision to conceal the identity of Huey Long in his novel *All the King's Men* was a missed opportunity:

> In *All the King's Men*, written in the mid-forties, Robert Penn Warren felt tightly bound to the traditions of conventional historical fiction. I don't think he could see his way toward the contemporary forms of the biographical novel, or else he would have called his protagonist Huey Long, not Willie Stark. I wish he had. I think he could have written a better novel if he'd actually dug into Long, because I know he was obsessed with him.[65]

For Parini, had something been different in Warren's thinking, he would have been able to imagine his way toward the biographical novel.

From the publication of *The Last Station* in 1990 until today, Parini has committed himself to the biographical novel—he is currently writing one about the apostle Paul. If Parini were an isolated author, we would have to establish textual links between him and other prominent novelists in order to suggest that he helped shape the contemporary American biographical novel. But Parini is the D. E. Axinn Professor of English and Creative Writing

Conversations with Jay Parini. Editor Michael Lackey. Jackson: University Press of Mississippi, ix–xx.

[64]Parini (1997), "Mentors," in *Some Necessary Angels: Essays on Writing and Politics*. New York: Columbia University Press, 3–17.

[65]Parini (2014), "Reflections on Biographical Fiction," in *Truthful Fictions: Conversations with American Biographical Novelists*. Editor and Interviewer Michael Lackey. London and New York: Bloomsbury, 213.

at Middlebury College, which is where the famous Bread Loaf Writing Conference is held—many prominent writers have taught at Bread Loaf. Parini has been involved with this conference for decades, and consequently, he has extensive contact with scores of famous writers. To put the matter bluntly, Parini is friends with some of the most prominent writers in the United States, and he has been engaging them in heated debates about and making the case for the biographical novel for decades. Writers who have told me about their experiences with Parini include Banks, author of the 1998 biographical novel *Cloudsplitter*; Oates, author of the 1999 biographical novel *Blonde*; and Edmund White, author of the 2007 biographical novel *Hotel de Dream*. These are three extraordinary biographical novels, and they were all written after the publication of Parini's *The Last Station* and *Benjamin's Crossing* (I do an extensive analysis of this novel in Chapter 3) as well as his essay "Fact or Fiction: Writing Biographies Versus Writing Novels." Based on these facts, is it possible to say that, if not for Parini, we would not have stellar biographical novels like *Cloudsplitter*, *Blonde*, and/or *Hotel de Dream*? I would not make such a bold declaration, but it is clear that there are strong lines of connection between Parini and some of the best American biographical novelists.

The contribution of Parini's that I want to underscore has more to do with attitude than content. One of the major stumbling blocks for biographical novelists has been managing and negotiating the competing and sometimes contradictory demands of biography and fiction, a problem that bedeviled Woolf. In her book *Victoriana*, which examines biographical novels about Henry James, Cora Kaplan, like Woolf, suggests that reconciling the two acts is not possible: "The 'bio' in biofiction also references a more essentialised and embodied element of identity, a subject less than transcendent but more than merely discourse. It implies that there is something stubbornly insoluble in what separates the two genres and that prevents them from being invisibly sutured; the join will always show."[66] Parini would contest this claim, not because he has discovered a way to magically blend the acts of representing (biography) and creating (fiction), but because he subordinates

---

[66]Kaplan (2007), *Victoriana: Histories, Fictions, Criticism*. New York: Columbia University Press, 65.

biographical representation to the writer's vision. Here is how he puts the matter in his 1997 essay about biofiction:

> Novels are about lives, after all: about pieces of lives or whole lives. Traditionally, these lives have been made up, with half-believable disclosures at the outset that read, "The characters in this novel are entirely fictitious and any relation to persons living or dead is entirely accidental." I would prefer that novelists of the future write: "Everything in the following pages is authentic, which is to say it is as true as I could make it. Take it or leave it."[67]

In the traditional disclaimer, authors made a statement disavowing or qualifying the relationship between the invented character and the real person. But in Parini's version of the disclaimer, the whole idea of the relationship disappears. All readers are left with is the creative writer's vision. In essence, Parini unapologetically asserts his authority as a novelist. What we get in a biographical novel, then, is the novelist's vision of life and the world, and not an accurate representation of an actual person's life. Put differently, biographical novelists differ from biographers, because, while authors of traditional and fictional biographies seek to represent the life (or a dimension of a life) of an actual historical figure as clearly and accurately as possible, biographical novelists use the biographical subject in order to project their own vision of life and the world. Here is how Banks puts the matter: "I'm using history in order to tell a story."[68] The goal is not to do biography. Rather, it is to use history and biography in order to construct a narrative:

> My real purpose is to generate and tell a story. It is not to correct history or write an addendum to the historical or biographical record. It is simply to appropriate the material that history has dropped at my door. . . . If history drops it on your doorstep, it's there to be used.[69]

---

[67]Parini (1997), "Fact or Fiction: Writing Biographies Versus Writing Novels," in *Some Necessary Angels: Essays on Writing and Politics*. New York: Columbia University Press, 250.
[68]Banks (2014), 45.
[69]Ibid.

Thus, Banks says that *Cloudsplitter* should not be read alongside or compared to biographies, but "should be read as a novel, and the books against which it should be measured are novels."[70] Accentuating the fact that they are writing novels rather than biographies liberates biographical novelists from the chokehold of biographical representation.

Within an American context, the year 1999 represents a key turning point in favor of the biographical novel. In this year, three novels were nominated for the Pulitzer. Two (Cunningham's *The Hours* and Banks' *Cloudsplitter*) were biographical novels, and Cunningham's *The Hours* won the award.[71] Cunningham's novel is significant because it addresses the literary establishment directly. The novel features a prominent writer (Richard) who receives an important literary award. For Cunningham's narrator, this prize "means that literature itself . . . seems to feel a need for Richard's particular contribution."[72] This is a wonderful way of articulating what happened with the Pulitzer committee. It felt a need at this time for the biographical novelist's contribution. After all, so many prominent American writers had published biographical novels by 1999 that it was impossible to ignore them.

Most encouraging, however, is the content of the Pulitzer's jury report, which indicates a shift in the literary establishment's aesthetic expectations and theory of knowledge. For instance, when discussing *The Hours*, the committee notes that a "fourth character is Woolf herself," which contributes to the novel's "four-person complexity."[73] Instead of assuming that a real person as a character would be a liability, as the 1980 Pulitzer committee did, the 1999 members recognize that such a literary choice could be a huge asset. What, in part, made this possible was the committee's acceptance of postmodernism. Before 1999, postmodernism was never mentioned in any Pulitzer jury report for fiction. But in the year that *The Hours* received the Pulitzer, the committee praised Cunningham for presenting "the floating post-modern world and generation that a number of contemporary writers have tackled, but none so artfully and movingly."[74] Rather than strictly demarcating

---

[70]Banks (2014), 50.
[71]Cunningham's *The Hours* also won the PEN/Faulkner Award.
[72]Cunningham (1998), *The Hours*. New York: Picador, 64.
[73]Fischer and Fischer (2007), 424.
[74]Ibid.

fact and fiction, biography and the novel, or a historical figure and a fictional character, postmodernists suggest that fact is fiction and that fiction is inseparable from fact. This postmodernist shift made the committee understand and appreciate a hybrid aesthetic form such as the biographical novel, which is why we could say that the biographical novel was becoming formally and officially recognized by 1999.

This year is also important because Martin Middeke and Werner Huber published *Biofictions*, a collection of essays focusing on biographical fictions of people from the Romantic period.[75] In the introduction, Middeke clarifies how the postmodern Zeitgeist set the stage for the rise of biofiction. Given that "fiction and historiographic/biographical discourse are not mutually exclusive"[76] in a postmodern age, hybrid forms of writing started to emerge. While Middeke acknowledges that the postmodern blending of fact and fiction resulted in hybrid forms of writing, he does not leave matters there, nor does he use this fact as an apologia for an "anything goes" approach to biofiction. Rather, he clarifies how biofiction enables us to formulate a more nuanced conception of a newly understood "factual world." To put the matter succinctly, Middeke claims that the authors of biofictions "may incorporate and reflect upon epistemological uncertainties caused by the aporias of time and language, *without* obliterating historical consciousness."[77] In other words, authors of biofiction do not get rid of the "historical" or "biographical" world. Instead, they provide more complicated ways of understanding the words "historical" and "biographical," and they subsequently use fiction to offer new ways of conceptualizing the historical and biographical. Middeke's introduction signals a decisive move in the right direction for scholars, as it brings rigor

---

[75]It might seem that I should also mention in this context Stephanie Bird's 1998 study *Recasting Historical Women: Female Identity in German Biographical Fiction*, as this work features biographical fiction in the subtitle. However, Bird's book is primarily about feminism rather than biofiction. And in those rare moments when she discusses the nature of biographical fiction, her terminology is muddled and confusing. Like Schabert, Bird treats biographical fiction and fictional biography as interchangeable. Consequently, she tends to use the criteria of biography rather than fiction to analyze and interpret the works.

[76]Martin Middeke (1999), "Introduction," in *Biofictions: The Rewriting of Romantic Lives in Contemporary Fiction and Drama*. Editors Martin Middeke and Werner Huber. Camden: Rochester, 3.

[77]Ibid.

to the conversation, recognizes that biofictions are fictions and not biography, and provides considerable insight into the origin and evolution of the literary form.

The year 1999 was clearly a watershed moment, but the news was not all good. So popular with prominent writers had the biographical novel become that the well-respected American editor and novelist Jonathan Dee published a scathing essay about it in *Harpers*. According to Dee, "there's no debating that the practice of conscripting flesh-and-blood people into novels has become a veritable epidemic in the last twenty-five years or so."[78] Dee considers this an "ominous"[79] sign, as he believes that it represents "a lowering of the literary bar."[80] To be more specific,

> Creating a character out of words and making him or her as vivid and memorable as a real person might be is perhaps the hardest of the fundamental tricks a novelist has to perform. Simply adopting or impersonating an already interesting real-life character— Lee Harvey Oswald, J. P. Morgan, Amelia Earhart—cannot be considered as substantial an achievement as creating a character who enters the reader's consciousness as a total unknown.[81]

For Dee, the rise of biofiction signifies our age's bankrupt imagination and perhaps the death of fiction.

In 2006, David Lodge published "The Year of Henry James," which tries to explain the mysterious confluence of biographical novels about Henry James in the year 2004. There were three Henry-James-inspired novels in that year, and two were biographical novels, Colm Tóibín's *The Master* and Lodge's *Author, Author*. Lodge wonders how it is possible to explain that James never appeared in a fictional work as a protagonist under his own name before Emma Tenant's 2002 novel *Felony*, but that in the year 2004, he was the primary subject of Alan Hollinghurst's *The Line of Beauty* and the protagonist in Tóibín's *The Master*, Lodge's *Author, Author*, and Michael Heyns' *The Typewriter's Tale* (Heyns' novel was submitted

---

[78]Dee (1999), "The Reanimators: On the Art of Literary Graverobbing," *Harpers Magazine* 298(1789): 77.
[79]Ibid.
[80]Dee (1999), 83–4.
[81]Dee (1999), 84.

to publishing houses in 2004, but because it was the last in the line of James-inspired novels, it was rejected until 2005).

Most fascinating in Lodge's essay is his claim that, even though he has "been reading, teaching and writing criticism about" James since he "was an undergraduate," he could not imagine until recently doing a biographical novel about him, because his "concept of what constituted a novel . . . did not include the possibility of writing one about a real historical person."[82] For Lodge, something has changed in the collective consciousness that has made the biographical novel not just possible but also a dominant literary form. Hence his astonishment "that the biographical novel—the novel which takes a real person and their real history as the subject matter for imaginative exploration, using the novel's techniques for representing subjectivity rather than the objective, evidence-based discourse of biography—has become a very fashionable form of literary fiction in the last decade or so."[83] After wondering "why the biographical novel should have recently attracted so many writers as a literary form," Lodge speculates that its rise "could be taken as a symptom of a declining faith or loss of confidence in the power of purely fictional narrative."[84] I want to briefly offer an alternative explanation for this intellectual development.

It is my contention that the rise of the biographical novel signaled the decline of what I refer to as the deductive imagination and the emergence of the inductive imagination, which converts a historically specific event into a literary symbol. This was the case because of the rise and legitimization of postmodernism, which, in its most basic form, means "incredulity toward metanarratives."[85] Given the growing skepticism about universals and metanarratives, there was a shift away from aesthetic models that started with an ahistorical precept, the basis for the deductive imagination, and a shift toward models that foregrounded the historically specific, the basis for the inductive imagination. This, I contend, explains why

---

[82]Lodge (2006), 10–11.
[83]Lodge (2006), 8.
[84]Lodge (2006), 9–10.
[85]Jean-François Lyotard (1991), *The Postmodern Condition: A Report on Knowledge.* Translated by Geoff Bennington and Brian Massumi. Minneapolis: University of Minnesota Press, xxiv.

the biographical novel became increasingly more popular with both average readers and prominent writers after the 1970s.

Developments in Oates' corpus will enable me to best chart the transformation in the literary imagination. In her fiction, Oates viciously criticizes white male liberals, especially the Kennedys and Bill Clinton. For instance, in her biographical novel *Blonde*, which is about Marilyn Monroe, Oates insightfully pictures the contradictory psychology of prominent American politicians. As a liberal, it would seem that JFK would have a progressive view of women. But in his relationship with Monroe, he is "a patrician patriarch."[86] Oates' JFK, however, is not merely a typical male of the 1960s. He also represents the contradictory psychology of a powerful male liberal of the 1990s. Notice how Oates draws a clear parallel between JFK and Clinton. Monroe enters the president's room while he is on the phone talking to "a White House adviser or cabinet member."[87] Oates describes what happens in a way that unmistakably recalls the Monica Lewinsky scandal: "Gamely the Blond Actress began to stroke the President's penis, as one might stroke a charming but unruly pet while its owner looked on proudly. Yet, to her annoyance, the President didn't hang up the phone."[88] Published in 1999, this novel was written at the height of the Lewinsky affair. But what is crucial to note is the transformation in Oates' writing during the nineties.

In this decade, Oates clearly targets the contradictory psychology of white male liberals in her fiction. For example, in 1992 Oates authored a work that required readers to use the deductive imagination to critique the American polity. That novella is *Black Water*, which is like Warren's *All the King's Men* in that it does not name the protagonist after the original figure. This novella is clearly based on the 1969 Chappaquiddick incident, when Senator Ted Kennedy had a car accident that resulted in the death of Mary Jo Kopechne, who is named Kelly Kelleher in the novella. But instead of naming her character Kennedy, Oates simply refers to him as The Senator. Also, the novel is set in the 1990s, after the first war in Iraq had already started, and the incident occurs on July 4th rather than July 18th, thus giving it much more political significance. These

---

[86]Oates (2009), 708.
[87]Oates (2009), 705.
[88]Ibid.

changes enable Oates to construct a symbolic character (a universal or metanarrative) that embodies the reckless patriarchal psychology of so many prominent political figures of the 1990s. And once this symbolic character is clearly defined, readers could then use the deductive imagination to illuminate the behavior of a wide range of powerful American males.

By 1999, with the publication of *Blonde*, Oates produced fiction that requires readers to use the inductive rather than the deductive imagination—Oates names her protagonist Marilyn Monroe. Through extensive research and expert artistic representation, Oates uses a historically specific example (the Monroe/JFK affair) to construct a literary symbol. That historical specificity functions as an argument confirming Oates' critique of the patriarchy. This is not the work of the fictive imagination, which can easily concoct a sexist character (the Senator as a literary symbol embodying a patriarchal mindset) that could be used to critique powerful males in the real world. In the postmodern age, we are more skeptical of such fictional abstractions because they resemble ahistorical precepts or traditional metanarratives. What we see in *Blonde*, therefore, is an empirical portrait of a known philanderer, whose reprehensible behavior contributed to the death of an actual woman. But Oates' concern is not just the patriarchal politics of the 1960s. By subtly using details from the Lewinsky case to describe JFK's treatment of Monroe, Oates invites readers to use the inductive imagination to draw a clear link between the patriarchal politics of JFK and Clinton. What JFK did in the 1960s, Clinton continued to do in the 1990s. Or, read the other way, we could use the records from the Lewinsky case in order to illuminate what occurred between Monroe and JFK. My point is this: the rise of the postmodern incredulity toward metanarrative necessitated a more empirically rooted and historically specific literary symbol, which, in part, explains the rise and legitimization of biofiction, an aesthetic form that requires readers to use the inductive rather than the deductive imagination in order to understand the author's social, political, and cultural critique. With regard to Oates' fiction, *Blonde* is a much more compelling critique of white male liberals than Oates' *Black Water*, because she avoids the charge of using the fictive imagination to concoct a sexist character (traditional literary symbol) that functions like an ahistorical Truth. By naming names and fictionalizing factual figures, Oates produces a searing portrait that is much more difficult to dismiss as the product of a paranoid or a runaway imagination. And by inviting readers to use the inductive imagination to link the white male liberals of the 1960s and the 1990s, Oates makes her implicit argument and cultural critique both persuasive and relevant. The shift from the deductive to the inductive imagination not only makes logical sense, but it is also a necessary aesthetic move in a postmodern age for contemporary writers who want to continue in their role as the culture's most insightful social critics.

We are now in a position to offer an alternative way of thinking about the emergence of biofiction. Lodge interprets its rise as a "declining faith or loss of confidence in the power of purely fictional narrative." But for many biographical novelists, given crucial developments in postmodernism, Lodge's belief in pure fiction is naïve and incoherent. To understand why, it is important to take into account the collapse of the fact/fiction binary. In the nineteenth century, when history became an institutionalized discipline that conceived of itself as a science, it distanced itself from literature by expanding and hardening the dichotomy between fact and fiction. Within this framework, historical fact became more dogmatically factual while imaginative fiction became more fantastically fictional.[89]

Postmodernists reversed this process, which we see most clearly in my interview with Cunningham about *The Hours*. Challenging the "questionable faith in the accuracy of history as written," Cunningham rejects the idea of something like categorical "*fact*," because "we're subjective, by nature."[90] As such, the human subjective always plays a role in the formation of fact, thus rendering fact more subjective and fictional than many previously thought or were willing to admit. It is worth noting that Cunningham is not solely interested in shattering the idea of hardcore fact. Given the embedded nature of the human condition, he also exposes the

---

[89]For a more detailed analysis of the history of history, see Hayden White's *Metahistory: The Historical Imagination in Nineteenth-Century Europe*; George G. Iggers' *Historiography in the Twentieth Century*; and Beverley Southgate's *History Meets Fiction*.
[90]Cunningham (2014), "The Biographical Novel and the Complexity of Postmodern Interiors," *Truthful Fictions: Conversations with American Biographical Novelists.* Editor and Interviewer Michael Lackey. London and New York: Bloomsbury, 89.

notion of pure fiction as incoherent nonsense. When discussing the construction of a fictional character, Cunningham says: "I don't see a particularly clear or easily-drawn line between fact and fiction."[91] This is the case because "fiction writers work from" their "experience of the world and the people who inhabit it."[92] Some writers, Cunningham continues, seek "to disguise that which" they have "seen and heard." But the reality is that "fiction can only arise out of what a writer has seen and heard." To be more specific: "The mother in a novel may be more like the writer's actual mother, or less like her, but she pretty much inevitably comes from the writer's relationship with a mother."[93]

This postmodern approach clearly poses a challenge to Dee's and Lodge's view that the rise of the biographical novel indicates a growing disbelief in pure fiction, because the collapsing borders between fact and fiction ultimately render the idea of pure fiction incoherent. So while Joseph Conrad's Kurtz in *Heart of Darkness*, F. Scott Fitzgerald's Daisy in *The Great Gatsby*, and Virginia Woolf's Mr. Ramsay in *To the Lighthouse* appear to be pure fictional creations, we in the postmodern era know that Kurtz is based on Léon Rom, that Daisy is based on Ginevra King, and that Mr. Ramsay is based on Leslie Stephen.[94] Disguising the figures by giving them different names produces the illusion that authors have invented purely fictional characters. But the postmodern reality is that these seemingly pure inventions are empirically rooted and historically based. Thus, when it comes to the construction of a fictional character, the major difference between Cunningham's creation of Virginia Woolf and Woolf's creation of Mr. Ramsay is that Cunningham named his character after the actual figure, while Woolf concealed the identity of the person on which the character is based by changing the name. In essence, biographical novelists are simply more transparent than most novelists in that

---

[91]Cunningham (2014), 90.

[92]Ibid.

[93]Ibid.

[94]For a discussion of Rom as the basis for Kurtz, see Adam Hochschild's *King Leopold's Ghost: A Story of Greed, Terror, and Heroism in Colonial Africa*, 140–9. For a discussion of King as the basis for Daisy, see James L. W. West's *The Perfect Hour: The Romance of F. Scott Fitzgerald and Ginevra King, His First Love*. For a discussion of Stephen as the basis for Mr. Ramsay, see my essay "Modernist Anti-Philosophicalism and Virginia Woolf's Critique of Philosophy."

they reveal the source of their characters by naming them after the actual historical figures.

While I have been trying to provide a definitional framework for the biographical novel in this introductory chapter, it would be a mistake to think that there is a Platonic form that can capture the essence of all biographical novels. A better way to think about the genre is in terms of a steady progression in the form's evolution, which we see most clearly through the biographical novels about Eliza Lynch, an Irish woman who was the companion of Francisco Solano López, president of Paraguay from 1862 until 1870. William E. Barrett authored the first biographical novel (*Woman on Horseback*) about Lynch in 1938, and in his foreword, Barrett insists that his work is faithful to the historical record: "In the preparation of 'Woman on Horseback,' I discarded many romantic legends which would have delighted a novelist and which would have outraged fact. In the writing, I have been faithful to time and place and sequence; in no case distorting the true chronology of events for dramatic effect."[95] Taking liberties with the established facts in his biographical novel is not an option for Barrett. But by the year 2002, Anne Enright has a much different epistemological orientation toward her subject matter. As she says in the acknowledgments to her biographical novel *The Pleasure of Eliza Lynch*: "Eliza Lynch seems to provoke in her English-speaking biographers all kinds of sneering excess. Some facts seem to remain constant and it is around these facts that this (scarcely less fictional) account has been built. This is a novel, however. It is Not True."[96] Facts, for Enright, partake of the fictional, which is why her novel is "scarcely less fictional" than the seemingly factual studies on which *The Pleasure of Eliza Lynch* is based. This is a postmodern move that Barrett's approach precludes. But more importantly, Enright feels free to assert her rights as a creative writer, to use the life of Lynch in order to create a "novel" that "is Not True." Lily Tuck makes a similar claim in her Eliza Lynch novel *The News from Paraguay*. In her "Author's Notes," Tuck claims that she "tried to keep to historical facts where" she found "them to be important and necessary." But given that many events that occurred "are complicated and, for the most part,

---

[95]Barrett (1938), *Woman on Horseback: The Biography of Francisco Lopez and Eliza Lynch*. New York: Frederick A. Stokes Company, viii.
[96]Enright (2003), *The Pleasure of Eliza Lynch*. London: Vintage Books, 231.

not well known," Tuck unapologetically invents. This leads her to make the following disclaimer: "What then, the reader may wonder, is fact and what is fiction? My general rule of thumb is whatever seems most improbable is probably true." To bring into sharp focus the philosophy undergirding her approach, Tuck quotes a friend of hers: "Nouns always trump adjectives, and in the phrase 'historical fiction' it is important to remember which of the two words is which."[97] The noun signifies what an object is, so if we call a work a "fictional biography," then we are talking about a biography. But as Tuck insists, what she writes is fiction. Problematic, of course, is that Tuck refers to her book as historical rather than biographical fiction. But if we attend to Lukács' definitions of the historical and the biographical novel and the evolution of the biographical novel over the last eighty years, then it would make more sense to call *The News from Paraguay* a biographical rather than a historical novel.

We can now say with confidence that the biographical novel has officially arrived. Consider, for instance, the stellar writers who have authored such works in just the last thirty years: Bruce Duffy, Jay Parini, Joanna Scott, J. M. Coetzee, Margaret Atwood, Julia Alvarez, Thomas Pynchon, Michael Cunningham, Russell Banks, Joyce Carol Oates, Colm Tóibín, Anne Enright, Lance Olsen, Emma Donoghue, Jerome Charyn, Colum McCann, Laurent Binet, and Hilary Mantel. However, despite the stunning output from such notable writers, we still struggle to understand why this aesthetic form came into being, what exactly it is, and how it uniquely pictures the historical and engages the political. Therefore, in the following pages, I provide some answers to these questions. In Chapter 2, I do a contrastive analysis of Ray Monk's *Ludwig Wittgenstein: The Duty of Genius* and Duffy's *The World As I Found It* in order to clarify how the traditional biographer and the biographical novelist engage their subject in radically different ways. In Chapter 3, I do an analysis of Parini's *Benjamin's Crossing* and Olsen's *Nietzsche's Kisses* in order to show how a rejection of positivism (historical, philosophical, psychological, and scientific) and the rise of surrealism necessitated a new form of the historical novel, which is the biographical novel. In Chapter 4, I illustrate how two of Hurston's biographical novels function to critique the

---

[97]Tuck (2005), *The News from Paraguay*. New York: Perennial, 247.

contemporary political situation in ways more profound than other political novels. In Chapter 5, I examine three biographical novels about slavery that expose the sociopolitical structures of oppression from both the past and the present. In the final chapter, I address the ethics of the biographical novel, and I develop a preliminary and provisional model for defining ethical and unethical usages of an actual figure's life.

It should be noted, however, that what I do in this book is not to be considered exhaustive. The contemporary biographical novel is one of the richest and most promising aesthetic innovations of the last fifty years, and we are still trying to come to terms with its uncanny power to simultaneously picture the past and the present and to critique the political. Contemporary writers have only started to harness the power of this aesthetic form, and it will take scholars years before they will be able to clearly document and assess the genre's value and importance in giving us an accurate picture of ourselves and advancing the democratic promise of social justice. My objective with this study has been to initiate a more focused conversation.

2

The fictional truth of the biographical novel: The case of Ludwig Wittgenstein

On the most basic level, the difference between a standard biography and a biographical novel is the usage of fictional techniques, characters, and scenes. The biographer seeks to represent the subject's life as accurately as possible, and while many writers of the late twentieth century readily acknowledge that all writing is fiction because it entails an arbitrary selection or organization of specific facts and a willful deletion or accentuation of certain details, there is a difference between the inevitable fictionalization inherent within all writing and the strategic invention in a novel.[1] For example, in the wonderful biography *Ludwig Wittgenstein: The Duty of Genius*,

---

[1] In literary circles, E. L. Doctorow made the case in 1977 that history is fiction most passionately and convincingly in his essay "False Documents," in which he claims "that there is no fiction or nonfiction as we commonly understand the distinction: there is only narrative" (231). This, of course, is the view of the historian Hayden White, whose books *Metahistory*, *The Content of the Form*, and *Tropics of Discourse* had such an enormous impact on scholars in a wide variety of disciplines. For scholarly studies that examine the epistemological developments that led to the view that history is fiction, see Barbara Foley's *Telling the Truth: The Theory and Practice of Documentary Fiction*; Linda Hutcheon's *A Poetics of Postmodernism: History, Theory, Fiction*; Beverley Southgate's *History Meets Fiction*; and Judith Ryan's *The Novel after Theory*. For a discussion of the way this development made the contemporary biographical novel possible, see my introduction to *Truthful Fictions*.

Ray Monk briefly discusses Wittgenstein's Viva (June 18, 1929), the oral examination that G. E. Moore and Bertrand Russell conducted in order to determine whether Wittgenstein's work (*Tractatus Logico-Philosophicus*) would qualify him for a Ph.D. There is no record of the discussion, so Monk's description of the event consists of a short paragraph that states only what documentary evidence permits.[2] By stark contrast, in the spectacular biographical novel *The World As I Found It*, Bruce Duffy gives readers eight dense pages of information describing the Viva, which includes tense exchanges among all three philosophers and comical depictions of Russell's sexual obsession with a young woman.[3] In this instance, what makes Duffy's work a novel instead of a biography is the fact that he consciously and strategically invents a scene, which is something that a prominent biographer like Monk would never do.[4]

Given this simple distinction, we could say that the two genres have radically different objectives (one to accurately represent what actually happened, the other to fictionally create an unknown scene), and consequently, there must be divergent criteria for assessing the quality and success of each. My task in this chapter is to define some of the distinctive features of the biographical novel, specifying what it is uniquely suited to picture and achieve. To that end, I will contrast Monk's biography and Duffy's biographical novel. I have selected these two because they are both exemplary. Duffy's novel was published in 1987, and it won the Whiting Writer's Award and was republished in 2010 as a New York Review Books classic. Monk's biography was published in 1990, and it won the John Llewellyn Rhys Prize and the Duff Cooper Award.

I

Doing an exhaustive, section-by-section contrastive analysis of both works would prove tedious and of limited value, so in what follows I focus on one striking feature of Wittgenstein's life, which

---

[2]Monk (1990), *Ludwig Wittgenstein: The Duty of Genius*. New York: The Free Press, 271.
[3]Duffy (2010), *The World As I Found It*. New York: New York Review Books, 463–71.
[4]For a clear statement of Monk's approach to biography, see his essay "Philosophical Biography: The Very Idea."

is of considerable importance for both Monk and Duffy. The issue is anti-Semitism. At two separate points in his life, Wittgenstein displayed a heightened consciousness about his Jewish heritage. The first period occurred in 1931, when Wittgenstein penned numerous comments about Jews, some of which are highly offensive. The second occurred in late 1936 and early 1937, when Wittgenstein made a confession to a number of his friends. One of his confessed "sins" was his failure to acknowledge that he was of Jewish descent.[5] Monk and Duffy offer radically different views of these two periods in Wittgenstein's life and, consequently, their works give readers divergent perspectives of the philosopher's life, culture, and time.

The difference is not just in terms of content, but also in the way the two engage and use primary source material. Take, for instance, one of the anti-Semitic passages from Wittgenstein's notebooks. According to the 1931 Wittgenstein, Jewish thinkers can be talented, but they cannot be geniuses: "Even the greatest of Jewish thinkers is no more than talented (Myself for instance.)."[6] This is the case because they lack the capacity to originate a new system of thinking. At most, Jews can only imitate and reproduce what others have thought. As Wittgenstein writes:

> I think there is some truth in my idea that I really only think reproductively. I don't believe I have ever *invented* a line of thinking, I have always taken one over from someone else. I have simply straightaway seized on it with enthusiasm for my work of clarification. That is how Boltzmann, Hertz, Frege, Russell, Kraus, Loos, Weininger, Sraffa have influenced me. Can one take the case of Breuer and Freud as an example of Jewish reproductiveness?[7]

Wittgenstein is not saying that Jews lack an intellectual capacity. He is merely saying that they can reproduce what others have said, but that they cannot invent a new or original line of thinking. To

---

[5]There has been much criticism regarding Wittgenstein's comments about Jews. For some of the most insightful work on this topic, see David Stern's "Was Wittgenstein a Jew?" and Bela Szabados' "Was Wittgenstein an Anti-Semite? The Significance for Wittgenstein's Philosophy."
[6]Wittgenstein (1984), *Culture and Value*. Translated by Peter Winch. Chicago: University of Chicago Press, 18e.
[7]Wittgenstein (1984), 18e–19e.

punctuate his point, Wittgenstein concludes the section by seemingly complimenting Jews: "It is typical for a Jewish mind to understand someone else's work better than he understands it himself."[8] For Wittgenstein, Jews excel with regard to basic comprehension, but as for originating a system of thought, they falter, which is why they cannot be geniuses.

To his credit, Monk does not gloss over or minimize Wittgenstein's anti-Semitic remarks. But he does circumscribe their range of reference by saying that they are only directed at Wittgenstein: "His remarks on Jewishness were fundamentally introspective. They represent a turning inwards of the sense of cultural decay and the desire for a New Order . . . to his own internal state."[9] In other words, there is evidence that Wittgenstein is an anti-Semite, but there is no evidence that his anti-Semitism impacted the way he understood or related to Jews other than himself.

Duffy engages the same primary source, but he puts it to a much different use. In the late twenties, after having turned his back on philosophy for nearly a decade, Wittgenstein briefly got involved with the Vienna Circle, a philosophical group that adopted what it considered some of the core ideas in Wittgenstein's *Tractatus*. The leader of the group was Moritz Schlick, who believed it was important to get the former Austrian philosopher's thoughts on paper and into print. Therefore, he introduced Wittgenstein to the young Jewish philosopher, Friedrich Waismann, whose job was to assist Wittgenstein in publishing his work. Duffy clearly uses the 1931 anti-Semitic passages from the notebooks to portray Wittgenstein's views of and interactions with Waismann. After working for a couple years on a book project with the Jewish philosopher, Duffy's Wittgenstein concludes that "Waismann was brilliant and capable, certainly, but otherwise unoriginal. But then this was not altogether surprising, since Waismann was a Jew. As Wittgenstein saw it, it was part of the Jewish nature to understand another man's work better than he himself understood it."[10] Duffy is certainly on solid ground in putting these anti-Semitic words into Wittgenstein's mouth. But if we accept Monk's reading of the primary source from which these comments are taken, then it would be inappropriate and even

---

[8]Wittgenstein (1984), 18e.
[9]Monk (1990), 316.
[10]Duffy (2010), 474–5.

THE FICTIONAL TRUTH OF THE BIOGRAPHICAL NOVEL   39

illegitimate for Duffy to have Wittgenstein apply them to a Jew other than himself.

At this point, let me briefly indicate one of the primary differences between the two genres. Through a close analysis of primary source material, the biographer (Monk) specifies what Wittgenstein's anti-Semitic remarks say (that Wittgenstein considered Jews incapable of originating a system of thought) and do not say (that Wittgenstein's anti-Semitism impacted how he understood and/or interacted with Jews other than himself). Monk does not rule out the possibility that anti-Semitism played a role in Wittgenstein's views of or relations with Jews. He merely claims that Wittgenstein's comments in the notebooks are directed exclusively at himself.

The biographical novelist (Duffy), by contrast, uses the primary source material in order to construct and define a character structure (Wittgenstein's). He subsequently uses that definition in order to imagine how that character (Wittgenstein) would have interacted with others. According to this framework, if Wittgenstein adopted anti-Semitic views, then it would only follow that such views would have colored his perceptions of and impacted his behavior with a particular Jew, such as Waismann. Therefore, when Duffy portrays Wittgenstein's relationship with Waismann, he uses the anti-Semitic comments from the notebooks to construct the scene.

Had Duffy merely used the comments from the notebooks to suggest that anti-Semitism affected Wittgenstein's relationship with Waismann, there would be little reason for objecting, for it is entirely plausible that Wittgenstein's anti-Semitic views impacted his relationship with and understanding of Waismann. After all, Wittgenstein speculates that his view of Jews could explain Josef Breuer and Sigmund Freud. But Duffy does not just suggest that Wittgenstein's anti-Semitism had a poisonous impact on a personal relationship. He goes much further by suggesting that Wittgenstein unwittingly aligned himself with or inadvertently contributed to the making of the Nazis. To do this, Duffy invents the captivating character of Max Einer, a friend of Wittgenstein's who becomes a Nazi late in the novel. Like Wittgenstein, Max was in the First World War, where he became enamored of "the mystical."[11] But unlike Wittgenstein, Max comes from a poor and uneducated background.

---

[11] Duffy (2010), 403.

It is in and through his conversations with Max about Waismann that Duffy's Wittgenstein has the most insidious effect. By this point in the novel, Max has expressed many of his anti-Semitic sentiments, which have been quickly dismissed. But when Wittgenstein explains to Max how Waismann's intellectual limitations derive from his Jewish nature, Wittgenstein gives Max a formal and comprehensive anti-Semitic discourse. Note how Duffy pictures this interaction:

> *Jewish reproductiveness*—this was how Wittgenstein termed this characteristic one day in conversation with Max. It was an ill-considered and irresponsible remark, and Wittgenstein immediately regretted having said it in Max's presence. Certainly, Wittgenstein did not mean for Max to view it as being in any way in sympathy with the various racial theories that were then surfacing with renewed vigor. But it was too late.[12]

What makes this episode so chilling and troubling is the fact that it is in a chapter titled "Heirs." The suggestion is this: Wittgenstein has many heirs, like Schlick, Waismann, and the Vienna Circle, but also Max. To underscore Wittgenstein's contribution to the making of the Nazis, late in the novel Duffy calls the reader's attention to Wittgenstein's influence on Max, who is by this time a member of the SS: "Wittgenstein's past was seeping over him with thoughts of Max, the radical, self-anointed Christian wearing SS death's heads."[13] For those who admire and respect Wittgenstein and his work, Duffy's decision to create Max in order to suggest that Wittgenstein contributed to the making of the Nazis could only be considered high-order blasphemy. But the real question that we need to pose at this point is this: Is there any substance or justification in Duffy's suggestion?

This is not an absurd question, for as Monk notes, Wittgenstein's anti-Semitic remarks in 1931 bear a striking resemblance to Hitler's comments about Jews in *Mein Kampf*.[14] What makes Duffy more extreme than Monk, however, is the idea that Wittgenstein contributed to the making of the Nazis, which is symbolically represented through the character of Max. To clarify why we should

---

[12]Duffy (2010), 475.
[13]Duffy (2010), 510.
[14]Monk (1990), 313–14.

take Duffy seriously, I need to provide a background framework for understanding the Nazis' particular version of anti-Semitism.

II

The most succinct formulation of Nazi anti-Semitism, and the one that makes most sense in relation to Wittgenstein, can be found in point 24 of the Nazi Party program, which reads: "The Party as such represents the standpoint of a positive Christianity, without tying itself to a particular confession. It fights the spirit of Jewish materialism within us and without us."[15] For those unfamiliar with Nazi ideology, the claim in this passage might strike them as totally irrelevant to Wittgenstein. But for those who know the ideology that went into the making of point 24, precisely how this claim directly relates to the Austrian philosopher will be clearly evident.

The idea in point 24 is central to the writings of many prominent Nazis, but in this chapter I will focus on only two: Dietrich Eckart and Adolf Hitler. Of crucial importance is the phrase "Jewish materialism" (den jüdisch-materialistischen Geist), the opposite of which is not German idealism, but Christian idealism.[16] To understand the way the Nazis defined Christian idealism, we need to trace the idea back to its source, which can be found in its most rudimentary form in the writings of Immanuel Kant. As an Enlightenment rationalist, Kant favored the rise of science and logic as a method for making sense of the world. But he rejected the view that science exhausted or could exhaust our understanding of the world. Therefore, Kant made a distinction between the mechanistic world and that which transcends the mechanistic laws of natural necessity. To be more specific, humans are determined by the mechanistic laws of natural necessity, and as such, they

---

[15]Quoted in Richard Steigmann-Gall (2003), *The Holy Reich: Nazi Conceptions of Christianity, 1919–1945.* Cambridge: Cambridge University Press, 14.
[16]For studies that examine the influence German idealism had on Nazi ideology, see Berel Lang's *Act and Idea in the Nazi Genocide*; Roderick Stackelberg's *Idealism Debased: From Voelkisch Ideology to National Socialism*; and Michael Mack's *German Idealism and the Jew: The Inner Anti-Semitism of Philosophy and German Jewish Responses.* For a discussion of the role Christian idealism played in the making of Nazi ideology, see my book *The Modernist God State: A Literary Study of the Nazis' Christian Reich.*

inhabit the empirical world. In the empirical world, the physical and psychological laws of existence predetermine how humans think and behave, which is why Kant argues in the *Critique of Practical Reason* that humans are subject to the "mechanism of nature."[17] In short, nature "is the existence of things under law," which is "the direct opposite of freedom."[18] While Kant believes that humans are, in large measure, determined by the inexorable laws inherent within the empirical world's mechanism of nature, he also holds that humans can, at times, experience "freedom and independence from the mechanism of nature,"[19] an act that enables them to access and enter the intelligible world. Humans achieve this by behaving as autonomous moral agents, behavior that is possible because humans are capable of experiencing two separate and distinct types of freedom. In Kantian terms, to be free, humans must restrain and even overcome their selfish and materialistic inclinations, for "inclination, be it good-natured or otherwise, is blind and slavish."[20] The moment humans overcome inclination, they experience what Kant refers to as negative freedom, an act that, in part, enables them to sacrifice self-interest (inclination) for a higher good. More difficult and demanding is positive freedom, which consists of acting as a self-legislating agent. Through positive freedom, humans can transcend the world of sense and thereby evade determinism by legislating to themselves the moral law. In essence, positive freedom implies a creative imposition upon the world, an act that enables people to overcome environmental determinism (the Nazis will define this as materialism) insofar as they determine their environment rather than being determined by it.

In his book *Religion within the Limits of Reason Alone*, Kant uses his empirical/intelligible distinction in order to define Judaism and Christianity in oppositional terms. For Kant, it is in the person of Christ that autonomy is born, which is why his birth symbolizes a total rupture with Judaism. As Kant claims, "Of all the public religions which have ever existed, the Christian alone is moral," because Christianity consists "not in dogmas and rites

[17]Kant (1993), *Critique of Practical Reason*. Translated by Lewis White Beck. Upper Saddle River, New Jersey: Prentice Hall, 101.
[18]Kant (1993), 29, 44.
[19]Kant (1993), 90.
[20]Kant (1993), 124.

but in the heart's disposition to fulfill all human duties as divine commands."[21] As the Nazis would do in the party program, Kant defines Christianity most clearly by pitting it against Judaism, which never rises to the level of a religion, because it is steeped in the empirical (the material) rather than the intelligible world:

> The *Jewish faith* was, in its original form, a collection of mere statutory laws upon which was established a political organization; for whatever moral additions were then or later *appended* to it in no way whatever belong to Judaism as such. Judaism is really not a religion at all but merely a union of a number of people who, since they belonged to a particular stock, formed themselves into a commonwealth under purely political laws, and not into a church.[22]

Nothing in Judaism inspires believers to behave as autonomous moral agents, because the faith is based on the Ten Commandments ("statutory laws"), which merely require blind obedience and "mechanical worship." In essence, Judaism is a purely materialistic faith (hence, not a religion), which can never rise above the world of sense and thereby enter the intelligible world. This explains why Christianity should be understood not as an extension of Judaism but as "completely forsaking the Judaism from which it sprang."[23] Christianity, as a form and instance of idealism, requires the ability to transcend the mechanistically determined world through morally autonomous action, whereas Judaism, as a form and instance of materialism, is totally determined by the mechanistic laws of being, which is why the birth of Christ signifies a decisive rupture with Judaism.

The strict distinction between materialism and idealism became the basis for determining who is fully human and who is not. In the *Critique of Practical Reason*, Kant explicitly claims that humans rise above animality, and thereby realize humanness, only insofar as they activate practical reason through negative or positive freedom. If humans, as beings belonging to the sensuous (empirical) world,

---

[21]Kant (1960), *Religion within the Limits of Reason Alone*. Translated by Theodore M. Greene and Hoyt H. Hudson. New York: Harper Torchbooks, 47, 79.
[22]Kant (1960), 116.
[23]Kant (1960), 118.

are animalistic insofar as they are mechanistically determined by the antecedent conditions of being and the inexorable laws of nature, then humans, as beings belonging to the intelligible world, are more than animal insofar as they activate practical reason and thereby transcend the antecedent conditions of being and the mechanistic laws of natural necessity. It is important to note that Kant does not just say that humans are more than animal because they have the *potential* to act as autonomous moral agents. His claim is stronger. A person must actually *activate the faculty of practical reason* in order to rise above animality and thereby realize humanness:

> That he [a person] has reason does not in the least raise him in worth above mere animality if reason serves only the purposes which, among animals, are taken care of by instinct; if this were so, reason would be only a specific way nature had made use of to equip man for the same purpose for which animals are qualified, without fitting him for any higher purpose.[24]

Activating practical reason through the moral law, thus allowing one to transcend the mechanistic laws of natural necessity, is what enables a person to realize full-fledged humanness, which is why Kant concludes that "the moral law reveals a life independent of all animality and even of the world of sense."[25] Contrariwise, those "humans" who never activate the faculty of practical reason by behaving as moral and, therefore, free agents, belong exclusively to the world of sense and are either totally animalistic or more animal than human.

Prominent Nazis such as Eckart, Alfred Rosenberg, and Adolf Eichmann read Kant,[26] but most people from the Nazi period,

---

[24]Kant (1993), 64.
[25]Kant (1993), 169.
[26]In *The Myth of the Twentieth Century: An Evaluation of the Spiritual-Intellectual Confrontations of Our Age*, Rosenberg claims that Kant's religious philosophy was so popular with the Germans that "Kant's words" about "the starry heavens above us and the moral law within us" (an allusion to the conclusion of *Critique of Practical Reason*) are in danger of being "reduced to triviality" (197). That Rosenberg's observation has some merit is clear from comments Adolf Eichmann made at his trial. During a police examination, Eichmann "declared with great emphasis that he had lived his whole life according to Kant's moral precepts, and especially according to a Kantian definition of duty" (qtd. in Arendt [2006], 135).

including Nazi elites, derived their view of Kant mainly from Houston Stewart Chamberlain, who is considered "the 'spiritual founder' of National Socialist Germany,"[27] which is why Paul Gilroy rightly claims that "we can interpret Chamberlain's work as he wanted it to be understood: as a strong bridge between Kant and Hitler."[28] It is this link between Kant and the Nazis that has led prominent scholars to say that the German philosopher bears some responsibility for the Holocaust. As Berel Lang says: "Certain ideas prominent in the Enlightenment [and he specifies Kant] are recognizable in the conceptual framework embodied in the Nazi genocide."[29] Or, as Charles W. Mills claims: "*The embarrassing fact for the white West (which doubtless explains its concealment) is that their most important moral theorist* [Kant] *of the past three hundred years is also the foundational theorist in the modern period of the division between* Herrenvolk *and* Untermenschen, *persons and subpersons, upon which Nazi theory would later draw.*"[30] In 1899, Chamberlain published *The Foundations of the Nineteenth Century*, a book that was subsequently hailed "as the 'gospel of the Nazi movement'"[31] in the Nazis' official newspaper, the *Völkischer Beobachter*. This two-volume work was immensely popular, selling more than a quarter of a million copies by 1938.[32] Given Chamberlain's comprehensive vision of religion, politics, and Germany, Rosenberg "hailed him as a pioneer and spiritual forerunner and viewed himself as Chamberlain's true successor."[33] In 1923, Joseph Goebbels read the *Foundations*, and when he met Chamberlain in 1926, he indicates in his diary how important Chamberlain was to National Socialism by referring to

---

[27]Shirer (1960), *The Rise and Fall of the Third Reich: A History of Nazi Germany*. New York: Simon and Schuster, 158.

[28]Gilroy (2001), *Against Race: Imagining Political Culture Beyond the Color Line*. Harvard University Press, 63.

[29]Lang (2003), *Act and Idea in the Nazi Genocide*. Syracuse: Syracuse University Press, 168–9.

[30]Mills (1997), *The Racial Contract*. Ithaca: Cornell University Press, 72. Mills' emphasis.

[31]Shirer (1960), 159.

[32]Shirer (1960), 156.

[33]Field (1981), *Evangelist of Race: The Germanic Vision of Houston Stewart Chamberlain*. New York: Columbia University Press, 1.

him as a "spiritual father," dubbing him a "Trail blazer, pioneer!"[34] Chamberlain's biographer, Geoffrey G. Field, notes that Hitler read the *Foundations*.[35] But more importantly, Field indicates how crucial Chamberlain was by describing Hitler's response to the famous writer's public endorsement. After getting word of Chamberlain's support, members at the Nazi Party headquarters in Munich were euphoric, and Hitler was so giddy that he was supposedly "'like a child.'"[36]

Chamberlain follows Kant by using the empirical/intelligible distinction to define Jews, and the consequences are dire. As Chamberlain claims: "Following up the differentiation Kant was enabled to make the epoch-making assertion: 'Religion we must seek in ourselves, not outside ourselves.' That means, when we change it to the terms of our definition: Religion we must seek only in the world which cannot be interpreted mechanically."[37] That Chamberlain considers this approach to religion the logical product of Kant's understanding of Christ and Christianity he makes clear in his book *Immanuel Kant*: "Kant's doctrine of religion is no more and no less than the proof in detail, and the methodical development, of Christ's doctrine—'Behold! The Kingdom of God is within you.'"[38] Within Christian idealism, the nonmechanically interpreted world is Kant's intelligible world, the very world that Jews can never access or inhabit because of their inability to transcend their biology or conditioning through negative or positive freedom. This mechanical/nonmechanical distinction explains the gaping abyss that separates Judaism from Christianity. Therefore, just as Kant claims that "the origin of Christianity" represents a "forsaking [of] the Judaism from which it sprang," Chamberlain says: "Whoever wishes to see the revelation of Christ must passionately tear this darkest of veils from his eyes. His advent is not the perfecting of the Jewish religion but its negation."[39] This is the case because Judaism is "the most materialistic—yes, assuredly the most materialistic—religion

---

[34]Goebbels (1962), *The Early Goebbels Diaries: 1925–1926*. Edited by Helmut Heiber. New York: Frederick A Praeger, 83.

[35]Field (1981), 452.

[36]Field (1981), 438.

[37]Chamberlain (1912), *The Foundations of the Nineteenth Century*. New York: John Lane Company, II.485.

[38]Chamberlain (1914), *Immanuel Kant*. New York: John Lane Company, II.411.

[39]Chamberlain (1912), I.221.

in the world."[40] In terms of Christian idealism, what Jews lack is the capacity to originate something new, for "the Jew has never distinguished himself by creative power, even in the limited sphere of religious legislation; indeed, what is most his own is borrowed."[41] Jews either passively allowed their religion to come into being or they imitated other religions, but they never exercised autonomy by creating a religion that was nonmechanistically determined, which is why Chamberlain draws the following conclusion: "Their [the Jews'] scanty mythically religious conceptions, indeed even their commandments, customs and ordinances of worship, they borrowed without exception from abroad, they reduced everything to a minimum which they kept rigidly unaltered; the creative element, the real inner life is almost totally wanting in them."[42] In essence, Chamberlain argues that, since the Jews have produced a purely materialistic "religion," we can infer that they are mere materialists. Therefore, Chamberlain concludes: "Wherever the Semitic spirit has breathed, we shall meet with this materialism. Elsewhere in the whole world religion is an idealistic impulse; Schopenhauer called it 'popular metaphysics'; I should rather call it popular idealism."[43]

According to the logic of this model, that which is mechanistically determined is nonreligious, while that which transcends the mechanistic universe is religious: "Science is the method, discovered and carried out by the Teutons, of mechanically looking at the world of phenomena; religion is their attitude towards that part of experience which does not appear in the shape of phenomena and therefore is incapable of mechanical interpretation."[44] What makes a human more than a mere machine is freedom in a Kantian sense. In other words, a being becomes more than animal when "he discovers in himself what Kant calls 'the spontaneity of freedom,' something utterly unmechanical and anti-mechanical."[45] Chamberlain's disciple, Rosenberg, best articulates the nature of Kant's distinction: "The Nordic spirit gained philosophical consciousness in Immanuel Kant whose fundamental achievement lies in the separation he established between forces of religion

---

[40]Chamberlain (1912), I.234.
[41]Chamberlain (1912), I.446.
[42]Chamberlain (1912), I.216.
[43]Chamberlain (1912), I.422.
[44]Chamberlain (1912), II.486.
[45]Chamberlain (1912), II.480.

and science. Religion is concerned with 'the kingdom of heaven within us,' true science only with physics, chemistry, biology and mechanics."[46] Science is concerned with superficial things such as the material world, and if science were the final word, then the human would be nothing more than a mechanized automaton or a mindless animal.

As I will demonstrate, this empirical/intelligible (materialism/ idealism) distinction had a decisive impact on Eckart, Hitler, the party program, and Otto Weininger, and it was through Weininger that Wittgenstein came to admire and adopt what would become the Nazis' anti-Semitic ideology, the very ideology expressed in point 24 of the party program and the 1931 passages in Wittgenstein's notebooks.

Eckart died in 1923, but he had a profound and lasting impact on National Socialism, which is seen most clearly from Hitler's decision to dedicate *Mein Kampf* to him (among the heroes of National Socialism, Hitler asserts in his concluding dedication, Eckart was "one of the best, who devoted his life to the awakening of his, our people, in his writing and his thoughts and finally in his deeds").[47] It would be safe to say that the phrase and content about the Jewish materialistic spirit in point 24 comes from Eckart. In 1919, Eckart published an essay in the journal *Auf gut Deutsch* (in plain German) with the title, "Das Judentum in und außer uns" ("Jewishness in and outside Us"). Here is how point 24 of the German program reads: "*Sie* [the Party] *bekämpft den jüdisch-materialistischen Geist in und außer uns*" ("the party fights the spirit of Jewish materialism in and outside us.") In his essay, Eckart argues that "*die Seele ist naturgemäß Christlich*" ("the soul is by nature Christian").[48] What enables him to draw this conclusion is Kant ("*wie Kant sich ausdrückt*"),[49] who has made a distinction between the empirical and the intelligible ("*in den empirischen und in den intelligiblen Charakter*").[50] As materialistic beings who lack any understanding of the intelligible world, Jews can only be

---

[46]Rosenberg (1993), 74.

[47]Hitler (1971), *Mein Kampf*. Translated by Ralph Manheim. Boston: Houghton Mifflin, 687.

[48]Eckart (1928), "*Das Judentum in und außer uns*," in *Dietrich Eckart: Ein Vermächtnis*. Editor Alfred Rosenberg. Munich: Franz Eher, 208.

[49]Eckart (1928), 206.

[50]Ibid.

categorized as enemies of that which transcends the material world. As Eckart claims:

> While the Jews still live among us, everything they do comes to this, and *must* come to this. Their goal is the despiritualization of mankind. Therefore they attempt to destroy every form behind which the living soul operates; because, as archmaterialists, they are of the insane opinion that the spiritual—only vaguely suspected by them—is connected as a matter of life and death with the form, and must be destroyed together with it.[51]

Within this framework, contact with materialistic Jews would do irreparable damage not just to individual Christians but to Christianity as such, which is why Eckart draws the following conclusion: "*Gerade aber die Vermanschung des christlichen Ideals mit dem jüdischen Materialismus schädigt, und zwar ganz allein, das **Christentum**"[52]* ("It is in particular the mish-mashing of Christian ideals with Jewish materialism that damages all by itself Christianity."). Given the particular effect Jewish materialism has on Christians and Christianity, the Nazis believe that they have only one choice, which is to expel the materialistic Jew from within and without. Hence, point 24 of the party program.

That Hitler considered National Socialism to be based on idealism and that he believed the movement successful because of its roots in idealism he makes clear in a 1935 speech. Many people, Hitler argues, fail to understand the reason why National Socialism rose to power so quickly, but this is because "they imagine that a people and a State are nothing but a lifeless machine."[53] Hitler obviously rejects this materialistic interpretation, for he believes that it is "the strength of idealism alone [that] has accomplished these acts which have moved the world." Indeed, he goes on to claim that the successes of National Socialism testify to the truth of idealism:

---

[51]Eckart (1978), "Jewishness in and around Us: Fundamental Reflections," in *Nazi Ideology before 1933: A Documentation*. Editors Barbara Miller Lane and Leila J. Rupp. Austin and London: University of Texas Press, 25. I cite Lane and Rupp because they have included excerpts from Eckart's essay in their book. The German passages that I cite and translate are not included in the Lane/Rupp edition.
[52]Eckart (1928), 204. Eckart's emphasis.
[53]Hitler (1941), *My New Order*. Edited by Raoul de Roussy de Sales. New York: Reynal and Hitchcock: September 13, 1935, 337.

"Were any yet greater proof needed of the might of idealism, it can be found in this Movement." So successful has National Socialism been that Hitler, when reflecting on the then-current situation in Germany, can only gush about idealism: "What idealism it was—but what a force lay in that idealism."[54]

Without understanding Hitler's commitment to idealism, it is simply impossible to grasp his anti-Semitic approach to history and politics. We first see this in a 1919 outline of an unpublished book, part of which would make its way into *Mein Kampf*. According to Hitler, the projected book would begin with the Bible, and here is how he characterizes the first part: "The Bible—Monumental History of Mankind—2. Viewpoints—Idealism—Materialism."[55] For Hitler, the Bible provides the world with a monumental history of humanity, for it pictures from beginning to end the two most decisive viewpoints, which are idealism and materialism. Later in the outline, Hitler translates this idealism/materialism binary into "Christianity and Bolshevism."[56] In essence, Hitler reads all of political history through the lens of Christian idealism, which leads him to believe that the battle in his day is between communist Russia and Christian Germany.

In defining idealism, Hitler is quick to distance it from any overly sentimental philosophy, claiming "that idealism does not represent a superfluous expression of emotion." Quite the contrary, it is "the premise for what we designate as human culture," which is why "it alone created the concept of 'man'!"[57] According to this model, humanness, in the strict sense of the word, is defined in terms of freedom. When Hitler first introduces the concept of idealism in *Mein Kampf*, he specifically defines it in relation to negative freedom. After briefly discussing how the German conception of duty means serving the community rather than the self, Hitler defines idealism by distinguishing it from egoism. Within this framework, animals are material beings, governed solely by egoistic inclination and desire, so sacrificing self-interest for the good of the community is simply out

---

[54]Hitler (1941), 338.
[55]Hitler (1974), *Hitler's Letters and Notes*. Edited by Werner Maser. Translated by Arnold Pomerans. New York, Evanston, San Francisco, and London: Harper & Row, 283.
[56]Hitler (1974), 286.
[57]Hitler (1971), 298–99.

of the question. Given the logic of Hitler's claim, those who cannot experience negative freedom are more animal than human, a point Hitler makes most clearly in a discussion about egoism: "Egoism, as we designate this urge, goes so far that it even embraces time; the moment itself claims everything, granting nothing to the coming hours. In this condition the animal lives only for himself, seeks food only for his present hunger, and fights only for his own life."[58] Immersed in and governed by the temporal, the animal can never imagine the world beyond the present moment. In other words, because the materialist ego embraces only the temporal now, time mechanistically determines the ego. Translated into Kantian terms, a being is defined as animalistic insofar as he or she is mechanistically and materialistically determined by the laws of nature and the environment, a situation that leads to a bondage in and to time.

For Hitler, if idealism "alone created the concept of man,"[59] then the Jews would either be the lowest form of human on the great chain of being or they would not qualify as human in the strict sense of the word, because they lack "the idealistic attitude."[60] On the topic of negative freedom, Hitler is direct: "In the Jewish people the will to self-sacrifice does not go beyond the individual's naked instinct of self-preservation," which is why Hitler concludes that the Jew "lacks completely the most essential requirement for a cultured people, the idealistic attitude."[61] If, as Chamberlain argues, negative freedom is a prerequisite for a community, culture, and/or state to function, then the Jews' lack of the "idealistic attitude" would render the formation of such a community, culture, and/or state impossible. Hitler makes this point forcefully when he argues, like Chamberlain, that the Jews' enslavement to inclination leads necessarily to anarchy: "The Jew is only united when a common danger forces him to be or a common booty entices him; if these two grounds are lacking, the qualities of the crassest egoism come into their own, and in the twinkling of an eye the united people turns into a horde of rats, fighting bloodily among themselves."[62] Instead of subduing or renouncing individual inclination for the good of the

---

[58]Hitler (1971), 296–97.
[59]Hitler (1971), 299.
[60]Hitler (1971), 301.
[61]Ibid.
[62]Hitler (1971), 302.

larger community, something that Aryans supposedly do, "the Jew," Hitler concludes, "is led by nothing but the naked egoism of the individual,"[63] thus resulting in endless strife and anarchic confusion when material rewards are not available for uniting the community.

Negative freedom, however, is ultimately not enough, for, like Kant and Chamberlain, Hitler argues that positive freedom is vital. After mentioning Aryan achievements, Hitler underscores the positive dimension of idealism, which is manifested in acts of originality and creativity: "Without his idealistic attitude all, even the most dazzling faculties of the intellect, would remain mere intellect as such—outward appearance without inner value, and never creative force."[64] What endows intellect with inner value is antimechanical activity. Were a person to mechanistically create something of dazzling beauty, it would still lack inner value, because what makes a monument of unaging intellect have value and worth is "creative force," that which determines the environment rather than being determined by it. Insofar as something is merely a mechanical reproduction, it cannot have "inner value."

This lack of positive freedom explains the Jews' inability to create "monuments of human culture."[65] For instance, Jews can mechanistically reproduce what other cultures have accomplished, but they cannot produce a legitimate and lasting culture of their own, for as Hitler claims: "The Jew possesses no culture-creating force of any sort, since the idealism, without which there is no true higher development of man, is not present in him and never was present."[66] It should, therefore, come as no surprise that Hitler draws the following conclusion: "Hence the Jewish people, despite all apparent intellectual qualities, is without any true culture, and especially without any culture of its own."[67] After rehearsing these arguments about the Jews' lack of negative and positive freedom, Hitler draws what he considers the logical conclusion, that Jews cannot technically be dubbed human:

To what an extent the Jew takes over foreign culture, imitating or rather ruining it, can be seen from the fact that he is mostly

---

[63]Ibid.
[64]Hitler (1971), 299.
[65]Ibid.
[66]Hitler (1971), 303.
[67]Hitler (1971), 302.

found in the art which seems to require least original invention, the art of acting. But even here, in reality, he is only a "juggler," or rather an ape, for even here he lacks the last touch that is required for real greatness; even here he is not the creative genius, but a superficial imitator, and all the twists and tricks that he uses are powerless to conceal the inner lifelessness of his creative gift.[68]

Wittgenstein and Hitler agree that a Jew cannot be a "creative genius," but Hitler goes much further by suggesting that the Jew is more animal ("an ape") than human, because he lacks the idealistic attitude, an attitude that is necessary for a person to experience positive freedom and thereby become a full-fledged human.

After doing an extensive analysis of the Jews' non- and/or anti-idealistic attitude, Hitler draws his most important conclusion: "The Jew cannot possess a religious institution, if for no other reason because he lacks idealism in any form, and hence belief in a hereafter is absolutely foreign to him. And a religion in the Aryan sense cannot be imagined which lacks the conviction of survival after death in some form."[69] This passage would be nearly incomprehensible were readers unaware of the Christian idealism of Kant and Chamberlain. But for those who have read the work of both of these writers closely and carefully, Hitler's claim makes perfect sense. For both Kant and Chamberlain, Christ represents the birth of a new idea and the death of an old one. The old one is mechanical obedience to statutory laws, such as the Ten Commandments. As mindless automatons, Jews behave as servile beings who merely follow orders. Christ awakened within humanity the capacity for negative and positive freedom, the abilities to restrain or sacrifice selfish and materialistic inclination in the name of a higher communal good and to determine the environment through an act of culture-creating force. Within this framework, Jews did not accept Christ, because they are, "by nature," incapable of negative or positive freedom, an idea that Hitler derived from Chamberlain, who in turn derived it from Kant. It is for this reason that Hitler concludes: "The Jews are members of a *people* and not

---

[68]Hitler (1971), 303.
[69]Hitler (1971), 306.

of a 'religion.'"[70] Let me repeat Kant's formulation, as it bears a striking resemblance to Hitler's: "Judaism is really not a religion at all but merely a union of a number of people."

There is no evidence that Wittgenstein was influenced by or even read Hitler's *Mein Kampf*, but we do know that he read and admired Weininger's *Sex and Character*, which was heavily influenced by Chamberlain's Kantian model found in *The Foundations of the Nineteenth Century*—Weininger mentions Chamberlain many times in his book.[71] This explains why Wittgenstein's anti-Semitism bears such a striking resemblance to that of the Nazis. Weininger's whole book is based on Kant's empirical/intelligible distinction, which takes the form of Jewish materialism and Christian idealism in Nazi ideology. For Weininger, the human is defined as "he who, in addition to the empirical, conditioned existence, possesses a free, intelligible ego,"[72] an ego that Kant defines as unconditioned. That which is determined by the mechanistic laws of natural necessity belongs to the empirical world, while that which can and does transcend the mechanistic laws of natural necessity belongs to the intelligible world. Within this framework, there are certain disciplines that are devoted exclusively to the study and depiction of the empirical dimension of human being, such as biology, physics, and chemistry. By stark contrast, there are certain disciplines that are devoted primarily to the study and depiction of the intelligible dimension of human being, such as religion, ethics, and aesthetics.

The concept of genius enables Weininger to bring into sharp focus the nature of the distinction between the two approaches. For Weininger, unconditioned creativity is the mark of the genius,[73] the indication that a person "becomes the really divine spark in mankind."[74] In other words, only those beings that can transcend

---

[70]Ibid.

[71]Wittgenstein scholars generally acknowledge that Weininger had a major impact on Wittgenstein. For the best work on this connection, see Monk's *The Duty of Genius*, 19–25; Brian McGuinnes's *Wittgenstein: A Life: Young Ludwig 1889–1921*, 40–3; Rudolf Haller's "What do Wittgenstein and Weininger have in Common?," 90–9; and the essays in David G. Stern's and Bela Szabados' *Wittgenstein Reads Weininger*.

[72]Weininger (1906), *Sex and Character*. New York and Chicago: A. L. Burt Company, 279.

[73]Weininger (1906), 138.

[74]Weininger (1906), 171.

the mechanistic laws of natural necessity and thereby inhabit the intelligible world can be geniuses. Notice how Weininger distinguishes the two: "The 'timeless' men [geniuses] are those who make history, for history can be made only by those who are not floating with the stream. It is only those who are unconditioned by time who have real value, and whose productions have an enduring force."[75] Implicit in Weininger's comments is the claim that those beings that lack the capacity for genius merely float with the stream. They are carried along by the dominant current of thought. As for those beings with the capacity for genius, not only can they stand above and/or outside the dominant current of the time, but they can also determine the direction of the intellectual and historical stream.

Following Kant and Chamberlain and anticipating the Nazis and Wittgenstein, Weininger defines the Jews as pure materialists who have no capacity to transcend the empirical world, which means that Jews could never be geniuses. What compels Weininger to define genius in this way is his specific approach to religious subjectivity, which, as is the case with Chamberlain and the Nazis, links Christianity with idealism. For instance, when discussing separate approaches to morality, Weininger claims that the dominant one in Germany is "ethical individualism," which is "taught by Christianity and German idealism."[76] According to the logic of this model, it is in the person of Christ that unconditioned freedom is most fully incarnated. Of course, the problem of linking this ethical individualism with Christianity is that it leads to a radical form of opposing and even negating Judaism and the Jew. Therefore, with stunning predictability, Weininger replicates the anti-Semitic model found in Kant's *Religion within the Limits of Reason Alone*, Chamberlain's *Foundations*, Eckart's "Jewishness in and outside Us," point 24 of the party program, Hitler's *Mein Kampf*, and Wittgenstein's notebooks.

Describing "the psychical peculiarity of the Jewish race" in a chapter titled "Judaism," Weininger concludes that Jews "do not live as free, self-governing individuals, choosing between virtue and vice in the Aryan fashion."[77] This is the case because they lack both the

---

[75]Weininger (1906), 138.
[76]Weininger (1906), 176.
[77]Weininger (1906), 303, 309.

desire and capacity for transcendence, which is why Judaism does not qualify as a religion in the strict sense of the word. Weininger makes this point in a section that could have been written by Kant, Chamberlain, or Hitler. As Weininger claims: "It is inevitable, then, that we should find no trace of belief in immortality in the Old Testament. Those who have no soul can have no craving for immortality." Hence, "the absence from the Jew of true mysticism—Chamberlain has remarked on this—has a similar origin."[78] In essence, Judaism is a purely materialistic religion, which explains why Weininger poses the following question: "Why is it that the Jewish slave of Jehovah should become so readily a materialist or a freethinker?" The answer: "When it is fully recognised that Judaism is to be regarded rather as an idea in which other races have a share, than as the absolute property of a particular race, then the Judaic element in modern materialistic science will be better understood."[79] Jews cannot have anything that is exclusively their own, because, as beings with no desire or capacity for transcendence, they have not created anything original or uniquely their own. Their culture and achievements have always and only been borrowed from others.

Given their *atranscendent* nature, it only makes sense that Jews would gravitate toward the sciences, and specifically positivism, for "Judaism in science, in the widest interpretation of it, is the endeavour to remove all transcendentalism." Thus, Weininger concludes: "The Jew is of all persons the least perturbed by mechanical, materialistic theories of the world."[80] To put the matter succinctly: "Because he [the Jew] believes in nothing, he takes refuge in materialism."[81] It is this materialism/idealism binary that separates not just Jews from Aryans, but also Judaism from Christianity: "Judaism and Christianity form the greatest possible contrasts; the former is bereft of all true faith and of inner identity, the latter is the highest expression of the highest faith."[82] Weininger concludes the chapter with an ominous proclamation that clearly anticipates the Nazi version of Christianity: "The decision must be made between Judaism and Christianity, between business and culture, between

---

[78]Weininger (1906), 314.
[79]Ibid.
[80]Ibid.
[81]Weininger (1906), 324.
[82]Weininger (1906), 325.

male and female, between the race and the individual, between unworthiness and worth, between the earthly and the higher life, between negation and the God-like. Mankind has the choice to make. There are only two poles, and there is no middle way."[83]

As should be obvious by this point, many of the core ideas and sentiments found in the work of Kant, Chamberlain, Eckart, and Hitler inform Wittgenstein's anti-Semitic remarks. Central to Wittgenstein's worldview is the belief that "what is good is also divine." By good, Wittgenstein means that which is beyond the empirical, that which "is outside the space of facts." This link between the good and the divine, Wittgenstein says, "sums up my ethics."[84] Wittgenstein has clearly adopted Kant's empirical/intelligible distinction, which defines the good as that which transcends the mechanistic laws of natural necessity, and the person who defines this idea most clearly is Weininger. In his "Judaism" chapter, Weininger says:

Of the divine in man, of "the God who in my bosom dwells," the true Jew knows nothing; for what Christ and Plato, Eckhard and Paul, Goethe and Kant, the priests of the Vedas, Fechner, and every Aryan have meant by divine, for what the saying, "I am with you always even to the end of the world"—for the meaning of all these the Jew remains without understanding. For the God in man is the human soul, and the absolute Jew is devoid of a soul.[85]

According to Weininger's logic, without the soul, humans are nothing more than empirical beings whose lives are totally determined by their biology and environment. As such, they are mindless animals.

Wittgenstein adopted this view, though he does not state the matter as crudely as Weininger. For Wittgenstein, Jews cannot be geniuses because they cannot inhabit the intelligible realm. They are like animals that are totally determined by their biology and environment: "It might be said (rightly or wrongly) that the Jewish mind does not have the power to produce even the tiniest flower or blade of grass; its way is rather to make a drawing of the flower or blade of grass that has grown in the soil of another's mind and to put

---

[83]Weininger (1906), 330.
[84]Wittgenstein (1984), 3e.
[85]Weininger (1906), 313.

it into a comprehensive picture." Given that the Jew cannot originate something new, "he has nothing that is peculiarly his."[86] Everything is borrowed. Hitler makes an identical point about Jews in *Mein Kampf*. The German dictator acknowledges that Jews possess a certain kind of intelligence, but it is a limited intelligence. They can imitate and reproduce what others have done, but they cannot produce something of their own, which is why Hitler concludes: "Since the Jew—for reasons which will at once become apparent— was never in possession of a culture of his own, the foundations of his intellectual work were always provided by others. His intellect at all times developed through the cultural world surrounding him."[87] Jews are skilled at imitating and reproducing what others have done. But as for the good and the divine, which presuppose a desire and capacity to originate and create, these are off limits to Jews, which is why they, according to Chamberlain, Weininger, and the Nazis, are more like animals than humans.

Like Kant, Chamberlain, Weininger, Eckart, and Hitler, Wittgenstein uses the Bible as evidence to buttress his anti-Semitic views. In a passage from either 1939 or 1940, Wittgenstein briefly describes how he understands the difference between the Old and New Testaments: "The Old Testament seen as the body without its head; the New Testament: the head. When I think of the Jewish Bible, the Old Testament on its own, I feel like saying: the head is (still) missing from this body."[88] If the head is the locus of thinking, then Jews would not be able to act according to the laws of practical reason, which means that they would not be able to act as free agents. In essence, Wittgenstein sees the Old Testament as representing the mindless body, while he sees the New Testament as representing the faculty that enables people to transcend biological impulses and environmental conditioning.

III

If we understand the nature of the Nazis' Christian idealism, which they used in order to define Jews as anti-Christian materialists,

---

[86]Wittgenstein (1984), 19e.
[87]Hitler (1971), 301.
[88]Wittgenstein (1984), 35e.

then Duffy's suggestion that Wittgenstein unwittingly contributed to the making of the Nazis and its anti-Semitic political agenda would make considerable sense. Duffy sprinkles hints throughout the novel that Wittgenstein's culture is profoundly anti-Semitic and that Wittgenstein and his family have internalized and adopted their culture's version of anti-Semitism. For instance, in one of the early chapters, when describing the dysfunctional Wittgenstein family, Duffy underscores the links between Wittgenstein and Hitler: "Hitler was born in Austria in the same year Wittgenstein was, 1889."[89] This is significant because the Wittgensteins' "Catholic Vienna was a cosmopolitan but anti-Semitic city, and around this time anti-Semitism was becoming an increasing force in its politics and consciousness."[90] Karl Lueger, a member of the Christian Social party and mayor of Vienna from 1897 until 1910, was instrumental in "whipping up a misty confection of democracy, social reform, anti-Semitism, Catholicism, concern for the little man and sheer personality."[91] Given this anti-Semitic environment, Wittgenstein's Jewish father, Karl, was "baptized a Protestant"[92] in an effort to expunge the "Jew within."[93] This desire to purge the family and self of Jewishness is not just an unconscious philosophy that Karl unwittingly adopted. It is a fully conscious decision. For instance, Wittgenstein's older sister, Gretl, wants to acknowledge her Jewish heritage, so she tries to put a Menorah on display in the Wittgenstein house. Her reason for doing so is to acknowledge that "there's a half believer in me."[94] But Karl demurs, claiming that his "is a Christian house."[95] For Karl, being a Christian leaves no room for the Jew.

While Karl seeks to overcome his Jewishness by becoming Christian, he recognizes that this is not entirely possible, because he is by nature a Jew, which has unfortunate consequences for his son. We see this most clearly when Ludwig tells his father that he wants to become a philosopher. Karl objects. For Wittgenstein's father, Christians have something that Jews lack, and that something

---

[89]Duffy (2010), 22.
[90]Duffy (2010), 22–3.
[91]Duffy (2010), 23.
[92]Duffy (2010), 24.
[93]Duffy (2010), 25.
[94]Duffy (2010), 136.
[95]Ibid.

equips them to be musicians and philosophers. As Karl says in a letter to his son:

> Again, I say, in the Jew, there is the dual tendency to understand and even crave art *in more or less direct proportion to his own inability to express himself as an artist*. Mahler is a good practitioner, with sometimes wonderful effects, but he has not, it seems to me, the depths of Christian artists. I would not presume to tell you why this is, but all the same—*it is*. It is quite empirically true, as you will readily see by simply asking yourself how many of our greatest artists have been Jews. Few. Precious few. And fewer still philosophers.[96]

Christians have the capacity to produce great art and philosophy, whereas Jews do not. Since Wittgenstein is a Jew, his father encourages him to abandon the futile desire to become a philosopher.

Wittgenstein defies his father by pursuing philosophy. Eventually, however, he not only accepts Karl's Christian anti-Semitic view, but also systematizes it into a much more coherent and comprehensive philosophy, which he uses in his conversation with Max to define Waismann's limitations as a Jew. But near the end of the novel, when Wittgenstein reflects on his life, he finally confronts his own Christian anti-Semitism. At this point, Wittgenstein discovers that he has unwittingly and subconsciously internalized Weininger's ideas from *Sex and Character*, which is described as "one of those books read in youth that, for better and worse, hold a lifelong and uneasy claim to one's moral and mental map." The narrator goes on to claim that the book entered Wittgenstein's "blood like a malaria, stimulating dreams that he now saw he would spend his life periodically sweating out."[97] What Wittgenstein specifically adopted is Weininger's model of Christian idealism, which pits Christians and Jews in mortal opposition to one another, for "Weininger maintained that Christ was the greatest man in the history of the world because he had conquered man's greatest enemy, the Jew within."[98] As I have already discussed, this idea of conquering and purging the "Jew within" is central to the Nazis'

---

[96]Duffy (2010), 61–2.
[97]Ibid.
[98]Duffy (2010), 514.

party program. Jewishness, as a communicable disease, is not an isolated, self-contained reality within specific beings. For Weininger and the Nazis, it is like a spreadable disease, which means that people could be infected by Jewishness. Hence, the Nazis' desire to fight "the spirit of Jewish materialism within us and without us." As such, Germans must work diligently to purge the country and themselves of all things Jewish. More specifically, Jewishness is a diseased mental orientation:

> Anyone could be a Jew, according to Weininger, Jewishness being not a race, people or creed but a tendency of mind that is most conspicuously evident in Jews. The Jew warned the true Aryan to guard himself against such traits: the rootlessness and irreverence, the lack of fixed beliefs and the resulting fixation on material things rather than spiritual values.[99]

Within this framework, Jews are materialists who neither understand nor appreciate that which transcends the material world.

If the capacity for transcendence, which manifests itself in an act of genius, is a prerequisite for overcoming Jewishness, then Duffy's Wittgenstein is doomed, for he "could feel Weininger's root sickness and revulsion in the face of his unforgivable Jewishness."[100] It is at this point that Duffy's Wittgenstein applies to himself the Weiningerian theory of Jewishness, which Weininger derived mainly from Kant via Chamberlain:

> Jewish lineage he had, but no true allegiance. He was philosophical. About Jews he could say, in echo of Weininger, that even the greatest of Jewish thinkers was merely talented. Certainly, he could say this about his own talent, which he thought was the useful but essentially unoriginal Jewish talent for clarifying the ideas of other men, Gentile men—men of authentic genius with original minds.[101]

This is a more sophisticated and nuanced version of Karl's claim that a Jew cannot be a philosopher, because he lacks the necessary

---

[99]Ibid.
[100]Ibid.
[101]Duffy (2010), 515.

capacity to produce a work of genius, and it is the same claim that Wittgenstein made about Waismann in his conversation with Max.

Duffy's Wittgenstein casts a critical glance on himself for having adopted this view, but what troubles him most is his realization that he has indoctrinated Max with his Christian anti-Semitism. In essence, Duffy's Wittgenstein gives Max a Weiningerian conceptual framework, one that is consistent with Nazi ideology, which explains Duffy's decision to make the fictional figure a Nazi. As a symbol, Max represents an anti-Semitic undercurrent in Wittgenstein's writings, philosophy, and person. Duffy clearly calls the reader's attention to Max's symbolic function within the novel through his interactions with the famous philosopher G. E. Moore, who was one of Wittgenstein's mentors at Cambridge, and his wife Dorothy. This is not surprising, since the actual Wittgenstein recommended Weininger's *Sex and Character* to Moore, which underscores the fact that Wittgenstein disseminated Weininger's work and thus potentially contributed to the anti-Semitic ideology that the Nazis adopted.[102] When Max first meets the Moores, he is described as "a man of the Gospels."[103] In most cases, such a description would be considered an honorific appellation. But within a Nazi context, this description could only mean anti-Semitic trouble, for the Nazis believed that "Christ was one of the greatest antisemites of all time."[104] To underscore the degree to which Max's Christ triumphs over and even negates Judaism and the Jew, Duffy pictures Max with his Bible, part of which has been removed. Dorothy comments on this: "It looks as if you lost part of your Bible." To this Max replies with indignation: "Not lost, said Max with a snort. I pulled it out. The Old Testament it was. Five years behind I see this is all

---

[102]Evidently, Moore did not have a positive response to Weininger's work, which prompted Wittgenstein to partially defend Weininger. For Wittgenstein's remarks, see his August 23, 1931, letter to Moore (Wittgenstein [2008], 193).

[103]Duffy (2010), 373.

[104]This citation comes from an issue of *Der Stürmer*, which is generally regarded as the most important and influential anti-Semitic newspaper in Nazi Germany. Julius Streicher was the founder and editor of the journal, and even though he never killed a Jew or ordered a Jew to be killed, he was convicted at the Nuremberg Trials for making the Holocaust possible through his newspaper. He was one of the first Nazis to be hanged. The passage I cite comes from a March, 1937 issue (no. 12). For an analysis of the distinct version of Christianity that Hitler and the Nazis used in order to justify their anti-Semitic political agenda, see my essay, "Conceptualizing Christianity and Christian Nazis after the Nuremberg Trials."

lies made by the desert Jew." Max goes on to detail the standard approach to the Bible that most Nazis took: "In these books are two Gods, the Jew God and the Christian. Both cannot be."[105] That Max would say such a thing to Dorothy is significant, for it is she who specifies the symbolic relationship between Max and Wittgenstein: "At first, Dorothy Moore couldn't quite picture them together. And yet there was an unspoken intimacy between them, as if their separate oddities had knitted together over the years like a human island, populated with its own peculiar flora and fauna."[106] On the surface, Wittgenstein and Max could not be more different— Wittgenstein is wealthy and well educated, while Max is poor and uneducated. But beneath the surface, they are inextricably linked, and it is their anti-Semitism, which is the logical consequence of their Christian idealism, that unifies them most.

To emphasize the links between Wittgenstein and the Nazis, Duffy has Max become a member of the SS and makes a significant date change. In late 1936 and early 1937, the actual Wittgenstein had a personal crisis, which led him to contact close friends and make a confession to them.[107] One of the things he confessed is that he failed to tell his friends that he is a Jew. Duffy's novel consists of four books, and the final one starts "in September of 1938, six months after the *Anschluss*."[108] It is during this period that Duffy's Wittgenstein makes his confession. Why? Duffy is clearly drawing a link between Wittgenstein and the Nazis. Therefore, Duffy's Wittgenstein confesses at this time because he finally considers how his anti-Semitic philosophy aligns with and perhaps contributes to the Nazis' agenda, thus joining (*Anschluss*) Austria (Weininger, Hitler, and Wittgenstein) and Germany (the Nazis).

What specifically prompts Duffy's Wittgenstein to reflect on his anti-Semitism at this time is the fact that Max visits Wittgenstein's sister in an unofficial capacity as a member of the SS in order to urge her to emigrate from Austria for her own safety. After meeting with Wittgenstein's sister, Max writes to his former friend, asking why he never told him that he had Jewish blood in him. Max goes on to claim that this fact about blood ultimately means nothing

---

[105]Duffy (2010),376.
[106]Duffy (2010), 373.
[107]Monk (1990), 367.–8.
[108]Duffy (2010), 499.

because he "learned from the wise Jew Weininger who knew that
the Jew is not simply a victim of his own blood."[109] Wittgenstein's
anti-Semitism is far more subtle and understated than Max's, which
is why he is so stunned by the letter. But it is this letter that leads
Wittgenstein "to see the truth of his life, no matter what the truth
was or what it cost him."[110] And what he discovers is this:

> Wittgenstein's past was seeping over him with thoughts of Max,
> the radical, self-annointed Christian wearing SS death's heads,
> and Otto Weininger, the sex-crossed, self-hating Jew who had
> written *Sex and Character*, a book that for Max had been an
> explosive. Yet here, too, Wittgenstein saw that he had nobody
> to blame but himself: it was he who had introduced Max to
> Weininger, having once shown Max a copy of *Sex and Character*
> while they were living in Trattenbach.[111]

The symbolism of Max should be clear: from his family (Karl
and Hans, Wittgenstein's brother, from whom Wittgenstein
got Weininger's *Sex and Character*) and culture (Lueger, Hitler,
Weininger), Wittgenstein inherited a version of Christian anti-
Semitism, which he bequeathed to his friend Max, who became a
Nazi. In essence, Duffy suggests that Wittgenstein was, like most
people of the time period, complicit in the making of the anti-
Semitic ideology that Hitler and the Nazis would adopt. But it
is the logic behind the symbolism that is most significant. What
prompted Duffy's Wittgenstein to confess to Moore after the
Anschluss that he had denied his Jewish heritage? If we accept the
symbolism of Duffy's novel, the answer is that Wittgenstein must
have been thinking about the role he played in the making of the
anti-Semitic ideology on which National Socialism is premised
when he made his confession to Moore. And there is good reason to
accept this interpretation. After all, Wittgenstein adopted a version
of Christian anti-Semitism that is strikingly similar to the Nazis', as
we see in his notebooks, and he disseminated those views through
his recommendation of Weininger to at least one person: Moore.
Hence, Wittgenstein's realization of "the fantastic delusion of his

---

[109]Duffy (2010), 509.
[110]Duffy (2010), 510.
[111]Ibid.

own life" when "thinking of Weininger then in that period after the *Anschluss*."[112] Given this discovery, it should come as no surprise that Duffy has Wittgenstein confess to Moore immediately after the *Anschluss*.

At this point, let me clarify what my interpretation implies. As a Nazi, Max is the visible manifestation of a dark undercurrent in Wittgenstein's philosophy, and as such, he reflects the degree to which Wittgenstein unknowingly and unintentionally contributed to the Nazis' anti-Semitic project. By 1938, Duffy's Wittgenstein finally comes to realize what he has unwittingly and inadvertently done. In short, he has adopted Weininger's "insane idealism, which," Duffy's Wittgenstein belatedly discovers, is "less a moral state than a self-imposed death sentence."[113] The empirical/ intelligible distinction, which is at the core of the philosophy of Kant, Chamberlain, Weininger, the Nazis, and Wittgenstein, is intellectually incoherent, not so much because it wrongly identifies Jews with materialism (the empirical), but because it is deadly unrealistic. For Duffy, the "insane idealism" of Weininger, Wittgenstein, and the Nazis has less to do with morality and genius than with political self-destruction, because the empirical/ intelligible distinction is totally unrealistic. Nobody, not even the Nazis' fictional Aryans, could live up to the ideals implicit in it. More sadly, as Duffy's Wittgenstein discovers, the philosophy ultimately leads to self-destruction, as we see with Wittgenstein, who develops a philosophy that presupposes the destruction of the Jew within himself and without. In short, a philosophy that leads to self-annihilation. In adopting Weininger's philosophy, Wittgenstein implicitly supports the Nazis' anti-Semitic political ideology and thereby sentences himself to death.

IV

Within the context of literary history, the symbolic function of a figure like Max is of crucial importance, as it enables us to clearly distinguish biographical from fictional truth. With clarity and precision, Monk

---

[112]Duffy (2010), 513.
[113]Duffy (2010), 512.

defines biographical truth in his essay "Philosophical Biography: The Very Idea." The biographer's objective is to understand the subject, to accurately depict the subject's life, and the way to do this is to picture (show) rather than theorize (explain) the life. Given this distinction, Monk concludes that biography "is a nontheoretical activity,"[114] which is why he condemns the biographies of Jean-Paul Sartre. To illustrate, Monk discusses Sartre's biography of Charles Baudelaire. When doing that biography, "Sartre had a theory that we are each of us entirely responsible for the kind of life we lead, and, in particular, that our lives are shaped by a decisive original choice that determines the kind of person we will be."[115] Sartre's theory has a distorting effect, for his "central interest in describing the events of Baudelaire's life, one feels, is to demonstrate the truth of this theory."[116] To put the matter simply, there is, for Monk, a "difference between revealing character through *description* and trying to *explain* it through theorizing."[117] Biographical "truth," as Monk conceives it, consists of descriptive representations of the subject's life, and if the author purposely or inadvertently uses a theory to explain a life, "then something has gone wrong."[118]

As I have demonstrated in the introduction, biographical novelists primarily consider themselves authors of fiction, not biography. Therefore, their relationship with and approach to their subjects differs considerably from those of biographers'. To clarify why this is the case, let me briefly return to the 1968 forum with Ellison, Warren, and Styron that I discussed in the first chapter. In that forum, Ellison praised Warren for changing the name of Huey Long to Willie Stark in his novel *All the King's Men*, because the writer's task "is to create symbolic actions which are viable specifically, and which move across all of our differences and all of the diversities of the atmosphere."[119] For Ellison, Warren engages history exactly right by changing Long's name to Stark, because Stark can clearly represent Long, but he can also symbolize so many other people

---

[114]Monk (2001), 5.
[115]Monk (2001), 7.
[116]Ibid.
[117]Ibid.
[118]Monk (2001), 14.
[119]Ellison et al. (Spring 1969), "The Uses of History in Fiction," *Southern Literary Journal* 1(2): 74.

across "differences" and "diversities." By stark contrast, Ellison thinks that Styron made a huge error by naming his protagonist after the historical figure in his novel *The Confessions of Nat Turner*. Ellison considers Styron's choice, and hence the biographical novel, a mistake for two separate reasons: it makes him vulnerable to criticism from historians and it renders his protagonist, because of its historical specificity, incapable of functioning as a symbolic instrument of sociopolitical critique.

Ellison's either/or approach, however, fails to take into account the way biographical novelists are able to strategically blend fact and fiction. No doubt, Duffy restricts himself somewhat to historical and biographical specifics by naming his protagonist Wittgenstein, but he also retains the freedom to create symbolic figures, such as Max, that can represent a wide variety of people and events across "differences" and "diversities." It is this construction of a multi-signifying symbolic figure that distinguishes fictional from biographical truth. To bring into sharp focus the difference between the two, let me define fictional truth by contrasting it with Monk's biographical truth. Monk opposes showing and explaining, the revelation of the subject through description versus the explanation of the subject through theory. In a sense, biographical novelists would agree with Monk, as they, too, favor showing. However, what they show is not always "true." For instance, there is no record of Wittgenstein passing out in a local Jewish theater. But to picture a central conflict within Wittgenstein, Duffy invents such a scene, as I discussed in Chapter 1. He does this because, after having lived in the Wittgenstein material for many years, Duffy extracts from the philosopher's life a theory about the nature of a distinct kind of internal conflict, which leads people to commit horrific acts of social injustice. Within this framework, showing and explaining are not in conflict with one another, as they are with Monk. Rather, Duffy starts by showing Wittgenstein's conflict. But based on what Wittgenstein experiences, Duffy then extends the conflict far beyond his protagonist by constructing a symbol that could explain much more than just Wittgenstein's life. In other words, Duffy converts the biographical subject into a literary symbol. Thus, the biographer's goal is to give readers biographical truth, which is an accurate representation of the subject's life, while the biographical novelist's goal is to give readers fictional truth, which is based on and rooted in the life of an actual historical figure but is then converted into a literary symbol that could be used to illuminate much more than just the individual subject's life.

It is this symbolic figure that is the biographical novelist's most important contribution to literature, as it can simultaneously illuminate political and intellectual history and function as an instrument of sociopolitical critique. Ellison was rightly concerned about subordinating artistic freedom to empirical fact, because creative writers do more than just translate historical figures and events into polished prose. They invent symbolic figures that can be used to represent the internal logic of historical individuals involved in major political events and historical collisions. As such, Duffy's fictional Max, who embodies an anti-Semitic undercurrent in Wittgenstein's psyche and philosophy, can also be used to represent the phenomenological reality of Austrian anti-Semites and Nazi ideologues and functionaries.

We can see how this functions by using *The World As I Found It* to illuminate something that Duffy does not mention, which is the assassination of Schlick. As a student of natural science and mathematics, Schlick completed his Ph.D. in 1904 under Max Planck, a theoretical physicist who originated quantum theory. Schlick taught courses in ethics and natural science, and by 1922, he became the chair of natural philosophy at the University of Vienna. In 1924, he organized a private discussion group, which would by the late twenties come to be known as the Vienna Circle. This group took much of its inspiration from Wittgenstein's *Tractatus*. As Duffy notes, "the group's early members looked to Wittgenstein to lead them toward an age of scientific philosophy based on logic and empiricism and, above all, freedom from the muddles of metaphysics."[120] To put the matter succinctly, the group used Wittgenstein's book in order to clarify and define the role of language and logic in relation to the positivist models in the natural sciences. Their empirical mantra, which they took from Wittgenstein's *Tractatus*, was this: if the content of a sentence cannot be empirically verified, then it has no meaning. Such an approach, they believed, delivered the deathblow to all things religious and metaphysical.[121]

---

[120]Duffy (2010), 473.
[121]According to Hans-Joachim Dahms, the Vienna Circle's "strong opposition to all religious doctrines and metaphysics entailed from the start certain enmities" (57).

Within the context of the Nazi paradigm, the philosophy of the Vienna Circle could only be categorized as Jewish, as that which is necessarily restricted to the empirical. And, indeed, numerous members were Jewish, a fact that explains many of Duffy's choices in *The World As I Found It*.[122] One of the questions that Wittgenstein scholars have not answered is this: Why did Wittgenstein become hyperconscious about Jewishness, and particularly his Jewishness, in 1931 and 1936? The answer has something to do with the Vienna Circle, which is when we first get a sense that Wittgenstein's anti-Semitism impacts others. But here I want to make a distinction. Hitler and the Nazis exerted a conscious and direct anti-Semitic influence. They strategically used Kant's empirical/intelligible distinction, as derived from and popularized by Chamberlain, in order to clearly and unambiguously define Jews as anti-Christian materialists, and they disseminated and promulgated that view in order to inspire anti-Semitic action. Duffy's Wittgenstein, by contrast, exerted what could only be considered a *Frankenstein*-type influence. He *unintentionally* gave birth to a "Jewish" monster, what has come to be known as logical positivism. And as Friedrich Stadler and Hans-Joachim Dahms convincingly demonstrate, the Vienna Circle members were characterized as "adherents of 'Jewish' neo-positivism" or "'subversive Jewish Positivism,'"[123] thus making it a Jewish monster.

Duffy's portrayal of Wittgenstein's relationship to the Vienna Circle brilliantly captures the essence of the dominant view of the group as a Jewish monster. While members of the group looked to Wittgenstein for direction and inspiration, he looked at them with sorrow and dismay: "The first time Wittgenstein encountered this little group, waiting for him to help them throw off the last heresies and lead them, clear-eyed, into a new day, he felt a deep sense of sadness. They were the heretics. They took up his logic but cast aside his mysticism, never understanding how inextricably the two were bound."[124] Wittgenstein's *Tractatus* certainly defines the limits

---

[122]In her essay, "'Wiener Kreise': Jewishness, Politics, and Culture in Interwar Vienna," Lisa Silverman says: "The fact that eight of the Vienna Circle's fourteen members had Jewish backgrounds . . . meant that the entire group was perceived as Jewish" (60).

[123]Stadler (1995), "The Vienna Circle and the University of Vienna," in *Vertreibung der Vernunft: The Cultural Exodus from Austria*. Wien and New York: Springer-Verlag, 46; and Dahms (1995), 62.

[124]Duffy (2010), 473.

of language, but the book was not supposed to dismiss or foreclose consideration of the metaphysical and the mystical, as many in the Vienna Circle thought. Therefore, to voice his objections to their appropriation of his work and their intellectual approach, Wittgenstein "read these antimetaphysicians the passionate metaphysical love poems of the Indian poet Rabindranath Tagore"[125] at the first meeting with them. If, according to Nazi ideology, what Jews cannot understand or appreciate is that which transcends the material world ("the absence from the Jew of true mysticism," as Weininger claims), then it would only follow that the Vienna Circle would be a distinctly Jewish group. To signify this, Duffy has his Wittgenstein explain to Max the "derivative nature" of the Jew at this point. As born materialists, Jews are at the mercy of their bodies and environment, which is why they are "unoriginal."[126]

All this occurs in the "Heirs" chapter. At first, it might seem that Wittgenstein's primary heirs are the members of the Vienna Circle, for Duffy underscores in this chapter Wittgenstein's impact on them: "In them Wittgenstein saw something else that nauseated him: it was the growing shadow of his own influence, as reflected in strong, sophisticated intellects surrendering not just to his ideas but to the sheer force of his personality."[127] But Max is another possible heir, for it is in this chapter that Wittgenstein first gives the future Nazi an anti-Semitic framework that bears a striking resemblance to the one found in the party program and the writings of Chamberlain, Eckart, Rosenberg, and Hitler. And since there is no mention of the Vienna Circle after the "Heirs" chapter and since Max becomes a dominant figure in the novel from this point forward, it would make most sense to say that Max, with his anti-Semitism, is Wittgenstein's primary heir. From the vantage point of an anti-Semite like Max, the Vienna Circle predictably understands the empirical part of the *Tractatus*, but the members lack the capacity to appreciate or value the "mystical," which Wittgenstein defines as "the feeling of the world as a limited whole."[128]

---

[125]Ibid.
[126]Duffy (2010), 474.
[127]Duffy (2010), 473.
[128]Wittgenstein (1988), *Tractatus Logico-Philosophicus*. Translated by C. K. Ogden. London and New York: Routledge & Kegan Pau LTD, 187.

Symbolically, Wittgenstein's alignment with the critics of the Vienna Circle rather than the members of the group becomes hugely important, because it explains the actual Wittgenstein's concern with Jews and his confessions about his Jewishness in 1936 and 1937. To clarify why this is the case, let me use Max as a symbol in order to illuminate the Schlick assassination. On June 22, 1936, Hans Nelböck assassinated Schlick, and when asked at the trial why he did so, "he claimed that Schlick's empirical critique of transcendental knowledge and rejection of metaphysics had caused him to lose all moral grounding and existential coherence." Nelböck also confessed "to have carried out the murder because he believed that Schlick was Jewish."[129] Indeed, he later claimed that he "had done a service to National Socialism by his deed and thereby effected the elimination of a teacher who spread Jewish teachings that were alien and detrimental to the people."[130] The Schlick assassination generated much attention in the Austrian press, but it was a publication in the Catholic newspaper *Schönere Zukunft* (A More Beautiful Future) that has most significance. Johann Sauter was one of Schlick's colleagues at the University of Vienna. He was a philosophy professor who published books about Kant and natural rights. In a July 12, 1936, article in *Schönere Zukunft*, under the pseudonym Prof. Dr. Austriacus, Sauter argued that Nelböck's murder of Schlick was not the act of a psychopath, for there were sensible "motives behind this terrible case." Specifically, Sauter notes that he knows many students who came under Schlick's influence and as a consequence "lost all faith in God, the world and humanity."[131] This occurred because Schlick taught a materialist philosophy that renders the ideas of God and metaphysics meaningless and incoherent. In a critical passage that could have been written by Chamberlain, Weininger, Eckart, or Rosenberg, Sauter says:

> Schlick was not a philosopher by training, but only a physicist. And he never intended to be anything more than a physicist even

---

[129]Silverman (2009), 59.
[130]Cited in Dahms (1995), 61.
[131]Austriacus (1997), "The Case of Professor Schlick in Vienna—A Reminder to Search Our Conscience," in *The Vienna Circle: Studies in the Origins, Development, and Influence of Logical Empiricism*. Vienna and New York: Springer, 871.

as the holder of the chair of philosophy, i.e., he always called it his profession to dissolve philosophy entirely and to present anything that could be grasped scientifically as a purely physical process. Thus, he considered psychology, ethics, and man as such to be nothing more than objects of physics. . . . Schlick ultimately owed his call to Vienna to his materialistic way of thinking.[132]

After making this claim about Schlick's materialism, Sauter notes only a couple of sentences later that "soon all elements hostile to metaphysics gathered around him, particularly all the Jews."[133] For readers today who are unaware of the link between materialism and Jews, the transition here would be considered confusing and forced. But if we understand that Jews are, according to Chamberlain, Weininger, and the Nazis, materialists who are drawn to materialist disciplines, then Sauter's claim makes perfect sense.

Just in case readers overlooked his point about Schlick's Jewishness, Sauter restates it later in the article from a slightly different angle. He briefly describes Schlick's work in a way that unmistakably echoes Wittgenstein's *Tractatus*:

His unshakable conviction was that all statements concerning metaphysics lacked any meaning. Since they did not correspond to any objects, it was utterly "meaningless" to even ask about them. For Schlick a statement was only "meaningful" if it was "verifiable on the basis of what can be perceived by the senses." This logistically embellished materialism was Schlick's basic doctrine.[134]

Sauter goes on to clarify how Schlick's anti-metaphysical philosophy ultimately undermines ethics and morality. All of this builds for his conclusion, which indicates the degree to which the Schlick case exposes "the Jews' dangerous intellectual influence."[135] As Sauter claims:

It is well-known that Schlick, whose research assistants were a Jewish man (Waismann) and two Jewish women, was the idol of

---

[132]Austriacus (1997), 872.
[133]Ibid.
[134]Austriacus (1997), 873–4.
[135]Austriacus (1997), 876.

Vienna's Jewish circles. And now the Jewish circles of Vienna are constantly celebrating him as the most significant thinker. This we understand very well. For the Jew is the born anti-metaphysician and loves Logicism, Mathematicism, Formalism and Positivism in philosophy—all of them qualities which Schlick possessed in abundance. Nevertheless we would like to call to mind that we are Christians living in a Christian-German state, and that it is we who will decide which philosophy is good and appropriate.[136]

With stunning precision, Sauter articulates here the dominant religious philosophy (Christian idealism) underwriting point 24 of the Nazi Party program.

Sauter's comments assume an even more haunting and pernicious form when we read them alongside his July 27, 1938, memo requesting clemency for Nelböck, who received a ten-year sentence for murdering Schlick. Written after the *Anschluss*, Sauter opens the letter to the National Socialist authorities by claiming that he has known Nelböck since 1929, when he took courses in his philosophy classes. He then abruptly shifts to Schlick, making two startling remarks. He minimizes the nature of the crime by saying that Nelböck "attacked" rather than murdered Schlick and by strategically indicting the murdered professor by saying that he "was an exponent of Jewry at the School of Philosophy." Having seemingly exposed Schlick, Sauter then establishes that Nelböck's political sympathies are in the right place, which shifts the burden of responsibility to the professor: "Nelböck, a man of strong national motives and explicit anti-Semitism, grew more and more outraged at Schlick." Anti-Semitism in this context is clearly considered a virtue. Given Nelböck's unassailable political convictions, Sauter concludes by suggesting that the wronged student had no moral or political choice but to act as he did: "I humbly ask you, Sir, to kindly and benevolently consider this plea for clemency, since the crime was committed in a state of excusable necessity—of ideological and political necessity."[137] The suggestion is that killing Schlick was not a criminal act; it was a political must for the health of the "Christian-German state." To underscore that Sauter's political sympathies are also in the right place, he concludes the letter with a "Heil Hitler!"

---

[136]Ibid.
[137]Austriacus (1997), 902.

Instead of mentioning the 1936 Schlick assassination, thereby suggesting that it prompted Wittgenstein's consciousness about his Jewishness and led to his confession (which I suspect is what really happened), Duffy shifts the focus to the 1938 *Anschluss*, and there is a clear reason why. The *Anschluss* signifies the extension of the Nazis' Christian anti-Semitic political agenda, which ultimately led to the negation of the Jew within and without on a massive scale. Therefore, the *Anschluss*, as a symbol, is big enough to encompass the political psychology that made more minor events possible, such as the Nelböck assassination of Schlick. Within this framework, Wittgenstein would have had more in common intellectually with Nelböck and Sauter than Waismann and Schlick. But once Wittgenstein witnessed the political implications and material manifestations of his anti-Semitic philosophy, as seen in the Schlick assassination in real life or the *Anschluss* in Duffy's novel, this led him to do a scorching self-analysis and self-critique. But most terrifying of all is the realization that he, in having internalized and disseminated Weininger's Jewish materialist/Christian idealist philosophy, has unwittingly contributed to the Nazi project, symbolically figured in and through the character of Max. As the philosopher queries: "Could Wittgenstein have been surprised that all these ideas found an immediate home in Max?"[138] This realization occasions an ambiguous form of guilt. On the one hand, he feels guilty for having contributed to the making of a Jewish monster such as logical positivism. His role in the making of this monster led to the death of Schlick, a man whom Wittgenstein admired and respected. On the other hand, he feels guilty because he sympathizes with those who dubbed logical positivism a Jewish monster, such as Nelböck and Sauter. In this instance, his guilt revolves around Max, who is a symbolic incarnation of a dark undercurrent in his thinking, which, in skeletal form, is consistent with Nazi ideology. According to this reading, Max symbolizes Nelböck and Sauter. In other words, Max incarnates the subconscious ideology informing Wittgenstein's philosophy. This realization leads Wittgenstein to a lengthy but insightful reflection on the nature of influence, identity, and responsibility:

> And here, when his own influence was mounting, Wittgenstein saw
> that he was not a single man but a composite—a concatenation

---

[138]Ibid.

of the various influences that went under the name or tag of fate known as Ludwig Wittgenstein. This was only a further burden, because with what he took, consciously or unconsciously, of another life to make a mental life of his own, he accepted also a portion of that person's fate, evading and accepting it at the same time. In this sense, then, Weininger was certainly a part of him, just as he and Weininger were both, in some way, a part of Max. This, he saw, was the burden and paradox of influence: to wonder what truly is yours while yet accepting responsibility for it.[139]

Accepting his place within the philosophical chain and owning his philosophy and its consequences, Wittgenstein takes responsibility for his intellectual contribution, which, in part, includes the making of the Nazi, Max, a figure who, like Nelböck and Sauter, seeks to eliminate the Jew within and without.

V

Understanding the function of a symbolic figure like Max enables us to make another crucial distinction between the traditional biography and the biographical novel. According to Monk, successful biographers attempt to describe (show) rather than explain (theorize) a life as clearly and accurately as possible. Within this framework, "self-effacement is a requirement,"[140] because good biographers resist the impulse to interject themselves or their views into the work by theorizing their subject. In other words, in order to represent as accurately as possible the life of their subject, the biographer must ignore or suppress the self. Now Monk, of course, understands that his own vision of life might inflect his representation of his subject. But that would be an inadvertent rather than an intentional act of representation.

By stark contrast, biographical novelists unapologetically project their own vision of the world, and they merely use the life of their subject in order to express that vision. In Duffy's case, his goal is not to efface himself in order to reveal Wittgenstein's character.

---

[139]Duffy (2010), 513.
[140]Monk (2001), 12.

Rather, it is to use Wittgenstein in order to picture a specific intellectual sickness within both Wittgenstein's culture and self as well as his own. However, it is important to note that Duffy wants to get Wittgenstein right. In fact, the success of his novel depends on it. But the ultimate objective is not to represent Wittgenstein. Rather, it is to use an accurate, piercing, and compelling dimension of Wittgenstein's life in order to communicate his own vision.

For instance, in my interview with Duffy, he told me that his "principal characters were, and are, damaged people."[141] This is not something Duffy neutrally observes from his healthy vantage point, for he draws a clear line of connection between himself and his characters by saying that he, too, comes "from a very damaged background."[142] Part of that sickness derives from living in a racist environment. When discussing his character Max, Duffy claims that he "was struck by how a man could be so charming and also so frightening, and such a racist: How could all these temperaments be present in the same person? How could such a person be blind to these alter egos? Forgive himself, in effect."[143] Max is not merely a fictional abstraction, for Duffy claims that he has had firsthand experience of such a character. When discussing Max's character, Duffy says:

> I think I also saw this—obviously, on a smaller scale—when I was growing up in the D. C. area. Maryland was a pretty redneck place in the sixties and seventies, or at least around where I was living. So I had several friends who were racist and free with the N-word. People like to forget it but this was common. I just grew up with it. So in writing, I was trying to come through that mess.[144]

Given the structural similarities of the racism in Vienna and DC, Duffy's task is to select a part of Wittgenstein's life that can symbolically picture the nature of these structures and the way they

---

[141]Duffy (2014), "In the Fog of the Biographical Novel's History," *Truthful Fictions: Conversations with American Biographical Novelists.* Editor and Interviewer Michael Lackey. New York and London: Bloomsbury, 118.
[142]Ibid.
[143]Duffy (2014), 122.
[144]Ibid.

spread. Duffy does this in the closing pages of *The World As I Found It* through a lengthy scene about Weininger's funeral. As he told me:

> Weininger expresses many of the pathologies and nightmares of his time, from race to sex. Novelistically, Weininger's funeral—after his suicide—was a very dramatic and concrete way to show the toxic ideas that the young Wittgenstein was exposed to, again, in a time in which ideas could literally be a matter of life and death. Weininger's funeral made all these conflicts stand out.[145]

For Duffy, the structures of racist pathology in Weininger's and Wittgenstein's Austria, the Nazis' Germany, and Duffy's DC share some common features, and as a novelist, his goal is to use Wittgenstein to clearly picture these structures—I refer to these as dual-temporal truths, which I discuss in much greater detail in Chapter 5.

This cross-cultural and cross-temporal model explains Duffy's decision to have Max visit New York City. In a discussion with Moore, Max seems to sympathize with blacks, who, he believes, are still treated like slaves in the United States. While in New York, he meets a sailor who says that many blacks want to go back to Africa, which leads Max to draw a parallel between blacks and Jews: "The little Jew, he wants to be the big Zion Jew. The Negro to be again African. Many peoples want their Zion land. Africa I think is their Negro Zion—in Africa I think will be better for them."[146] These reflections lead Max to ask some African Americans "if they will go back to Africa, to their hot Negro Zion."[147] But to Max's surprise, the blacks run away from him. Max, as a symbol of a dark undercurrent in Wittgenstein's philosophy, is not just an anti-Semitic reality in Europe, but also an anti-black reality in the United States (I will discuss this link between Jews and blacks in much more detail in Chapter 4). In essence, Max has two symbolic functions within the novel: he brings into sharp focus the self-destructive, anti-Semitic conflict within Wittgenstein and he symbolizes the

---

[145]Duffy (2014), 124.
[146]Duffy (2010), 378.
[147]Ibid.

racist ideology at work in Europe and the United States, an ideology inherent within Wittgenstein's notebooks.

Given this reading of *The World As I Found It,* is Duffy suggesting that Wittgenstein is directly responsible for either Schlick's assassination or, more horrifically, the Holocaust? For someone like Duffy, this question is too simplistic. On the one hand, it would be naïve to think that Wittgenstein, a prominent philosopher who had a significant impact on a wide range of people, would have had no influence on the cultural ethos of his day. On the other hand, it would be nearly impossible to demonstrate or say that he directly impacted Nazi ideology—we have no evidence that Hitler, Goebbels, or Rosenberg read Wittgenstein's work. But this begs the question: What is the orientation toward history of a biographical novelist like Duffy? In an interview about the uses of history in the biographical novel, Duffy says that he rejects the approach of someone like Lukács, who "demands" from literature "this imposed, matrix-like system, this historical overlay over the character."[148] For Duffy, this usage of history within the novel leads necessarily to a falsification of character. Millions of Europeans contributed to the cultural ethos that made the Nazis and the Holocaust possible. As a biographical novelist, Duffy's goal is to picture characters caught up in the historical events and ideologies of their day: "Most of us live in the fog of the day to day. We're not aware of giant sweeps of history around us in which we are the cogs. As a novelist, I want to put my characters into the fog of the day to day—into what is really going on right around them."[149] Within this framework, characters are governed by immediate desires, intellectual predispositions, and emotional orientations, all of which entail certain limitations. The task of the biographical novelist, therefore, is not to indicate how the writings of a Weininger or a Hitler dictated the way people or a person thought. Rather, it is to clarify the historical and intellectual conditions that made people or a person read and appreciate writings by someone like Weininger or Hitler, whose works were read by a large segment of the population. As Duffy claims: "For a writer, the trick is not to open *Sex and Character* or *Mein Kampf* with contempt. The trick is to clear your mind and read *Mein Kampf,* say, as an out-of-work

---

[148]Duffy (2014), 114.
[149]Duffy (2014), 115.

carpenter with a hungry family might have in 1929. That is my job as a fiction writer."[150] For rational contemporary readers, *Sex and Character* and *Mein Kampf* feel like totally insane texts. How could someone of Wittgenstein's intellectual stature read a book like *Sex and Character*, which bears such a striking resemblance at so many points to *Mein Kampf*, with rapture, admiration, and respect? This is the question Duffy seeks to answer in *The World As I Found It*, and in doing so, he suggests that Wittgenstein was a part of and even contributed to a cultural ethos that made Hitler and the Nazis a nightmarish possibility from which we are still trying to awake. And, to the horror of Duffy's Wittgenstein, it is this question that must have troubled the Austrian philosopher after the *Anschluss*, which perhaps explains the timing of the Jewish confession of Duffy's Wittgenstein. Immediately after reflecting on Weininger, the *Anschluss*, and Max, Duffy's Wittgenstein has a crucial realization:

> He thought he had been vigilant, no sleeper in the hay, but he saw that each vigilance was not good enough. Flicking his cane before him, switching through the sharp grass, he told himself how he had been an ass deep in hay, and deeper still in his own evil-smelling fool's honey. What had ever led him to believe that character would tell and protect? What had ever led him to believe that genius would prevail over a flawed character and thereby keep one from being snatched by the sleeve into that fulsome, earthbound machinery that grinds up the generations, then stamps them out again into fresh abominations?[151]

Note how Duffy's Wittgenstein uses questions to underscore the nature of the crisis. In essence, Duffy has brought into sharp focus two terrifying historical possibilities: that Wittgenstein unwittingly contributed to the making of the Nazis' ideology, an ideology that necessitates the negation of the "materialist Jew" within and without, and that Wittgenstein wondered if, in fact, he was complicit in the Nazis' horrific political program, which manifested itself at the time in the form of the *Anschluss*. Duffy does not emphatically state that either of these is a textual, biographical, or historical fact. He merely suggests that they are very real historical and biographical

---

[150]Duffy (2014), 124.
[151]Duffy (2010), 513.

possibilities, a troubling outcome of Wittgenstein's thinking that probably bedeviled him after he heard about Schlick's assassination and the *Anschluss*.

And herein lies both the unique effectiveness and success of the biographical novel. Ellison suggests that using actual historical figures would implicitly divest novels of their power to symbolize and thereby critique the body politic. Biographical novelists base their novels on actual historical figures, which seems to limit the symbolic function of the novel, but they then invent characters or scenes that embody the symbolic meaning and significance of the historical figure's ideas and life, and it is these invented figures that can represent so many other figures across "differences" and "diversities." Put more concretely, while Duffy's novel focuses on an actual historical figure's life, it can also represent and even illuminate something not mentioned in the text like the Schlick assassination. Indeed, what makes Duffy's novel so powerful is that his symbolic figure can depict something about which he has never heard. It is exactly this capacity of the novel to do sociocultural critique that Ellison so desperately sought to preserve, for he believed that the novelist has a crucial role to play within the culture. What he could not anticipate was the way the biographical novelist would strategically blend the factual and the fictional, the historical and the symbolic, Wittgenstein and Max.

Let me conclude by indicating the nature and significance of Duffy's achievement as a biographical novelist by contrasting it with Monk's. When discussing anti-Semitic comments in Wittgenstein's writings that bear a resemblance to Hitler's, Monk says: "Though alarming, Wittgenstein's use of the slog of racist anti-Semitism does not, of course, establish any affinity between himself and the Nazis. His remarks on Jewishness were fundamentally introspective."[152] What leads Monk to draw this conclusion is textual evidence. Since he can find no evidence that establishes a clear cause and effect relationship between Wittgenstein and the Nazis, he claims that there is, "of course," no affinity between the two. Duffy's approach is very different. He uses textual evidence to construct a character structure, and based on that character structure, there are compelling reasons to entertain the possibility that there are

---

[152]Monk (1990), 316.

causal and/or interactive relationships between Wittgenstein and the Nazis. For Duffy, given Wittgenstein's admiration for Weininger, adoption of Weinigner's "insane idealism," anti-Semitic remarks in his notebooks, and recommendation to Moore to read Weininger, it would only be logical to assume that Wittgenstein adopted and even disseminated what would become some of the crucial tenets of the Nazis' anti-Semitic political project. Thus it would be reasonable to say that Wittgenstein contributed in some way to a European ethos that required millions of unwitting and ordinary anti-Semites to execute. But to be clear, this does not mean that Duffy makes any absolute claim about Wittgenstein's role in the making of Hitler and the Nazis. Duffy's position is that we cannot know for certain one way or the other, and he would say that neither can Monk. But therein lies the true horror at the core of Duffy's novel. Was Wittgenstein right to think that he unwittingly contributed to the making of Europe's death-bringing anti-Semitism? This is the horrific question that the anti-Semitic Wittgenstein must have lived with after the Schlick assassination and the *Anschluss*. What makes Duffy's novel so brilliant is how he vividly pictures this real but unresolved (unresolvable) possibility in and through Max, whose being intelligently symbolizes a racist structure that exists in a wide variety of peoples, places, and times.

3

Surrealism, historical representation, and the biographical novel[1]

Many prominent biographical novelists know Lukács' critique of the biographical novel, but they reject it, not so much because of his faulty understanding of the aesthetic form, but because of his approach to history. In a recent interview, Jay Parini told me that he read *The Historical Novel* as a young man but "came to realize that Lukács had it wrong." For Parini, there are two separate problems with Lukács' approach to history. First, Lukács considers history nonfiction. But as Parini claims, "There's no appreciable difference between history and fiction in terms of narrative technique. It's all narration."[2] Therefore, he argues that "history should acknowledge its debt to fiction. History should understand that no matter how much it protests, it remains a form of fiction."[3] Second, Parini considers Lukács' positivist approach to history false and obsolete. In a round-table forum titled "The Uses of History in the Biographical Novel," Parini says that Oswald Spengler, Erich Auerbach, and Lukács have all adopted the same approach to history, which he rejects: "I find historical positivism, like philosophical positivism,

---

[1]A truncated version of this chapter has been published in the the journal *a/b: Auto/Biography Studies* under the title "The Rise of the Biographical Novel and the Fall of the Historical Novel," 31, no. 1 (2016), 33–58.

[2]Parini (2014a), "Reflections on Biographical Fiction," in *Truthful Fictions: Conversations with American Biographical Novelists*. Editor and Interviewer Michael Lackey. New York and London: Bloomsbury, 205.

[3]Parini (2014a), 207.

somewhat old hat and false."[4] Lance Olsen lodges a similar critique. In a recent interview, Olsen told me that he rejects "Lukács' assumptions," because he is "working with a set that makes me uncomfortable—the quaint notion, for instance, that there is some kind of transcendental truth; the one that we can easily define what history is; the one that we can easily define what the novel is."[5] As I will argue in this chapter, the rejection of objective history and historical positivism explains, in part, why the biographical novel has eclipsed and even supplanted the historical novel.

For contemporary biographical novelists, there are compelling reasons for shifting the novel's focus from what Lukács refers to as the "objective weight" and "objective proportion"[6] of history to the subjective consciousness of a prominent historical figure. At this point, let me briefly discuss some concurrent developments in history and literature that made the biographical novel acceptable to contemporary academics and popular with the general public. In the nineteenth century, history became an institutionalized discipline that conceived of itself as a science. As such, it distanced itself from literature by expanding and hardening the dichotomy between fact and fiction. Within this framework, historical fact became more dogmatically factual while imaginative fiction became more fantastically fictional. There were, to be sure, prominent nineteenth-century detractors, like Friedrich Nietzsche, who rejected the fact/fiction dichotomy by exposing the degree to which the scientific historian's established fact is really an anthropomorphic construction, thus suggesting that a (personal or communal) power interest played a much more crucial role in the formation of historical fact than the seemingly neutral and objective observers of history were willing to admit. But it was not until the 1960s, with the linguistic turn in multiple disciplines, the provincialization of Western thought, the deconstruction of the correspondence theory of truth, and the valorization of postmodernism, that the fact/fiction binary was systematically and comprehensively

---

[4]Parini (2014b), "The Uses of History in the Biographical Novel," in *Conversations with Jay Parini*. Editor Michael Lackey. Jackson: University Press of Mississippi, 133.
[5]Olsen (2014), "The Biographical Novel's Practice of Not-Knowing," in *Truthful Fictions*, 193.
[6]Lukács (1983), 290.

dismantled.[7] Perhaps no writer, with the exception of Nietzsche, anticipated the postmodern fusion of history and fiction more than Walter Benjamin, which explains why Parini's narrator makes the following claim in his biographical novel *Benjamin's Crossing*: "Benjamin believed that the equivalent of a Copernican revolution in thinking must occur. Fiction would replace history, or become history."[8] By 1997, the Copernican revolution in thinking was well underway, which is why Parini could publish a biographical novel that simultaneously discusses and enacts that revolution.

Put simply, radical shifts in our theories of knowledge and consciousness necessitated and inspired new literary forms. As Mas'ud Zavarzadeh claims, the mounting post–Second World War incredulity toward metanarratives, which is the most basic definition of postmodernism, gave rise to a new form of fiction. For instance, in 1965, Truman Capote published *In Cold Blood*, which has been misleadingly referred to as a "nonfiction novel," a phrase that Capote, in his self-promoting way, coined in interviews about his book.[9] For Zavarzadeh, the fictive novel provides an overarching interpretation of the world, an "epiphanic vision" that illuminates "the ultimate structure of reality."[10] But given the postmodern exposure of such metavisions as phantoms of an overheated imagination, the traditional approach to the novel no longer made sense, so the nonfiction novelists created a work with a "noninterpretive stance"[11] to the world.

---

[7]For discussions about the history of history, see Hayden White's *Tropics of Discourse*, *The Content of Form*, and *Metahistory: The Historical Imagination in Nineteenth-Century Europe* and Georg G. Iggers' *Historiography in the Twentieth Century*. For a discussion of the linguistic turn, see E. L. Doctorow's "False Documents," Richard Rorty's *Contingency, Irony, and Solidarity* and Judith Ryan's *The Novel after Theory*. For discussions of the provincialization of Western thought, see Dipesh Chakrabarty's *Provincializing Europe* and Edward Said's *Culture and Imperialism*. For discussions of the deconstruction of the correspondence theory of truth, see Rorty's *Philosophy and the Mirror of Nature* and Michel Foucault's *The Archaeology of Knowledge* and *The Order of Things*. For discussions about the rise of postmodernism, see Jean-François Lyotard's *The Postmodern Condition*; Linda Hutcheon's *Poetics of Postmodernism*; and Ryan's *The Novel after Theory*.
[8]Parini (1997), *Benjamin's Crossing*. New York: Henry Holt, 62.
[9]John Hollowell (1977), *Fact & Fiction: The New Journalism and the Nonfiction Novel*. Chapel Hill: The University of North Carolina Press, x.
[10]Zavarzadeh (1976), *The Mythopoeic Reality: The Postwar American Nonfiction Novel*. Urbana: University of Illinois Press, 42.
[11]ibid.

With regard to literary history, and specifically the rise and legitimization of the American biographical novel, the Capote case has done more to muddle and confuse than anything else, which is clear from Beverley Southgate's recent study *History Meets Fiction* (2009). This is a superb work of scholarship that clarifies the intellectual developments that led to the blending of fact and fiction, history and literature. Less compelling, however, is Southgate's discussion of *In Cold Blood*, which he uncritically refers to as a nonfiction novel. If we think of a novel as fiction, then we could say it invents a world that is not required to accurately represent historical events and persons. And if we think of history as nonfiction, then we could say it seeks to represent as accurately as possible the events and persons that exist in the world outside the text. Given these two separate activities, Capote's work would be considered nonfiction, as he makes clear in his acknowledgments: "All the material in this book not derived from my own observation is either taken from official records or is the result of interviews with persons directly concerned, more often than not numerous interviews conducted over a considerable period of time."[12] These prefatory remarks have led Southgate to say of Capote's book: "One could hardly better that as a statement of correct procedures for a contemporary historian."[13] But while Southgate considers the book typical history, he also calls it fiction. Startling, however, is Southgate's implicit definition of a novel, which is based not so much on an author's act of fictional creation as the reader's experience of a particular text: "*In Cold Blood* is a novel—*fiction*—inasmuch as it is an imaginative construction written to hold the attention of its readers, and make them want to keep on reading."[14] Given this description, novelists are different from historians and biographers because they know how to write in an engaging way. By this logic, if a historian or biographer were to write a captivating work, it would cease to be history or biography and would, therefore, become fiction. This obviously is a dubious definition of fiction, because it defines the novel on the basis of a reader's subjective response rather than a writer's creative act. Given

---

[12]Capote (1965), *In Cold Blood: A True Account of a Multiple Murder and Its Consequences*. New York: Random House, Acknowledgments.
[13]Southgate (2009), *History Meets Fiction*. Harlow: Longman/Pearson Education Limited, 34.
[14]Southgate (2009), 35.

Capote's approach to the material and what *In Cold Blood* actually does, it would be more accurate to refer to it as a page-turning history or biography than a nonfiction novel.

At stake here is not just what writers are doing but also the scholarly definition of writing in the postmodern age, and few works have done more to bring clarity to the discussion than Linda Hutcheon's 1988 study *A Poetics of Postmodernism*, which is subtitled *History, Fiction, Theory*. It was this triad that enabled Hutcheon to formulate her most enduring contribution to literary history, which is the idea of historiographic metafiction. The postmodern theorist's recognition that history and fiction are human constructs enables writers to rethink and revise accepted versions of the past. Historiographic metafiction incorporates historical events into a literary work, but given its awareness of crucial developments in theory, it also reflects in a critical way on the questionable process of converting those events into an official version of history. Significantly, Hutcheon's model can also be used to explain a major development from Capote's *In Cold Blood* to Mailer's *The Executioner's Song*. In *The Politics and Poetics of Journalistic Narrative*, Phyllis Frus claims that Capote's *In Cold Blood* and Mailer's *The Executioner's Song* are the first to take the label of the "nonfiction novel."[15] However, she argues that Mailer's novel goes beyond Capote's in that it contains critical self-reflections that call attention to the narrative construction of history and thereby tacitly undermines its own narratorial authority,[16] which is why Mailer's work is much closer to Hutcheon's historiographical metafiction than Capote's *In Cold Blood*. But because Mailer insists that he resisted the impulse to invent characters and scenes, as I have discussed in Chapter 1, it would actually be more accurate to refer to it as historiographic metabiography than historiographic metafiction.

Like Hutcheon, many contemporary biographical novelists question and challenge traditional approaches to history, but instead of merely using the novel to foreground a hermeneutics of suspicion, they have developed an aesthetic form that is better suited to engage and represent the forces that gave rise to major

---

[15]Frus (1994), *The Politics and Poetics of Journalistic Narrative: The Timely and the Timeless*. Cambridge: Cambridge University Press, 181.
[16]Frus (1994), 181–4.

historical collisions. In this chapter, I discuss Olsen's *Nietzsche's Kisses* and Parini's *Benjamin's Crossing* because these works best clarify why the biographical novel had to come into being. My main claim in this chapter is that the biographical novel has supplanted the classical historical novel, as Lukács defines it. Though seemingly unrelated, it is significant that a number of biographical novels reference twentieth-century anti-Semitism and/or the Holocaust: Joanna Scott's *Arrogance*, David Mamet's *The Old Religion*, Duffy's *The World As I Found It*, Zora Neale Hurston's *Moses, Man of the Mountain* and *Herod the Great*, Paul Russell's *The Unreal Life of Sergey Nabakov*, Ron Hansen's *Hitler's Niece*, and Irvin Yalom's *The Spinoza Problem* are just a few that immediately come to mind. Why are so many biographical novelists particularly fixated on anti-Semitism and/or the Holocaust? And why did the first major surge of biographical novels emerge in the 1930s, when Hitler and the Nazis came to power? Or, to pose the question from a slightly different angle, what is it about modern anti-Semitism and the Holocaust that mandated the rise of the biographical novel? As I will demonstrate in this chapter, the classical historical novel and the biographical novel presuppose two radically different conceptions of consciousness, one premised on positivism, the other premised on surrealism. For biographical novelists, the problem with the classical historical novel is not just that it is incapable of representing some of the key factors that made the Holocaust possible; it is that the model of consciousness that the classical historical novel presupposes necessarily misrepresents some of the key historical factors that led to something like the Holocaust. Given this logic, if we want to get a better sense of the ideology that made the Holocaust possible, turning to the biographical novel would not just be useful. It would be one of the only intellectual forms to adequately illuminate the structures of consciousness that made the horrific event possible.

I

A staunch critic of psychological fiction and modernist literature, Lukács favors the classical historical novel, because it accurately represents "history as a process,"[17] that is, the way historical

---

[17]Lukács (1983), 21.

concreteness functions according to rigorous and objective laws in shaping and determining the great sociopolitical collisions of a particular age. Rather than focusing on typical Romantic heroes, historical novelists center their narratives on "the mediocre, prosaic hero as the central figure,"[18] who ultimately incarnates a historical-social type. Should a great person be the focal point of a historical novel, this figure would be treated as more important than the historical transformation, which would necessarily lead to a distorted image of the society and the age. Hence Lukács' critique of the biographical novel.

What Lukács takes as a given is that the biographical novel "views human progress exclusively or predominantly in ideal terms and sees its bearers as the more or less isolated great men in history."[19] Accordingly, the biographical novel glorifies the protagonist by underscoring the role he or she plays in making history, and thus, the hero's "character is inevitably exaggerated, made to stand on tiptoe."[20] However, a cursory glance at the prominent biographical novels of the last thirty-five years does not support Lukács' contention. In *Nietzsche's Kisses*, for instance, Olsen effectively counters Lukács' model by revising the classical historical novel's approach to "the mediocre." For Lukács, a mediocre individual embodies a historical-social type, and in a momentary flash of greatness, commits a truly spectacular act, which has an enormous historical impact. But in Olsen's novel, mediocre individuals are society's primary culprits, the individuals who contribute most to catastrophic historical events because of their mindless acceptance of their culture's ideology, undisciplined and faulty forms of thinking, and uninformed and irresponsible types of action. While Olsen targets many prosaic characters, three are most important (Nietzsche's sister, Elisabeth; her husband, Bernhard Förster; and Nietzsche's mother, Franziska), as they play a crucial role in shaping history.

Olsen's Nietzsche can find little to redeem his mother's character. This is made most clear in an inner monologue in which Nietzsche, after sniffing his mother's pillow, wonders "what a lifetime's failure

---

[18]Lukács (1983), 34.
[19]Lukács (1983), 317.
[20]Lukács (1983), 314.

of the imagination smelled like."[21] Had Franziska's failings only impacted herself, Olsen's characterization would be considered petty and mean-spirited. But Olsen's depiction makes total sense when we realize that Franziska's mediocrity made possible one of the most criminal forms of intellectual misappropriation in political history, specifically the Nazi adoption of Nietzsche's work. To understand the historical link connecting Nietzsche's work and Nazi ideology, we first need to examine why this connection is incoherent.

In recent years, scholars have demonstrated that Hitler and the Nazis considered themselves Christian, which I have discussed at some length in my chapter about Wittgenstein.[22] As Hitler says in one of his first speeches after coming to power: "It is Christians and not international atheists who now stand at the head of Germany."[23] Given its commitment to Christianity, the Nazi Party, Hitler claims, "stands on the ground of a real Christianity," because it is based on "Christian principles."[24] Within Hitler's framework, there is only one "true Christianity,"[25] and for a truly Christian nation to flourish, it cannot and must not compromise its Christian principles. There is an inextricable link between Hitler's Christian faith and his virulent anti-Semitism, for as he claims in *Mein Kampf*: "*By defending myself against the Jew, I am fighting for the work of the Lord.*"[26] This is, as I demonstrated in Chapter 2, the version of Christianity articulated in the Nazis' party program: "The Party as such represents the standpoint of a positive Christianity, without tying itself to a particular confession. It fights the spirit of Jewish materialism within us and without us."[27] According to Hitler and the Nazis, to be a true Christian is to be an anti-Semite.

---

[21]Olsen (2006), *Nietzsche's Kisses*. Normal/Tallahassee: FC2, 172.

[22]See Richard Steigmann-Gall's *The Holy Reich*; Robert Michael's *Holy Hatred: Christianity, Antisemitism, and the Holocaust*; and Michael Lackey's *The Modernist God State: A Literary Study of the Nazis' Christian Reich*.

[23]Hitler (1941), *My New Order*. Editor Raoul de Roussy de Sales. New York: Reynal and Hitchcock, February 15, 1933, 148.

[24]Hitler (1942), *The Speeches of Adolf Hitler: April 1922–August 1939*. Translated by Norman H. Baynes. London, New York, and Toronto: Oxford University Press, August 26, 1934, 386, 387.

[25]Hitler (1971), *Mein Kampf*. Translated by Ralph Manheim. Boston: Houghton Mifflin, 307.

[26]Hitler (1971), 65.

[27]Quoted in Richard Steigmann-Gall (2003), *The Holy Reich: Nazi Conceptions of Christianity, 1919–1945*. Cambridge: Cambridge University Press, 14.

For anyone with just a casual knowledge of Nietzsche's works, and Olsen has much more than that, it should be clear that Nietzsche's writings would have set him in direct opposition to Hitler and the Nazis. Nietzsche's vicious critique of Christianity is well known. In *Twilight of the Idols*, he claims that "Christianity is a hangman's metaphysics," which "has up till now been mankind's greatest misfortune," because it is founded on a "*ressentiment against* life."[28] As such, Christianity depletes the human of his or her vitality, thus transforming him or her into "the domestic animal, the herd animal, the sick animal man—the Christian!"[29] This is the case because "sickness belongs to the essence of Christianity."[30] With regard to anti-Semitism, Nietzsche makes his position unambiguously clear in a letter to his sister: "It is a matter of honor to me to be absolutely clean and unequivocal regarding anti-Semitism, namely *opposed*, as I am in my writings."[31] So opposed was Nietzsche to his sister's anti-Semitism that he actually threatened to cut off contact with her for a period of time because of it.[32]

Given Nietzsche's unambiguous condemnation of Christianity and unequivocal hatred of anti-Semitism, how can we explain that Hitler visited the Nietzsche Archive three times; awarded Nietzsche's sister a monthly allowance to preserve and publicize Nietzsche's works; and commissioned the architect Albert Speer to build a memorial hall at the Nietzsche Archive? *Nietzsche's Kisses* provides answers to these questions. One of the most poignant scenes in the novel occurs when Nietzsche declares to his family that he can no longer believe in Christ or Christianity. Applying to the Bible the exegetical method he learned in his philology seminars, the twenty-two-year-old Nietzsche tells his mother and sister that God is a "bogeyman."[33] This marks a decisive rupture in the family.

---

[28]Nietzsche (1989a), *Twilight of the Idols*, in *Twilight of the Idols/The Anti-Christ*. Translated by R. J. Hollingdale. New York: Penguin Books, 65, 113, 121.
[29]Nietzsche (1989a), 128.
[30]Nietzsche (1989a), 181.
[31]Quoted in Walter Kaufmann (1974), *Nietzsche: Philosopher, Psychologist, Antichrist*. Princeton: Princeton University Press, 45.
[32]For an excellent discussion of the tension between the Nietzsche siblings on the topic of anti-Semitism, see Carol Diethe's *Nietzsche's Sister and the Will to Power*. To indicate the degree to which Nietzsche opposed his sister's anti-Semitism, Diethe cites a letter in which Nietzsche says that Elisabeth's alliance with the anti-Semites "is about the most radical method of 'finishing' with me" (69).
[33]Olsen (2006), 71.

Using a rigorous method of reading and analysis would be the only way to persuade someone with Nietzsche's intellectual capacity to reconsider his apostasy. But Elisabeth and Franziska number among the mediocre in terms of not just the content of their beliefs but also the functions of their intellect. Therefore, they deploy intellectually sloppy and morally reprehensible strategies for transforming the willful infidel into a Christian believer.

For instance, one scene in *Nietzsche's Kisses* portrays Elisabeth taking Rudolf Steiner, one of the early admirers and editors of Nietzsche, on a tour of the first Nietzsche Archive, which was in the Nietzsche house in Naumburg. At this point, Nietzsche has already had his mental collapse, so Elisabeth could talk about Nietzsche's work without fear of being contradicted. When characterizing the nature and content of Nietzsche's work, Olsen's Elisabeth makes claims that would confuse, embarrass, and infuriate her brother: "He [Nietzsche] has spoken of endless light and minds above minds merging without the encumbrance of mortal fabric. The beings inhabiting this Golgotha of Absolute Spirit speak to us in our dreams. When babies die, this is where they go."[34] According to Elisabeth's mythic version, Nietzsche is not a blasphemous Antichrist. Rather, he is a born-again Christian Hegelian, who can communicate with the dead in and through dreams. Significantly, what leads Elisabeth to draw this outlandish conclusion is her mother's comment that Nietzsche "reestablished his nourishing relationship with God Beyond God."[35] Later in the novel, we learn that Nietzsche made this comment when he was already insane—he does not even know that his mother is his mother at this point. But to make this interpretation of Nietzsche as a believer sound plausible, Elisabeth assures Steiner that Nietzsche articulated such ideas in his final work: "Herr Professor Nietzsche's final volume of thoughts and meditations, which as you know I am currently editing with Herr Gast, will, I am quite sure, prove as much."[36]

In Nietzsche's middle (1882–85) and late (1886–89) work, there is no evidence to suggest that he ultimately embraced any form of belief in God and/or religion. But this gets to the heart of the scandal regarding Nietzsche's work in relation to Hitler

---

[34]Olsen (2006), 82.
[35]Ibid.
[36]Ibid.

and the Nazis. To clarify what made it possible for the Nazis to seemingly appropriate Nietzsche and his writings, we first need to understand Elisabeth and her husband. Elisabeth was a Christian anti-Semite, and she married Bernhard Förster, who was a part of Richard Wagner's inner circle.[37] Like Hitler and the Nazis, Förster argued that there is an inextricable link between Christianity and Germanness. As he claims in his 1881 book *Das Verhältniss des modernen Judenthums zur deutschen Kunst* (The Relationship of Modern Jewry to German Art), it is a fact that Christianity and Germanness have become so completely united that were one to decline, so too would the other. Within this framework, that which is non-Christian is not just indifferent to Christians and Christianity. It is in mortal opposition to that which is Christian, which, in part, explains Förster's anti-Semitism.

Based on Förster's books, we could say that he is a logical link in the Christian anti-Semitic chain between Kant and the Nazis.[38] Like prominent Nazis, Förster consistently blends Christianity and idealism, which enables him to define Jews as anti-idealists (materialists) who stand in mortal opposition to that which is German and, therefore, Christian.[39] For instance, in his 1883 book *Parsifal-Nachklänge* (Parsifal Reminiscences) Förster argues that Christianity is the product of the Aryan Geist, and the central component of Aryan character is idealism. Given this definition of and approach to Christianity, Jesus could not have been a Jew. As Förster claims: "Based on his origins, Jesus was *no Jew*, rather he was a Galilean. Also, he was not a 'Semite,' rather he was the 'son of

---

[37]In *Nietzsche, God, and the Jews*, Weaver Santaniello notes how Nietzsche opposed Christian anti-Semitism, which was dominant in Richard Wagner's circle (139). Elisabeth met her future husband in this circle, which served to reinforce her Christian anti-Semitism.

[38]Olsen rightly suggests that the version of Christianity that Hitler and the Nazis would adopt emanated from the Wagner circle. Chamberlain was Wagner's publicist, and it was during his time working with the Wagner Circle that he arrived at most of the ideas in *The Foundations of the Nineteenth Century*. Förster's books are clumsy and overwrought, but they are similar to Chamberlain's *Foundations* in terms of their version of Christianity, which could be defined as Christian idealism. This version of Christianity mandates the supersession and even negation of what is referred to as the materialistic Jew.

[39]In *Das Verhältniss*, Förster claims that Germanness and Christianity were wed in the second phase of Christianity's development (19).

God,' the fulfillment of all yearnings of Aryan humanity."[40] Hence, there can only be an antagonistic relationship between Judaism and Christianity, Jews and Christians:

> The loyalty of the Aryan contrasts with the proverbial perfidy of the Semites. The Aryan's heroic bravery is the opposite of the Semite's (at most) passive courage, the Aryan's idealism the opposite of the Semite's realism. The Semite demands a reward for his deed, he strives for tangible goals; he honors only change within sight, that which can be rewarded "here on earth" within his lifetime. That which is beyond the grave and death is closed off to him. The uncorrupted Aryans just want to do good for itself, "for God's sake."[41]

It is this link between Christianity and idealism that so worried Olsen's Nietzsche. Note how Olsen intelligently calls his reader's attention to the connection. When explaining to his family some of the flaws and dangers implicit in Christianity, Olsen's Nietzsche specifically emphasizes how Christian thought led to Kantian idealism: "Christ may have been Plato's fault, of course, but weren't Descartes, Locke, Kant, and the rest Christ's?"[42] To conclude the paragraph, Olsen strategically underscores the degree to which Kant is the primary culprit because he fused Christianity and idealism: "Look at the Königsberg clock-setter translating the Messiah into the gabble of German idealism."[43] Olsen's characterization here is certainly rooted in reality, for as Nietzsche claims in *On the Genealogy of Morals*: "I also do not like these latest speculators in idealism, the anti-Semites, who today roll their eyes in a Christian-Aryan-bourgeois manner and exhaust one's patience by trying to rouse up all the horned-beast elements in the people by a brazen abuse of the cheapest of all agitator's tricks,

---

[40]Förster (1883), *Parsifal-Nachklänge: Allerhand Gedanken ueber Deutsche Cultur, Wissenschaft, Kunst, Gesellschaft*. Leipzig, 22. My translation. Chamberlain makes this same claim in the *Foundations of the Nineteenth Century*. This is clearly an idea circulating in the Wagner Circle.
[41]Förster (1883), 25. My translation.
[42]Olsen (2006), 71.
[43]Olsen (2006), 72.

moral attitudinizing."[44] In a very haunting way, Nietzsche, as Olsen so aptly pictures, anticipated with stunning clarity and precision what would become one of the centerpieces of the Nazis' Christian anti-Semitic ideology.

What probably made Nietzsche so fully conscious of the looming danger of Christian idealism was Förster's April 13, 1881 petition to Bismarck, which was signed by nearly 270,000 people.[45] It is this petition with which Olsen introduces his readers to Förster:

> The first he [Nietzsche] heard about Bernhard Förster was as the crackpot teacher in a Berlin gymnasium who had organized a petition demanding the limitation of Jewish immigration, registration of all Jews, and the exclusion of Jews from positions of authority in government and education.

> Förster called the appeal *a cry from the conscience of the German people.*

> Friedrich called it a joke.[46]

Striking about this petition is how closely it resembles and anticipates point 24 of the Nazi Party program. The petition begins: "The Jewish hypertrophy conceals within itself the most serious dangers to our national way of life. This belief has spread throughout all the regions of Germany. Whenever Christian and Jew enter into social relations, we see the Jew as master and the native-born Christian population in a servile position."[47] Notice how the petition frames the conflict in religious rather than racial terms. The oppressed in Germany are the Christians, who are presumably Germans. Therefore, the petition goes on to argue, "if the inward connection between German custom and morality and the Christian outlook and tradition is to be maintained, then an alien tribe may never, ever

---

[44]Nietzsche (1989), *On the Genealogy of Morals* in *On the Genealogy of Morals and Ecce Homo.* Translated by Walter Kaufmann and R. J. Hollingdale. New York: Vintage Books, 158.

[45]This petition "received over 250,000 signatures and became the subject of a debate in the Prussian Parliament" (Levy 122).

[46]Olsen (2006), 163–4.

[47]Förster (1991), "Antisemites' Petition," in *Antisemitism in the Modern World: An Anthology of Texts.* Lexington, MA and Toronto: D.C. Heath and Company, 125.

rise to rule on German soil."[48] The implication is that, to correct the current problem in Germany, eliminating the "alien tribe" (Jews) is necessary.

Nietzsche detested Förster, mainly because of his anti-Semitism.[49] So in a letter to his sister, Olsen's Nietzsche spends considerable time critiquing her choice in a man. Specifically, Nietzsche focuses on Förster's anti-Semitism. As Olsen's Nietzsche says in the letter, "antisemitism was a mutiny of the mediocre. People like Förster were motivated by envy, resentment, and fury in the face of their own intellectual inferiority. He [Förster] was dangerous in that way only severely obtuse people can be dangerous."[50] Olsen's reference to and focus on Förster as mediocre is important for understanding not just *Nietzsche's Kisses* but the contemporary biographical novel more generally. According to Lukács, the biographical novel glorifies a certain personage, and as such, distorts our picture of history. For Lukács, this is not just something the biographical novelists have done; it is the inevitable consequence given the form of the biographical novel. Olsen certainly portrays Nietzsche in a favorable light at times, though he also portrays him in a negative light at others. But the novel spends considerable time focusing on the large cast of mediocre people surrounding Nietzsche, thus shifting the focus from the larger-than-life hero to the ordinary person. In terms of historical representation, this is an incredibly significant move, for biographical novelists such as Olsen suggest that to understand great historical collisions, knowledge of the inner workings of the culture's mediocre individuals is of utmost importance. The great historical personage, Nietzsche in this case, is important not because of the inherent quality of his ideas, nor because of *his influence*, but because of the way the mediocre engage, misappropriate, and disseminate his ideas. As Olsen's Nietzsche says: "It was a terrible thought to contemplate: how an immense number of mediocre minds were occupied with remarkably influential matters."[51] Within the context of Olsen's novel, to understand the genocidal politics of the Nazis, knowledge of mediocre individuals such as

---

[48]Förster (1991), 126.
[49]Many scholars mention Nietzsche's hatred of Förster. See Santaniello (139), Diethe (57–60), and Julian Young (364).
[50]Olsen (2006), 164.
[51]Olsen (2006), 95.

Elisabeth and Förster is of monumental significance, because such knowledge clarifies the conditions that made it possible for Hitler and the Nazis to seemingly accept and promote Nietzsche's writings and ultimately to come to power.

We see this most clearly in the way that Elisabeth puts Nietzsche and his writings at the service of Hitler and the Nazis. Like Förster and the Nazis, Elisabeth adopts an eliminationist Christian ideology, which holds that purging Germany of all things Jewish is necessary for true Christian Germanness to emerge. To indicate that Elisabeth adopted this ideology, Olsen pictures her firing Peter Gast, a Jewish friend of Nietzsche's and one of the first editors of his work. Historically, Olsen's representation of Gast is not entirely accurate. Elisabeth fired Gast as editor in the early 1890s, but she re-hired him in the late 1890s, and she ultimately came to like him.[52] The novel is significantly different. The year is 1900, and Elisabeth is examining the manuscripts that Gast edited. Displeased, she suggests that Gast "has been unable to perceive the Fritz within Fritz," which leads her to fire "the Jew"[53] and to move the Nietzsche Archive from Naumburg to Weimar.

Olsen's decision to alter historical facts is common, for biographical novelists frequently stratify truth. Superficial externals, such as the exact details regarding the years Gast edited Nietzsche's texts, are subordinate to more significant historical truths, such as the intellectual factors and ideological forces that enabled the Nazis to seemingly appropriate Nietzsche's work in support of their political agenda. Therefore, in the aesthetic service of articulating a vital historical truth about the Nazi appropriation of Nietzsche, Olsen alters less significant truths. On its own, the firing scene brilliantly captures one of the core precepts at the heart of Nazi ideology, which is the desire to purge Germany of all things Jewish. As the Nazi Party program says, which I have discussed in Chapter 2, the goal is to eliminate Jewishness "within us and without us." So when Elisabeth fires "the Jew," she sets into motion the necessary dejudification of Nietzsche's work, which has

---

[52]When it comes to Gast, Elisabeth had little choice in the matter. He was one of the only people who could read Nietzsche's handwriting. Also, subsequent editors noted that Elisabeth was altering Nietzsche's texts, and they expressed their concern. Gast was willing to overlook Elisabeth's unscrupulous behavior.

[53]Olsen (2006), 191.

a two-fold effect: it makes Nietzsche's work more popular with the largely anti-Semitic German public and it sets Nietzsche's work against himself. As Olsen's Elisabeth says: "Fritz's books are selling better than they ever sold when he was himself."[54]

Given the link between the Nazis' version of Christianity and their anti-Semitism, it was imperative not just that Elisabeth eliminate positive references to Jews in Nietzsche's text, but that she also eliminate his atheistic critique of God and religion. Olsen intelligently pictures how and why this happened through one of Elisabeth's internal monologues. While reading and editing some of Nietzsche's blasphemous and atheistic texts, Elisabeth follows her mother's lead by persuading herself that Nietzsche was actually a believer, despite the overwhelming evidence in his writings to the contrary: "All this godless talk simply won't do."[55] For Elisabeth, the problem is that "Fritz isn't saying what Fritz means to say, and it is up to Lisbeth to make sure he does."[56] Therefore, she takes it upon herself to set matters straight by revising and even forging some of Nietzsche's texts: "She releases a sheet of paper from the sheaf, and commences recopying Fritz's letter in a reasonable facsimile of his handwriting, crafting it into the thing that it wants to be deep down inside itself."[57]

Having made Nietzsche a Christian anti-Semite, Elisabeth is now ready to present her brother to Hitler and the Nazis, which is why the narrative quickly shifts to October 1934, when Olsen has Hitler visit the Nietzsche Archive in Weimar.[58] In Elisabeth's imagination, this scene represents the passing of the torch, the culmination of more than four decades of her hard work. But Olsen brilliantly underscores the ambiguous nature of the torch she is passing. The scene occurs on Nietzsche's ninetieth birthday and begins with

---

[54]Ibid.

[55]Olsen (2006), 192.

[56]Ibid.

[57]Ibid. In *Nietzsche, God, and the Jews*, Santaniello claims that Elisabeth "forged, altered, or destroyed Nietzsche's documents to cover up his negative remarks concerning Wagner, herself, Christianity, and antisemitism" (40).

[58]According to Diethe, Hitler visited Elisabeth at the Nietzsche Archive in Weimar three times: November 2, 1933; July 20, 1934; and October 2, 1934 (151). Elisabeth invited Hitler to the Archive on the occasion of Nietzsche's birthday (152), which is when Olsen dates the Hitler visit in his novel (206), but I have found nothing to verify that he attended that celebration.

Elisabeth giving Hitler Nietzsche's walking stick. So the torch she is supposedly passing is the great thinking of Nietzsche. But here is how the narrative reads shortly after Elisabeth hands Hitler the walking stick:

> She is passing the torch, and there has been, she understands as she inhabits these glorious ticks of the clock, so much life in life.

> The furious sun falling through the foliage out front of the main lodge at the New Germania compound.[59]

Surrealistically layered into this 1934 scene with Hitler is a previous experience that occurred nearly fifty years ago. But nothing in this scene has prepared the reader for it (no reference to the New Germania compound was made in this section), so it can only strike the reader as misplaced. However, if we understand that Elisabeth is passing not her brother's but her dead husband's torch, the scene makes perfect sense.

In the 1880s, Elisabeth's husband tried to establish a utopian German community in Paraguay, which was called New Germania. In *Nietzsche's Kisses*, Olsen mentions how Elisabeth and Förster "would move to Paraguay together to build the New Germania, a utopian community where pure Germans with pure ideals could reinvent the country."[60] This is significant, because when Elisabeth passes the torch to Hitler, what she is actually passing to him is Förster's New Germania, which is built on the edifice of Christian anti-Semitism, and not Nietzsche's thought, which opposes Christianity and anti-Semitism. Put simply, Olsen suggests that Elisabeth reconfigured and then used Nietzsche to pass her husband's torch of a Jew-purified Christian utopia to a man who was then in the process of constructing a Jew-purified Christian Reich. And to signify this, Olsen describes how Elisabeth feels while directing the Nietzsche Archive: "Her effort reminds her of those exciting early days in the New Germania with Bernhard."[61] Intentionally or not, Elisabeth's mission with Förster impacts her work on Nietzsche.

---

[59]Olsen (2006), 207.
[60]Olsen (2006), 166.
[61]Olsen (2006), 191.

There is good reason to accept Olsen's approach to Elisabeth. For a period of time, Elisabeth lived with her brother and served as his secretary. But after Nietzsche's turn against Christianity, Elisabeth started to reject her brother. Actually, her response was more specific. She wanted to make her brother into a man like Förster. As she claims in an April 4, 1883, letter to her mother: "I simply wish Fritz had Förster's opinions. If people would support and follow his ideals, they would be better and happier."[62] This is the case because Förster is "one of the best Germans."[63] Elisabeth's admiration and respect for Förster was not just a fleeting experience. After his death in 1889, Elisabeth devoted her life to bringing Förster's political vision to reality—she refers to his Paraguay colonization project as her foster child (*Pflegekind*). As she claims in an 1894 plea ("*Aufruf*") on behalf of Neu-Germania, her holiest obligation ("*meine heiligste Pflicht*")[64] and innermost wish ("*innigste Wunsch*")[65] is to realize her husband's dream of creating a pure-German colony ("*rein-deutsche Kolonie*").[66]

What makes Elisabeth's 1894 plea so troubling for Nietzsche scholars is the fact that she established the Nietzsche Archive in that same year.[67] We know that Nietzsche explicitly and unambiguously denounced his sister's involvement with the New Germania project because of its anti-Semitism. As Nietzsche says in a letter to his sister: "You say that Neu-Germania has nothing to do with anti-Semitism, but I know for certain that the colonization project has a distinctly anti-Semitic character from that 'Correspondence circular' that is only sent out secretly and only to the most reliable members of the party."[68] For Nietzsche, any association with Förster would be considered a profound violation of him and his work. And yet, when Hitler visited the Nietzsche Archive for the first time, Elisabeth presented him with Nietzsche's walking stick and Förster's petition to Bismarck, which is based on the same anti-Semitic agenda that appears in the Nazis' party program

---

[62]Quoted in Daniela Kraus (1999), "Bernhard und Elisabeth Försters Nueva Germania in Paraguay: eine antisemitische Utopie." Diss. University of Vienna, 106.
[63]Ibid.
[64]Förster-Nietzsche (1894), "Aufruf," *Bayreuther Blätter* 17(4–6): 175.
[65]Förster-Nietzsche (1894), 176.
[66]Ibid.
[67]As early as 1932, Erich F. Podach expressed frustration with Elisabeth's irresponsible and dishonest handling of Nietzsche's works (125–76).
[68]Quoted in Diethe (2003), 59.

and Hitler's writings. Therefore, the transition in Olsen's novel from Elisabeth's passing of the torch to the reference to the New Germania makes perfect sense. Elisabeth did not just alter Nietzsche's writings. She Försterized them.

Olsen intimates that this is Elisabeth's objective in the novel when he describes her as *"förstering a new idea that will cull us all"*[69]—this is the most haunting passage in the novel. The scene in which this claim is made is of crucial importance not just because of its intellectual content but also because of its surrealist form. The chapter opens with Nietzsche at a Wagner opera. Irritated with "Wagner's over-the-top bits," Nietzsche's "mind is wandering."[70] During his reverie, he reflects on history, which he "must overcome" by "swimming against history's current."[71] The problem is that people like Wagner, Förster, and Elisabeth have crafted entertaining works of art and systems of thought to win the masses over to their Christian anti-Semitic side. So while Nietzsche casts a very skeptical and even condescending eye on the operatic spectacle he is witnessing, he is painfully aware that the audience is totally enthralled: "The audience loves it this is the good stuff this is the gold."[72] In the midst of this experience, Nietzsche has an apocalyptic vision of the future, which will end in *"calamity,"*[73] an obvious allusion to the Nazis' great death-happening given all the references to *Deutschland Deutschland über alles.*

What makes this passage so powerful and poignant, and totally unacceptable to someone like Lukács, is the surrealist representation of time and ideas. Reflecting on the past, Nietzsche diagnoses the present in order to project the future, and what he sees is the way his sister will surrealistically transform him into his polar opposite and, thereby, create the conditions for the twentiethcentury's political nightmare. More specifically, just as his sister will Försterize Nietzsche by transforming him into a Christian anti-Semite, she will Försterize us all by putting her brother's Försterized ideas at the service of the Nazis. In essence, Hitler's Nietzsche is Elisabeth's Försterized construct. These surreal blendings and fusions coalesce

---

[69]Olsen (2006), 179, Olsen's emphasis.
[70]Olsen (2006), 177.
[71]Olsen (2006), 178.
[72]Olsen (2006), 179.
[73]Ibid.

in a temporal current moving toward the Holocaust, and though Nietzsche saw where all this was going and sought to shift the historical current in a different direction, there was nothing he could do. History is not at the behest of the right or the just. This is the type of scene that distinguishes the biographical novel's surrealism from the historical novel's realism.

Given Elisabeth's Försterization of Nietzsche, it would be wrong to suggest that she did this in order to ingratiate herself with the Nazis. The Nazis first came together in 1919, so it would be anachronistic to read her intentions in that particular way. Rather, it would be more accurate to say that she was part of a Christian anti-Semitic political movement that would eventually find its fullest manifestation in National Socialism. Olsen's scandalous historical suggestion is this: Hitler did not use Elisabeth and/ or Nietzsche to further the objectives of the Nazi Party. Instead, Elisabeth Försterized Nietzsche, and in the process, contributed to the making of Hitler and the Nazis.

But what led her to do this was not intellectual brilliance. It was simple mediocrity, and this is one of the reasons why the biographical novel is so important for illuminating history. Olsen does not present Elisabeth as an evil genius, who skillfully manipulates people and events in order to further her ideological agenda. He presents her as the quintessential mediocre person, someone who mindlessly absorbs her culture's view that Jews are by nature inferior, who relies epistemologically on hearsay (her mother's claim that Nietzsche re-embraced his faith) in order to justify modifying and even forging Nietzsche's texts, and who fails to critically interrogate the basis for her views. Put simply, what made Hitler and the Nazis possible was mass mediocrity, which Franziska, Elisabeth, and Förster incarnate. Indeed, it was this kind of mediocrity that allowed the Nazis to wrongly believe that Nietzsche would have supported their political agenda.

With regard to the uses of history in the biographical novel, history does not emanate from or revolve around a great historical figure, which is why *Nietzsche's Kisses* effectively refutes one of Lukács' key critiques of the biographical novel. For Lukács, the biographical novel drains literature of its power to represent history because "the sole embodier of the great historical idea"[74]

---

[74]Lukács (1983), 301.

makes all other characters appear like "planets revolving around the sun of the biography's hero."[75] But Olsen suggests that Lukács' representation of the biographical novel is inaccurate, because the biographical novel actually focuses more on the mediocre than the hero. Specifically, Olsen underscores how a mediocre person such as Elisabeth helps "her brother into history."[76] As Olsen claims in an interview about *Nietzsche's Kisses*, what interested him was the way "Elisabeth had begun to rewrite her brother, gain control over him by narrativizing him."[77] Significant in this framework are the ways the mediocre fail to understand the biographical hero and the ways they manipulate and misappropriate the great person's ideas. In *Nietzsche's Kisses*, history is the logical product of a combination of narcissistic "thinking" (Franziska's naïve belief (wish) that Nietzsche re-embraced his Christian faith), uninformed convictions (Förster's and Elisabeth's anti-Semitism), and irresponsible actions (Elisabeth's revisions and forgeries of Nietzsche's writings). Bumbling simpletons, ignorant bigots, biased "scholarship," accidental encounters, and coordinated hate—this is the mediocre stuff that a historical collision such as the Nazi misappropriation of Nietzsche was made of. Hence, Elisabeth's response to Hitler's visit to the Nietzsche Archive: "This is how events feel falling into history."[78] For Lukács, the biographical form of the novel necessitates a portrayal of the way the autonomous hero's brilliant ideas directly advance the Enlightenment narrative of progress. But for Olsen, Lukács' model is premised on naïve and optimistic thinking about the relationship between the intellectual hero and ordinary people. What really occurs is just the opposite: the biographical novel pictures the inner workings of the mediocre, specifically the way they shape history through their interactions with and response to a great historical figure. Lukács's active hero who creates history must give way to Olsen's mediocre, who, in their misappropriation of the biographical hero, passively watch their history-making actions come into disastrous being.

---

[75]Lukács (1983), 321.
[76]Olsen (2006), 191.
[77]Olsen (2014), 195–6.
[78]Olsen (2006), 209.

II

In *The Historical Novel*, Lukács, who recognized that the aesthetic form was in decline, argues that "the classical type of historical novel can only be aesthetically renewed if writers concretely face the question: how was the Hitler regime in Germany possible?"[79] Many prominent contemporary writers would certainly agree that novelists must play a crucial role in deciphering and picturing what led to the emergence of major historical and political events, such as the rise of National Socialism in Germany, but they would reject the view that this can be achieved through the classical historical novel, because they hold that the only way to answer the question would be through the biographical novel. This is the case because, for biographical novelists, to understand major historical collisions, knowledge of a culture's dominant structures of consciousness is imperative. Now, of course, Lukács would agree with this claim, but he and the biographical novelists have radically different conceptions of consciousness. As I intend to show in this section, the biographical novelists consider Lukács' approach too narrow and reductive.

Central to *Benjamin's Crossing* is the issue of identity. Benjamin and his close friend Gershom Scholem, the famous Jewish scholar, discuss the issue many times, and it is a primary source of tension between the two. On the surface, it would seem that the problem derives from Benjamin's reluctance to embrace his Jewish heritage and identity. But as the novel progresses, we discover that there is a much deeper issue dividing the two thinkers. Scholem introduces the theme of identity early in the novel, when he says that "Benjamin had not yet awakened to a sense of his own Jewishness then, in those innocent years before the Great War."[80] Scholem's phrasing makes it seem like Benjamin will eventually embrace his Jewishness. But this is not the case, not because Benjamin is hostile toward Jews or Jewishness, but because he considers such signifiers to be provisional fictions.

What differentiates the two is their view about the ontological status of that which language signifies. Scholem holds that the word Jew signifies a being with a definite and definable nature.

---

[79]Lukács (1983), 344.
[80]Parini (1997a), *Benjamin's Crossing*. New York: Henry Holt and Company, 5.

Within this framework, Jewish identity takes primacy over all other provisional identities. For instance, during a conversation with his wife Dora, Benjamin notes how many Czechs, Poles, Americans, and Spaniards are in France. Referring to her and her husband, Dora says that Benjamin forgot the Germans. But Benjamin retorts: "'Our friend Scholem would say that we are Jews.'"[81] For Scholem, Jewishness is an ontological fact of one's being, while Germanness is a provisional and, therefore, negligible part of one's identity. Benjamin rejects this view, for he holds that the self is composed of many contradictory and provisional identities, so he would refer to himself as both German and Jewish, among other things. This becomes most obvious when he has a thought about his own identity: "My selves are many, he thought. One by one they emerge in my letters. They are all true, even when contradictory. I embrace them all."[82] There is no single identity that subsumes all others. Rather, the self is composed of many identities, some that are even in conflict with each other.

What ultimately leads the two to draw such radically different conclusions is their religious orientation. As a religious Jew, Scholem believes that humans possess a God-created nature, one that humans must discover if they are ever going to know themselves. In a heated argument with Scholem, Benjamin defines his friend's position: "'I feel no need to make my ideas and my life conform to some external law. I am not a rabbi, thank goodness.'"[83] Scholem does not appreciate Benjamin's comment, which is why he replies: "'You make me strangely uncomfortable, Walter.'"[84] Scholem should be uncomfortable, for as Benjamin says in a letter to his wife, he has adopted Nietzsche's atheistic view of language: "Nietzsche insists that God is dead, by which he suggests that all forms of centralized or centralizing meaning have been called into question. You could say I am the embodiment of this death, this loss of determined meaning. I no longer believe in it myself, or wish for it nostalgically."[85] Instead of thinking of language as something that can and does accurately represent an object's pre-given conceptual essence, Benjamin, like Nietzsche, concludes that language brings

---

[81]Parini (1997a), 223.
[82]Parini (1997a), 130.
[83]Parini (1997a), 91.
[84]Ibid.
[85]Parini (1997a), 20.

into conceptual (not physical) being the reality that it names. As Benjamin says in a lecture to some fellow inmates in a work camp: "'Language brings reality into being; it is, as it were, a bridge between what happens in the mind and what occurs in the world. Perhaps I will try to put this more boldly: Unless one frames reality in words, the reality does not exist.'"[86]

Like Olsen, Parini suggests that Nietzsche's works are incompatible with Nazi ideology. But whereas Olsen focuses on the specific content of Nietzsche's writings (his anti-Christian atheism and his opposition to anti-Semitism), Parini focuses more on the deep-level consequences of Nietzsche's atheistic view of language. So immediately after detailing Nietzsche's view of language to Dora, Benjamin says by way of contrast: "The Nazis are coming, bringing their own kind of determined meaning, their hatred of all ambiguity."[87] As an atheist, Nietzsche's world consists of anthropomorphic constructions, which necessarily contain ambiguities and contradictions.[88] This contrasts sharply with the believer's world, which can authoritatively distinguish the pure German from the pure Jew.

If it is true that Nietzsche's atheistic view of language sets him directly against the Nazis, then it would only follow that Scholem's religious view of language would align him with the Nazis. This is a radical and disconcerting claim, but Parini does not shy away from it. The key moment of realization and confirmation comes late in the novel. After taking a bottle of morphine, Benjamin surrealistically imagines that he sees people "in Hitler's camps now, their slumping shoulders, rank-and-file; his brother, Georg, was among them,"[89] along with many others. After describing these Jews, Benjamin's thoughts immediately shift—not coincidentally—to Scholem, specifically his belief that there is an essential difference between Jews and Christians:

Scholem has passionately maintained a belief in difference. Gentiles, he argued, are the opposite of Jews. Their God is, after

---

[86]Parini (1997a), 75.
[87]Parini (1997a), 20–1.
[88]As Nietzsche claims in *The Gay Science*: "Above all, one should not wish to divest existence of its *rich ambiguity*" (335).
[89]Parini (1997a), 279.

all, a human being, terrestrial man—an incarnation. The God of the Jews is beyond mortality, not inhuman but definitely nonhuman. *Totaliter aliter*—Wholly Other. Neither man nor woman, but utterly sexless and beyond reproduction. Because, for Christians, God can be man, therefore, men can be as gods; they can do superhuman things. Thus greatness of any kind appeals to them; tyrants and destroyers are revered as well as heroic painters, poets, musicians.[90]

The abrupt shift from the Nazi concentration camp to Scholem is certainly no accident. The suggestion is that Scholem has unwittingly adopted the Nazis' view of a distinct and clearly definable identity, the kind that made the concentration camps possible.

But to understand why and how this is the case, we must briefly define Benjamin's conception of history. Chapter 4 begins with an epigraph taken from Benjamin's "On the Concept of History." The passage offers a unique perspective of history, which "is the subject of a structure whose site is not homogeneous, empty time, but time filled by the presence of the Eternal Now."[91] To clarify what is meant, Benjamin references the way the French Revolution patterned itself on the Roman Empire: "Thus, to Robespierre, ancient Rome was a past infused with the time of the Now, which he blasted out of the continuum of history. The French Revolution viewed itself as Rome reincarnate."[92] Instead of thinking of history as the logical product of a series of temporally contiguous external happenings, a "sequence of events like the beads of a rosary,"[93] Benjamin defines history primarily in terms of a precedent-setting utopic fantasy of the ruling class. This surrealist fantasy takes the form of an imagined metaphysical constellation, a truth defined in terms of relations that stand outside time and are, thus, true for all time. Specifically, this constellation determines the shape a revolution in the present should and must take. It enables leaders to identify the ideal to which all within the in-group must aspire, but it also enables the leaders to identify the enemies of the ideal. Using

---

[90]Ibid.

[91]Parini (1997a), 57.

[92]Ibid.

[93]Benjamin (1968), "Theses on the Philosophy of History," in *Illuminations.* Translated by Harry Zohn. New York: Schocken Books, 263.

this framework, the effective historian will be able to identify and define the utopic fantasy that structures the political constellation in the present, thus clarifying why specific relations have taken their particular form. As Benjamin claims, the historian "grasps the constellation which his own era has formed with a definite earlier one. Thus he establishes a conception of the present as the 'time of the now' which is shot through with chips of Messianic time."[94]

Chapter 4 of *Benjamin's Crossing* sheds specific light on the nature of Benjamin's model. For Parini's Benjamin, traditional historians sought to understand the past by transposing themselves into the minds of historical figures. This is what Lukács expects and wants historical novelists to do. But according to Benjamin, this was a mistake. Referring to himself as an "anti-historian," Parini's Benjamin argues that the goal should be "to render visible the utopian element in the present, working backward toward the past."[95] Applying Benjamin's model to Hitler and the Nazis, the task is to identify and define the utopic ideal of the past that inhabits the present as a revolutionary chip of Messianic time. With Benjamin's antihistorical approach in mind, what makes Scholem's remarks about the essential differences between Christians and Jews so profoundly disturbing is that they are consistent with the Nazis' utopic fantasy, which is premised on a metaphysical constellation that distinguishes Christians from Jews.

We can see why this is the case by briefly examining the works of a few Nazi elites. Eckart articulates the Nazis' Messianic constellation in his 1924 book *Bolshevism from Moses to Lenin*, which consists of an imagined conversation between Eckart and Hitler. The work is totally didactic, consisting of statements and subsequent clarifications to define the nature of the burgeoning Nazi ideology. According to Eckart, "'we [National Socialists] want Germanism, we want genuine Christianity,'"[96] a rhetorical formulation that equates Germanism and Christianity. But if true Germanism necessarily implies genuine Christianity, then true Jewishness necessarily implies genuine anti-Christianity, which is why Eckart's Hitler concludes that Christ and the Jew belong to

---

[94]Ibid.
[95]Parini (1997a), 63.
[96]Eckart (1999), *Bolshevism from Moses to Lenin: A Dialogue between Adolf Hitler and Me*. Hillsboro, WV: National Vanguard Books, 36.

"'two fundamentally different worlds [which] were opposed to one another.'"[97] To support this view, Eckart references the New Testament, which justifies the Nazis' view that Christianity signifies a decisive rupture with Judaism and the Jew: "Christ was not so tolerant. With a whip he put a stop to the business of the 'children of the devil.'"[98] For Eckart, Christ was justified in taking this stance, because the Jews have a propensity to undermine governments, specifically Christian nations. Indeed, this is exactly what the Jews are doing today in Germany, for as Eckart's Hitler says: "'And the game they're playing today, they have been at for two thousand years.'"[99] Put simply, Christ defined the constellation of relations between Christians and Jews two thousand years ago, and that metaphysical model still holds true for today, thus explaining why the Nazis must take decisive action against the Jews in the present.

   Worth noting is that Eckart's Hitler and Hitler himself understand Christ in identical ways. As Hitler claims in an April 12, 1922, speech:

In boundless love as a Christian and as a man I read through the passage which tells us how the Lord at last rose in His might and seized the scourge to drive out of the Temple the brood of vipers and of adders. How terrific was His fight for the world against the Jewish poison today, after two thousand years, with deepest emotion I recognize more profoundly than ever before in the fact that it was for this that He had to shed His blood upon the Cross. As a Christian I have no duty to allow myself to be cheated, but I have the duty to be a fighter for truth and justice.[100]

Hitler opposes the Jews, and in doing so, he believes that he is obeying Christ and even being like Christ. And if Hitler were not to oppose the Jews, the situation could be dire, for human society could "suffer the same catastrophic collapse as did the civilization of the ancient world some two thousand years ago—a civilization

---

[97]Eckart (1999), 33.
[98]Eckart (1999), 35.
[99]Eckart (1999), 21.
[100]Hitler (1969), "Speech of 12 April 1922," in *The Speeches of Adolf Hitler: April 1922–August 1939*. Translated by Norman H. Baynes. Vol. I. New York: Howard Fertig, 19.

that was driven to its ruin through this same Jewish people."[101] In short, the imagined metaphysical constellation that was established two thousand years ago is the same one operating in the twentieth century. Consequently, if the Nazis do not follow Christ's injunctions and act as Christ did, then modern Christian civilization is destined to collapse.

Propaganda minister Joseph Goebbels penned in 1923 a novel (published in 1929) titled *Michael* that defines the Nazis' constellation of Christian anti-Semitic thought with stunning precision. The main character is Michael, a disillusioned German who wants to restore Germany's greatness. Significant is his conception of Christ, who gives modern Germans the needed framework for instituting their Christian Reich. According to Michael, "Christ is hard and relentless," which is why "He drives the Jewish money-changers out of the temple."[102] Setting Christ against the Jews is crucial, for it allows Goebbels' Michael to suggest that negating Jews is a prerequisite for establishing the Nazis' Christian Reich. As Michael claims: "We modern Germans are something like Christ Socialists."[103] Within this framework, Christians and Jews are in irreconcilable conflict: "Christ is the genius of love, as such the most diametrical opposite of Judaism, which is the incarnation of hate."[104] This conflict epitomizes the way history has functioned for two millennia: "The Jew is the lie personified. When he crucified Christ, he crucified everlasting truth for the first time in history. This was repeated dozens of times during the next twenty centuries and is being repeated again today."[105] The logic of this model is pernicious and deadly. For Michael, a "nation without religion is like a man without breath," and since the "German quest for God is not to be separated from Christ,"[106] this means that Germans have no alternative but to take decisive action against the Jews, for "Christ is the first great enemy of the Jews."[107] Established

---

[101]Hitler (1969), 20.
[102]Goebbels (1987), *Michael*. Translated by Joachim Neugroschel. New York: Amok Press, 39.
[103]Goebbels (1987), 65.
[104]Ibid.
[105]Goebbels (1987), 65–6.
[106]Goebbels (1987), 120.
[107]Goebbels (1987), 65.

two thousand years ago, this model is the imagined metaphysical constellation that determines the pattern of relations in the present.

While it is certainly impossible to understand the Nazi demonization and subsequent violation of the Jews without taking into account their specific version of Christianity, defined as a metaphysical constellation that sets Christ and the Jews in an eternal battle, it is not really the religious content of the constellation that concerns either Benjamin or Parini. Rather, it is the imagined metaphysics underwriting the constellation that matters most. When Scholem distinguishes between Jews and Christians, and it is significant that he frames the identities in religious rather than racial terms, he tacitly acknowledges and legitimizes the metaphysical constellation to which the Nazis appealed in order to generate the pattern of revolutionary relations in National Socialist Germany. This whole constellation presupposes a clearly definable metaphysical identity, which ontologically distinguishes Christian from Jew. Scholem differs from the Nazis because he perceives the metaphysical constellation from the vantage point of a Jew rather than a Christian.

But it is precisely this metaphysical conception of identity that Nietzsche identifies as intellectually incoherent. There are two separate reasons why this is the case. First, Nietzsche, like Benjamin, does not think that language neatly signifies objects in the world. As he says in a famous passage from his notebooks: "'Thinking,' as epistemologists conceive it, simply does not occur: it is a quite arbitrary fiction, arrived at by selecting one element from the process and eliminating all the rest, an artificial arrangement for the purpose of intelligibility."[108] Language does not accurately signify a pre-given conceptual reality. Rather, it brings into conceptual existence the epistemic reality that it names. In this case, language makes people believe that there is this thing called thinking going on inside a human's head, and it is separate and distinct from remembering, imagining, fantasizing, and feeling, among other things. But Nietzsche holds that this is just a deception and

---

[108]Given that Elisabeth collected the materials in *The Will to Power*, which consists of passages taken from Nietzsche's notebooks, I have reservations about using this text. However, I only cite passages that confirm ideas found in the works Nietzsche prepared for publication. This passage is particularly important, for it is one that Paul de Man discusses in his groundbreaking study *Allegories of Reading* (129).

seduction of language. What actually occurs in the human mind is a blending of many activities. But for the sake of communication, language falsifies that which it signifies. In other words, language is implicated in a necessary but useful lie.

Second, Nietzsche rejects the idea of a transcendental signifier. In a passage that brilliantly articulates the governing idea in his genealogical approach to knowledge and truth, Nietzsche says: "All concepts in which an entire process is semiotically concentrated elude definition; only that which has no history is definable."[109] The obvious implication is that, since all things have a history, nothing is definable. Put in concrete terms, to think that the Jew from the time of Christ has the same nature as the Jew in Nazi Germany is simply incoherent. Over the centuries, Jews and Christians have mingled, thus making it impossible to disentangle the Jewish from the Christian, the Christian from the Jewish. Moreover, given the evolution of ideas and people, it would make no sense to say that what was established two thousand years ago is the same as that which exists today.

What makes this whole system of the Nazis possible is an implicit and naïve belief in metaphysics, the view that there are truths (a metaphysical definition of the Christian, a metaphysical definition of a Jew, or a metaphysical constellation relating the two) which are valid for all people in all places at all times. Having understood not just the absurdities but also the dangers of metaphysics, it only makes sense that Parini's Benjamin rejects it. And he does this after having a conversation with Bertolt Brecht, in which Brecht makes the case for a nontechnical form of simplified thinking. Reflecting on Brecht's claim, Benjamin says to himself: "The elaborate metaphysical turns that had become second nature to him through long years of philosophical study must be sacrificed now."[110] Benjamin rejects Scholem's work, primarily because Scholem's characterization of the conflict between Christians and Jews is premised on an imagined metaphysics (for Nietzsche, Benjamin, and Parini, all metaphysics are imagined), which holds that Christians and/or Christianity have a nature that is distinguishable from and in opposition to the nature of Jews

---

[109]Nietzsche (1989), 80.
[110]Parini (1997a), 131.

and/or Judaism.[111] Benjamin opposes this view, not just because he rejects the idea of metaphysics, but because he understands that there is a link between metaphysical religious thinking and the Nazi extermination of the Jews.

As an anti-metaphysical thinker in the tradition of Nietzsche, Benjamin subscribes to a crossing approach to concepts and identities, which is why the title of Parini's book is so important. We get the best definition of crossing through a reference to a character named Meir Winklemann, who desired to become a rabbi, but because of a bad marriage, became a salesman. Given his career, Winklemann is described as "crossing borders so blithely that he no longer believed in the existence of separate countries."[112] In *The Gay Science*, Nietzsche identifies those who subscribe to this idea of crossing as the "homeless,"[113] those individuals who understand that they "are too manifold and mixed racially"[114] to be reduced to a singular identity. The intellectually homeless people "do not feel tempted to participate in the mendacious racial self-admiration and racial indecency that parades in Germany today as a sign of a German way of thinking."[115] With a clear understanding of European history and conceptual crossing, the idea of pure and fixed identities is totally absurd. Fluid, intermingling, blending— these are the things of which human and conceptual identity are composed, and necessarily so. For Scholem and the Nazis, to think that they could disentangle and/or differentiate Christian from Jew is more an adolescent fantasy than an incoherent fiction, for such distinctions are premised on the neat and tidy thinking (metaphysics) of a bygone era. And were Scholem or the Nazis to understand

---

[111]Parini acknowledges that Jacques Derrida influenced his thinking. One of the specific ideas that had a major impact was Derrida's suggestion that the rise of ethnology led to a radical deconstruction of metaphysics. As Derrida says in his lecture "Structure, Sign, and Play in the Discourse of the Human Sciences": "One can assume that ethnology could have been born as a science only at the moment when a decentering had come about: at the moment when European culture—and, in consequence, the history of metaphysics and of its concepts—had been *dislocated*, driven from its locus, and forced to stop considering itself as the culture of reference" (qtd. in Ryan, 53). For a wonderful analysis of Derrida's impact on contemporary creative writers, see Ryan's chapter "Structure, Sign, and Play" in *The Novel after Theory*.

[112]Parini (1997a), 72.

[113]Nietzsche (1989b), 338.

[114]Nietzsche (1989b), 340.

[115]Ibid.

the implications of living in a post-metaphysical age, in the age of conceptual crossing, the whole religious project underwriting the Nazi agenda would be exposed as nonsense.

What makes Benjamin's approach to history so incompatible with Lukács' and suitable for a biographical novel is his profound understanding of psychology, modernism, and surrealism, all of which Lukács detests. As an heir of Enlightenment rationalism, Lukács favors a form of historical positivism that uses deterministic models to foreground a logical and rational causal nexus. Put simply, Lukács seeks "a clear understanding of history as a process, of history as the concrete precondition of the present."[116] Consequently, here is the right way to do the historical novel:

> A writer who deals with history cannot chop and change with his material as he likes. Events and destinies have their natural, objective weight, their natural, objective proportion. If a writer succeeds in producing a story which correctly reproduces these relationships and proportions, then human and artistic truth will emerge alongside the historical. If, on the other hand, his story distorts these proportions, then it will distort the artistic picture as well.[117]

There is a natural and intrinsic weight to events and destinies, and within Lukács' positivist framework, Gobineau's *Essay on the Inequality of Human Races* (1853–55) would, as a matter of temporal and deterministic fact, carry more epistemic weight in defining the Nazis' racist ideology than the New Testament, for Gobineau's work is much closer in time than the Gospels.

But modernists reject the idea that there is a natural and objective weight to concepts, for the modernist mind is in part characterized by the anarchic, non-predictable distortions of surrealism. Closest to Robespierre were not necessarily the temporally contiguous works of Voltaire and Rousseau but rather the temporally distant writings of the ancient Romans. By wrenching out of the continuum of history an imagined metaphysical constellation, a leader such as Robespierre could generate a revolutionary fervor that shaped

---

[116]Lukács (1983), 21.
[117]Lukács (1983), 290.

the constellation of relations in his present. For the Nazis, Christ's brutal whipping of the Jews is their dominant constellation, for it ontologically distinguishes Christianity from Judaism, Christians from Jews. While the content of this imagined constellation is important, as Olsen so intelligently demonstrates, what really concerns Benjamin is the metaphysics underwriting it, as Parini so skillfully illustrates. So long as a metaphysics of meaning remains a legitimate possibility, conceptual crossing and evolution are seen as threats to a phantom ideal of purity, such as the true Christian, the true German, or the true Jew. This distinction between crossing and metaphysics is what separated Benjamin not just from the Nazis but also from his dear friend Scholem, who, as a Jewish scholar and an opponent of the Nazis, unwittingly and very ironically adopted one of the core assumptions inherent in Nazi ideology.

III

To conclude this chapter, I want to explain why the contemporary biographical novel has supplanted the classical historical novel. It is my contention that the classical historical novel, as defined by Lukács, is based on and takes too literally and seriously Marx's claim that "it is not the consciousness of men that determines their being, but, on the contrary, their social being that determines the consciousness."[118] Prominent biographical novelists accept the view that the material conditions of being contribute to the structures of consciousness, and they would certainly not want to go back to the naive Enlightenment idea of the autonomous subject. But they reject the view that too heavily weights the material conditions of being, because it renders humans empty ciphers within a historical context and it fails to take into account the anarchic, mysterious, unpredictable, and surrealist dimension of human consciousness. The issue here is not an either/or, as in Marx's formulation above. Rather, it is a question of a conception of consciousness and its relative weighting, and that weighting would differ from one context and age to the next. But to

---

[118]Marx (1977), *"Preface" to A Critique of Political Economy in Karl Marx: Selected Writings*. Editor David McLellan. Oxford: Oxford University Press, 389.

access that weighting, it was necessary to develop an aesthetic form that foregrounded a less deterministic and a more surreal consciousness. To put the matter succinctly, modernism's newly emerging concept of and approach to consciousness mandated the rise of a more suitable aesthetic form to signify and engage the historical and the political, which turned out to be the biographical novel.

We can see this most clearly through the kinds of biographical novels that have emerged over the last thirty years in order to represent the factors that led to the Nazis' anti-Semitic political agenda. In an effort to generate a communal fervor to inspire revolutionary action, people of a given historical period are governed not exclusively or even mainly by that which is most spatially or temporally contiguous, the deterministic and mechanistic laws deriving from the material conditions of being. Rather, they appropriate and are oftentimes subsequently governed by a myth that most suits their ideological agenda, no matter how distant in time and space. For the Nazis, the dominant myth was premised on a specific version of Christianity, one that projects Christ as the first and most extreme anti-Semite. Thus, the realization of the Nazis' modernist God state mandates the negation of that which is the antithesis of or opposes Christ or Christianity. Within this framework, what made the Nazis' anti-Semitic political agenda historically possible was a specific type of consciousness, one based on a metaphysical approach to human identity (as we see in *Benjamin's Crossing*) and an anti-Semitic version of Christianity (as we see in *Nietzsche's Kisses*). For many contemporary writers, picturing that historical consciousness can best be achieved in and through the biographical rather than the historical novel, through a surrealist rather than a realist aesthetic.

To understand why this is the case, let me briefly discuss an important debate about realism and surrealism that took place in the 1920s and the 1930s. André Breton published his first "Manifesto of Surrealism" in 1924, and the strangest thing about this work is the degree to which it shares common assumptions with writings from prominent Nazis, who were authoring some of their most important work at roughly the same time. Like the Nazis, Breton laments the rise and dominance of positivism, because it is reductive and dehumanizing. More specifically, he opposes "the realistic attitude," which he says is "inspired by positivism," because he believes that it is "hostile to any intellectual or moral advancement."[119] For Breton, when positivist models come to dominate, then humans and their humanity become captive to the mechanical and the formulaic, thus destroying the desire and vitiating the capacity for imagination and freedom. As he goes on to explain, his present is in thrall to rationalism: "We are still living under the reign of logic: this, of course, is what I have been driving at."[120]

While Breton and the Nazis consider positivist models limited, reductive, and formulaic, they have radically different counter-approaches. As I argued in Chapter 2, to the threat of positivism the Nazis adopted a Kantian model that charts a space within the human that is insusceptible to positivism's reductive calculations. More specifically, the Nazis hold that German Christians, unlike materialistic Jews, can transcend positivism's deterministic laws through negative and positive freedom. The Nazis do not question or challenge the reality or value of positivism. In fact, they consider positivism important. But they consider it only one dimension of the human, and a lesser one at that. The other dimension, which Kant refers to as the intelligible, is that part of the human that can transcend the mechanistic laws of natural necessity. When people adopt the view that a positivist model could explain everything about the human, they have then become materialists—this is why Schlick and the Vienna Circle were dubbed a Jewish organization, as I have shown in Chapter 2. And since Jews, according to the Nazis, are by nature materialists, they can neither understand nor experience that which belongs to the intelligible realm of being.

What separates Breton from the Nazis is his surrealist view of the human and the world, which calls into question and even deconstructs the empirical/intelligible distinction. While the Nazi model presupposes a neat and tidy distinction between the empirical world, which can be pictured in terms of positivism's strict laws of cause and effect, and the intelligible world, which transcends those laws, Breton's model presupposes a hazy and artificial distinction between reality (that which obeys the logical laws of reason) and dream. His solution to the reign of logic is to combine "these two

---

[119]Breton (1972), "Manifesto of Surrealism," in *Manifestoes of Surrealism.* Translated by Richard Seaver and Helen R. Lane. Ann Arbor: The University of Michigan Press, 6.
[120]Breton (1972), 9.

states, dream and reality, which are seemingly so contradictory, into a kind of absolute reality, a *surreality*."[121] The problem with his age is that the rise of realism and positivism has led many to valorize and reify the rational and logical and, in the process, to marginalize and neglect the dream (imaginative) dimension of thought. Surrealism is the answer, which Breton defines thus: "Psychic automatism in its pure state, by which one proposes to express—verbally, by means of the written word, or in any other manner—the actual functioning of thought. Dictated by thought, in the absence of any control exercised by reason, exempt from any aesthetic or moral concern."[122] According to this definition, positivism's "thought," which is dictated by reason, is not really thought, because within a surrealist framework, "there is a sentence unknown to our consciousness which is only crying out to be heard."[123] It is only by entering the world of dream that one can hear that sentence. The epistemological task, therefore, is to access actual thought by limiting reason's role so that the mind can finally understand and appreciate the "luminous phenomenon"[124] of the surrealist's world, which combines dream and reality.

In 1929, Benjamin published an essay that examines the impact of surrealism on epistemology, literature, and literary analysis. This essay is important because Benjamin, who has Marxist proclivities that would seemingly align him with Lukács, ultimately has a positive view of surrealism, which, as I will discuss shortly, Lukács considers incompatible with Marxism. As is the case with Nazi ideological elites, of central concern for Benjamin and the surrealists is the reductive nature of positivism. When setting the intellectual stage for the rise of surrealism, Benjamin, following Breton, suggests that it is a modern response to a realist approach to life. Detailing Breton's view, Benjamin says that "the philosophical realism of the Middle Ages was the basis of poetic experience."[125] To clarify the logic of Breton's position, Benjamin briefly defines realism and then

---

[121]Breton (1972), 14.
[122]Breton (1972), 26.
[123]Breton (1972), 30.
[124]Breton (1972), 37.
[125]Benjamin (1978), "Surrealism," in *Reflections: Essays, Aphorisms, Autobiographical Writings*. Translated by Edmund Jephcott. New York: Schocken, 184.

clarifies how contemporary artistic movements arose in response to the reductive nature of realism:

> This realism, however—that is, the belief in a real, separate existence of concepts whether outside or inside things—has always quickly crossed over from the logical realm of ideas to the magical realm of words. And it is as magical experiments with words, not as artistic dabbling, that we must understand the passionate phonetic and graphical transformational games that have run through the whole literature of the avant-garde for the past fifteen years, whether it is called Futurism, Dadaism, or Surrealism.[126]

Benjamin utilizes an ahistorical approach here to explain the rise of a variety of models. Over the ages, poetry has responded to the hegemony of a form of realism by underscoring the magical and mysterious within the human. What happened in the Middle Ages is now happening in the twentieth century, though the models of realism have become splintered and multifarious, assuming the forms of scientific, historical, and/or logical positivism. Challenging the reign of contemporary positivisms is of crucial importance, for as Benjamin says on the opening page, the major intellectual crisis for Germany is "that of the humanistic concept of freedom."[127] And as far as Benjamin is concerned, the surrealists have the most compelling answer: "Since Bakunin, Europe has lacked a radical concept of freedom. The Surrealists have one."[128] But for the surrealists, freedom is not to be considered primarily an individual experience. Rather, it must be linked with revolution, a massive experience of communal autonomy. As Benjamin claims: "To win the energies of intoxication for the revolution—this is the project about which Surrealism circles in all its books and enterprises."[129]

Ironically, for the pro-surrealist, quasi-Marxist Benjamin, one of the primary obstacles to revolution and autonomy is Marxism, which has embraced a literary form of positivism known as realism—this is the basis for Lukács' model in *The Historical*

---

[126]Benjamin (1978), 184.
[127]Benjamin (1978), 177.
[128]Benjamin (1978), 189.
[129]Ibid.

Novel. We can best see the limitations of Marxism through Lukács' critique of surrealism. Lukács defines his anti-surrealist, Marxist approach to literature in his 1938 essay "Realism in the Balance." For Lukács, "the main trend" of surrealism "is its growing distance from, and progressive dissolution of, realism."[130] This is a major problem because Marxist "literature is a particular form by means of which objective reality is reflected."[131] Since surrealism "denies that literature has any reference to objective reality,"[132] it is in irreconcilable conflict with the very purpose and meaning of the Marxist concept of literature, which has as its objective the task of picturing "how thoughts and feelings grow out of the life of society and how experiences and emotions are part of the total complex of reality."[133] Given surrealism's rejection of "reality" and its narcissistic focus on the "purely subjective,"[134] it can play no role in advancing a political revolution.

How can we explain that surrealism seeks to marshal energies for revolution, according to Benjamin, while it renders revolution impossible, according to Lukács? The answer has something to do with their divergent understandings of and approaches to consciousness and history. For Lukács, "what matters in the novel is fidelity in the reproduction of the material foundations of the life of a given period, its manners and the feelings and thoughts deriving from these."[135] Exposing these material foundations would enable the general population to better understand the nature of their situation within society and subsequently to formulate a strategy to escape. By stark contrast, surrealists, who focus on immediate subjective experiences and the fragmentariness of being, "fail to pierce the surface to discover the underlying essence, i.e., the real factors that relate their experiences to the hidden social forces that produce them."[136] To put the matter succinctly, great realists create literature that prophetically anticipates and even inspires "future developments,"[137] while surrealists, no matter how gifted, can do

---

[130]Lukács (1992), "Realism in the Balance," in *Aesthetic and Politics*. Translation editor, Ronald Taylor. London and New York: Verso, 29.
[131]Lukács (1992), 33.
[132]Ibid.
[133]Lukács (1992), 36.
[134]Lukács (1992), 40.
[135]Lukács (1983), 166–7.
[136]Lukács (1992), 36–7.
[137]Lukács (1992), 48–9.

nothing of the sort, and this is because they fail to understand what really matters, which are the material conditions of being that form and shape consciousness.

Benjamin has reservations about Marxism because of its positivist approach to history, which he expresses most clearly in his last essay "On the Concept of History." In the opening section of the work, Benjamin imagines a mindless puppet that represents historical materialism in that it can have a total perspective of the structures of capitalist exploitation. As a good Marxist, Benjamin certainly values a comprehensive picture of the economic and political laws that shape and determine a particular society. But as a critic of positivism, he thinks that historical materialism is narrow and limited and would benefit were it to enlist "the services of theology."[138] According to Benjamin, the positivist discourse of historical materialism, which could be expressed by a mindless puppet, would only appeal to people who also lack the desire and/or ability to be more than an automaton. Therefore, for historical materialism to be effective, it needs to acknowledge and respect that part of the human that cannot be defined by the reductive discourse of positivism, so it would benefit considerably were it to wed itself to a conceptual system that has as its focus that which transcends the laws of positivism, such as theology. Put simply, historical materialism needs to form an alliance with theology for two separate reasons: it would more accurately picture the autonomous dimension of the human and it would appeal to a wider range of people by preserving a sense of human mystery.

And yet, it is important to note that Benjamin invokes theology with some qualifications and reservations. Benjamin recognizes that theology, while valuable in that it valorizes the mysterious within persons and preserves a limited concept of human autonomy, also runs the risk "of becoming a tool of the ruling classes," for "the Messiah comes not only as the redeemer, he comes as the subduer of Antichrist."[139] Benjamin's observation here about the Messiah perfectly pictures the Nazis' utopian fantasy, a political ideology that sets the idealist Christ (Messiah) against the materialist Jew (Antichrist). The image that best embodies the metaphysical constellation underwriting the Nazi project can be found in Julius

---

[138]Benjamin (1968), 253.
[139]Benjamin (1968), 255.

FIGURE 1 Image entitled *Resurrection (Auferstehung)* in a 1929 issue of *Der Stürmer*.

Streicher's *Der Stürmer*, a publication that the Nuremberg Tribunal concluded did more to spread the Nazis' death-bringing anti-Semitism than any other publication in Germany.[140] In this image (see Figure 1), Nazi soldiers salute the crucified Messiah, but since this is an Easter image, it is titled *Resurrection (Auferstehung)*, which is as

[140]For discussions of the role Streicher's publication played in Nazi Germany, see my essay "Conceptualizing Christianity and Christian Nazis after the Nuremberg Trials" and Chapters 6 and 7 of *The Modernist God State*.

much political as it is religious. Symbolized by the soldiers' salutes to Christ and the waving Nazi flags, the political implication is that the risen Messiah will bless and redeem National Socialist Germany. Within this framework, the Messiah does not just redeem; he also subdues the Antichrist (the Jew), which explains why the Jew is pictured retreating in fear. He realizes that the resurrection of the Christian Messiah in Nazi Germany entails his negation.

We are now in a position to clarify the unique way in which the biographical novel engages history and to explain why it has supplanted the historical novel. The classical historical novelist skillfully pictures the rational and logical nexus of causal relations that shape a particular consciousness into being, the deterministic laws of socioeconomic being that can be objectively represented through literary realism. By stark contrast, the biographical novelist, while picturing the logical nexus of causal relations, also depicts the nondeterministic structures of human consciousness, the indeterminable laws of psychopolitical being that can only be represented through surrealistic literary techniques. To be more specific, the Nazis' anti-Semitic agenda, based as it is on a Messianic theology that sets Christians and Jews in mortal opposition to one another, could only succeed when a huge segment of the population finally internalized the view that Christ was the first and greatest anti-Semite, an imagined metaphysical constellation that defines Jews as the enemy of all things Christian and, therefore, mandates their negation. That version of Christianity, which Förster promulgated in his writings and through his petition, significantly impacted the ideology and actions of Elisabeth and thus explains how and why she Försterized Nietzsche in such a way that he (the Försterized Nietzsche) contributed to the making of Hitler and the Nazis. But when exactly did that virulently anti-Semitic version of Christianity come to dominate among Nazi elites? When did it become the dominant structure of consciousness among ordinary citizens of Nazi Germany? These questions cannot be answered in any clear and distinct way. They can only be intimated and suggested.

And this brings me to the main question I want to answer in this chapter. In my interview with Olsen, he said that "every genre exists because it can do things other genres can't."[141] What can the biographical novelist give readers that the classical historical novelist

---

[141]Olsen (2014), 197.

cannot? And why has the biographical novel become so popular in recent years? To answer these questions, I want to follow Parini by making a distinction between the historian and the anti-historian. For many Holocaust historians, knowing something exactly, such as what happened and what was said at the Wannsee Conference in 1942, would enable us to understand what led to the death camps. Biographical novelists, of course, consider knowledge of empirical specifics extremely valuable, but they complicate the Marxist picture by taking into account a surreal dimension of human consciousness. Of crucial importance to them is the imagined metaphysical constellation that surrealistically underwrites a major historical collision. To be more specific, prominent biographical novelists who focus on the Nazis consider the emergence of the anti-Semitic Christ the crucial element in the making of the Holocaust. For instance, Olsen vividly pictures how Elisabeth used her husband's ideology (the metaphysical constellation of Christ negating the Jew) to remake Nietzsche into a Christian anti-Semite, thus clarifying how Elisabeth's Försterized Nietzsche contributed to the making of National Socialism, a political organization that Nietzsche would have relentlessly mocked and totally condemned. Duffy clearly depicts how the Jewish Wittgenstein internalized a Christian idealist philosophy that inadvertently aligned him with Nazi sympathizers (Nelböck and Sauter) and the Nazis (Anschluss), thus embroiling Wittgenstein in a contradictory and self-negating ideology. Parini brilliantly images the surrealist subconscious of Scholem, which was structured in relation to the Nazis' metaphysical constellation that clearly defines Jews and Christians and pits them in mortal opposition to one another. Not one of these texts gives us a precise moment when the imagined metaphysical constellation came into being, because they cannot. For biographical novelists, empirical evidence is hugely important for the construction of their narratives. But even more important is what the documents cannot give, which is the imagined metaphysical constellation that functions at the level of the communal subconscious and determines how documentary evidence will be understood and assessed.

However, projecting that imagined metaphysical constellation in exact ways is not possible, because what we are dealing with here is a matter of a provisional surreal consciousness rather than a documentable textual fact. To illustrate my point, let me complicate my own interpretation. I am saying that the Streicher image from *Der Stürmer* best pictures the imagined metaphysical constellation underwriting Nazi ideology. But that image was published in March 1929. Given that the Nazis had not yet become the dominant political force in Germany, it would be inaccurate to say that the imagined metaphysical constellation in that image was the dominant one in the collective consciousness of the people at that time. So when exactly did it become the dominant structure of consciousness in Germany? Biographical novelists simply refuse to supply an answer to that kind of question, because they consider it deceptive to use a rigidly demarcated discourse to define the surreal consciousness of a people. This explains Parini's decision to picture Scholem's metaphysical constellation through the lens of a person who is in a drug-induced state. After taking a bottle of morphine, "scenes flickered before"[142] Benjamin's eyes: the chaotic jumble of a slaughterhouse, "Hitler's camps,"[143] and Scholem's metaphysical constellation. This surrealist scene is not depicted in a linear or logical way. But that is the point. There is a part of human consciousness that can be defined by the mechanistic laws of cause and effect, and most of the novel is organized along those lines—this is what the classical historical novel depicts, and for Lukács, it is all that such a novel should depict. But there is another dimension of human consciousness that can only be represented through the anarchic and unpredictable "laws" of surrealism, and it is in this surrealist moment that we get the most incisive portrayal of the imagined metaphysical constellation that made "Hitler's camps" possible. If a novelist wants to picture both the material conditions and the psychological structures that made mass oppression as seen in the Holocaust possible, the best way to do that would be through the surrealism of the biographical novel rather than the realism of the historical novel.

---

[142]Parini (1997a), 279.
[143]Ibid.

4

Zora Neale Hurston and the art of political critique in the biblical biographical novel

References to the Holocaust abound in twentieth- and twenty-first-century American literature. Now, of course, someone could easily correct me by saying, "knowledge of the Holocaust did not really surface until the mid-1940s. Therefore, it would be more accurate to say that literary references to the Holocaust could have only come into being in the mid-forties, at the earliest." But this issue of temporally restricting literary signification cuts to the heart of what is most important for many prominent writers. For instance, in 1957, William Faulkner refers to his *Light in August* character Percy Grimm, who brutally murders Joe Christmas in the name of God and the state, as "a Nazi Storm Trooper," even though Faulkner admits that he had not "heard of Hitler's Storm Troopers" in 1932 when he published the novel. Faulkner could make this claim because he holds that Grimm "exists everywhere." In other words, you can find Grimm "in all countries, in all people."[1] Put more concretely, the political psychology that led Grimm to violate Christmas is strikingly similar to the one that

[1] Faulkner (1958), *Faulkner in the University: Class Conferences at the University of Virginia, 1957-1958*. Editors Frederick L. Gwynn and Joseph L. Blotner. New York: Vintage Books, 41.

allowed Irma Grese to violate Jews in the Nazi death camps.[2] Therefore, Faulkner's novel is successful because Grimm effectively symbolizes a political psychology operational in other cultures and times, even if the author is totally unaware of other instantiations. Symbolizing something not directly known is hugely important, for as I discussed in Chapter 2, we assess the quality of a biographical novel's symbolism on the basis of its function to accurately signify unknown historical characters and events. So Duffy's *The World As I Found It* is an extremely successful and effective work, I argue, because the character of Max, who symbolizes a dark undercurrent in Wittgenstein's philosophy and thinking and thus aligns the Austrian philosopher with the Nazis, can illuminate something that Duffy does not mention or even seem to know, such as the Schlick assassination.

This desire to clearly define a political psychology, which can symbolically illuminate unknown historical figures and events in the past, present, or future, explains why so many mid-twentieth-century black authors frequently engage and reference the Holocaust. For many prominent black writers, the Holocaust is the most flagrant and extreme manifestation of political oppression. Therefore, if we want to understand the theological, political, and psychological conditions that made other atrocities possible, a close analysis of the Holocaust would be useful, because it is an extreme example illustrating the necessary conditions for violating certain groups of people with emotional, psychological, and legal impunity. For instance, in *The Fire Next Time*, James Baldwin notes that many "white people were, and are, astounded by the holocaust in Germany," because "they did not know that" white people "could act that way."[3] "But," Baldwin goes on to claim, he "very much doubt[s] whether black people were astounded,"[4] because blacks have been watching whites do to non-whites what the Nazis

---

[2]Irma Grese was a blond beauty who sadistically humiliated, brutalized, tortured, and murdered an untold number of Jews in Nazi concentration camps. After the court sentenced her to death, the unrepentant Grese wrote letters to her parents and siblings, telling them not to mourn because she has no regrets. In fact, she insists that she faithfully fulfilled her duty to her country and has a clean conscience. There are striking similarities between Grimm and Grese when it comes to their justifications for their brutal treatment of the racially-other "alien."

[3]Baldwin (1993), *The Fire Next Time*. New York: Vintage International, 52–3.

[4]Baldwin (1993), 53.

have recently done to the Jews. Therefore, blacks understand the conditions and structures that have made mass-scale political oppression possible. Given that these conditions and structures have been operational for ages, Aimé Césaire chides the white West for its indignation about the Nazis:

> People are surprised, they become indignant. They say: "How strange! But never mind—it's Nazism, it will pass!" And they wait, and they hope; and they hide the truth from themselves, that it is barbarism, the supreme barbarism, the crowning barbarism that sums up all daily barbarisms; that it is Nazism, yes, but that before they were its victims, they were its accomplices; that they tolerated that Nazism before it was inflicted on them, that they absolved it, shut their eyes to it, legitimized it, because, until then, it has been applied only to non-European peoples; that they have cultivated that Nazism, that they are responsible for it, and that before engulfing the whole edifice of Western, Christian civilization in its reddened waters, it oozes, seeps, and trickles from every crack.[5]

Knowing the theology, psychology, and politics on which Western ideology is premised, Césaire is not at all surprised by the Nazis, and he believes that whites should not be surprised either. Indeed, he goes on to claim that what really angers white Westerners about Hitler is not so much his criminal behavior, but "the fact that he applied to Europe colonialist procedures which until then had been reserved exclusively for the Arabs of Algeria, the 'coolies' of India, and the 'niggers' of Africa."[6] Zora Neale Hurston makes a similar claim in a bowdlerized chapter of her 1942 book *Dust Tracks on a Road*:

> All around me, bitter tears are being shed over the fate of Holland, Belgium, France, and England. I must confess to being a little dry around the eyes. I hear people shaking with shudders at the thought of Germany collecting taxes in Holland. I have not heard a word against Holland collecting one twelfth of poor people's wages in Asia. That makes the ruling families in Holland

---

[5]Césaire (2000), *Discourse on Colonialism*. New York: Monthly Review Press, 36.
[6]Ibid.

very rich, as they should be. What happens to the poor Javanese and Balinese is unimportant; Hitler's crime is that he is actually doing a thing like that to his own kind.[7]

The logic of Baldwin, Césaire, and Hurston could be stated thus: white people should not be surprised by the Nazis, because they have established the very same conditions and structures that have justified the violation of a wide variety of peoples throughout the world. Given this model, black writers suggest that we could examine what happened in the Holocaust to illuminate the psycho-political structures and the sociopolitical conditions that enabled white Westerners to violate non-whites in the past and present with emotional, psychological, and legal impunity.

Important to note, however, is that the focus of many black writers is not just on the past and the present. They believe that a close analysis of the Holocaust would enable them to predict the future violation of other groups, which makes them extremely nervous, because they realize that, since the structures and conditions for violating designated "inferiors" are already in place, they could easily be targeted. For example, when discussing what happened to Jews in Nazi Germany, Baldwin claims:

> For my part, the fate of the Jews, and the world's indifference to it, frightened me very much. I could not but feel, in those sorrowful years, that this human indifference, concerning which I knew so much already, would be my portion on the day that the United States decided to murder its Negroes systematically instead of little by little and catch-as-catch-can.[8]

This is an idea that is central to Richard Wright's *The Outsider*. In the novel is the character Langley Herndon, a fascist who wants to bring about a revolution in the United States. In his depiction of Herndon, Wright brilliantly exposes the political desire that ultimately inspires, necessitates, and justifies violence against certain groups of people. For Herndon, because blacks, like Jews, have been created by God as sub- or half-human ("Herndon's world

---

[7]Hurston (2006), *Dust Tracks on a Road*. New York, London, Toronto, and Sydney: HarperPerennial, 260–1.
[8]Baldwin (1993), 53.

considered him [a black man] half-human"),[9] the United States could easily adopt Hitler's approach in order to exterminate people of African descent. This is why Herndon "welcomed Hitler and publicly lauded his extermination of the Jews. Said that America should use the Negro as a scapegoat around which to unify the nation."[10] According to this system, it is permissible to violate culturally designated inferiors when they question, challenge, or threaten the dominant political order. When such a condition is met, the systematic annihilation of the "inferior" is necessary. By linking Hitler and Herndon, Wright suggests that what really motivates fascists is national unity, which is achieved by consolidating the interests, needs, desires, and identity of the dominant group. Within this framework, "the Negro was America's ace in the hole if the nation ever experienced any real internal stress. You could say that the nigger was the cause of it and get the rest of the nation to forget its problems and unite to get rid of the niggers . . . ."[11]

Attempting to define the structures and conditions that make massive political oppression possible is a dominant concern of many first-rate novels of the mid-twentieth century. Indeed, this approach is central to Ellison's *Invisible Man*, which brilliantly explores the political epistemology at work in "tyrant states."[12] As I discussed in Chapter 2, the writer's task, according to Ellison, "is to create symbolic actions which are viable specifically, and which move across all of our differences and all of the diversities of the atmosphere."[13] This describes perfectly what Ellison does in *Invisible Man*. To illuminate the psychological epistemology that enables political leaders to justify their violation of the culture's designated "inferiors," Ellison creates the Brotherhood. The political agenda of the Brotherhood is of ultimate importance for both the members and the leaders. According to this model, if individuals cannot advance one of the Brotherhood's objectives, they exist outside history. As such, they can be used and abused with impunity. The problem is that, given the construction of their

---

[9]Wright (2008), *The Outsider*. New York and London: HarperPerenial, 334.
[10]Wright (2008), 354.
[11]Wright (2008), 355.
[12]Ellison (1995), *Invisible Man*. New York: Vintage Books, 577.
[13]Ralph Ellison, William Styron, Robert Penn Warren, and C. Vann Woodward (Spring 1969), "The Uses of History in Fiction," *Southern Literary Journal* 1(2): 74.

inner eyes, the political leaders do not see those who exist outside of their history-making agenda. Within this framework, as soon as a political agenda is established within a person's body, the psychological epistemology will determine what can and cannot be seen, what does and does not belong to history.

From the time it was first published, readers have suggested that the Brotherhood is really the Communist Party. But as Arnold Rampersad notes, Ellison pointed "out repeatedly that the Brotherhood is an invention. It is, indeed, no more the Communist Party than Invisible's college is Tuskegee Institute."[14] Ellison was adamant on this score because he held that specific characters should be able to symbolically represent a wide range of political figures. Once Ellison details the way a psychological epistemology functions within the Brotherhood to render certain people and groups invisible, that model could be applied to many groups, such as the Republican Party, the Democratic Party, and the Communist Party. This same approach informs Wright's *The Outsider*, which pictures "'the psychological origins of tyranny,'"[15] and William Styron's *Sophie's Choice*, which depicts "a mind swept away in the rapture of totalitarianism."[16]

Hurston was just as concerned as Faulkner, Ellison, Wright, and Styron about the political structures and psychological conditions that made massive oppression possible, but she differed from these writers because she believed that the best literary form for exposing, countering, and disabling oppressive political structures was the biblical biographical novel. In the American context, Hurston originated the biblical biographical novel, which has become incredibly popular in recent years, resulting in the publication of Friedrich Buechner's *The Son of Laughter*, Anita Diamant's *The Red Tent*, David Maine's *The Preservationist*, and Rebecca Kanner's *Sinners and the Sea*, just to mention a notable few. What accounts for Hurston's desire to write a biblical biographical novel is her conviction that so many political leaders of her day used or referenced the Bible to justify their oppressive political agendas. Like Frantz Fanon, Hurston believes that "all forms of exploitation resemble one another. They all seek the source of their

---

[14]Rampersad (2008), *Ralph Ellison: A Biography*. New York: Vintage Books, 245.
[15]Wright (2008), 378.
[16]Stryon (1992), *Sophie's Choice*. New York: Vintage International, 160.

necessity in some edict of a Biblical nature."[17] It was from the late 1930s until her death in 1960, when writing biblical biographical novels about Moses and Herod, that Hurston focused most of her attention on the degree to which the Bible contributed to the making of the twentieth century's political horror show and on the best aesthetic form for countering and disabling oppressive political systems. In the following pages, I argue that, while scholars have generally understood how Hurston's work strategically references and critiques Hitler and the Nazis, they have failed to appreciate the nature of her intellectual contribution and political critique, because they have not recognized the unique ways in which the biographical novel historicizes and engages the political.

I

There are two separate critiques of the Bible that Hurston develops in two very different biblical biographical novels. The first is *Moses, Man of the Mountain*, which strategically alludes to Hitler and the Nazis. When the novel was first published, the reviewer Richard Greenleaf noted the link between "the plight of the Hebrews in the days of Pharaoh and their plight now in the day of Hitler."[18] More specifically, Deborah E. McDowell claims that Pharaoh's order to kill "Hebrew male babies" indicates that the "shadow of Nazism is cast from the beginning of *Moses*."[19] For Barbara Johnson, the connection is based more on a parallel concern than a direct allusion: "At a time when Hitler had cornered the market on blood-and-soil nationalism, it is not surprising to find Hurston questioning the grounding of nationhood on racial identity."[20] Of all the studies to note the references to the Nazis, Mark Christian Thompson has done the most extensive work. For

---

[17]Fanon (1967), *Black Skin, White Masks*. Translated by Charles Lam Markmann. New York: Grove Weidenfeld, 88.
[18]Quoted in M. Genevieve West (2005), *Zora Neale Hurston & American Literary Culture*. Gainesville: University Press of Florida, 161.
[19]McDowell (1991), "Foreword: Lines of Descent/Dissenting Lines," in *Moses, Man of the Mountain*. Editor Zora Neale Hurston. New York: HarperPerennial, xv.
[20]Johnson (1997), "Moses and Intertextuality: Sigmund Freud, Zora Neale Hurston, and the Bible," in *Poetics of the Americas*. Editors Bainard Cowan and Jefferson Humphries. Baton Rouge and London: Louisiana State University Press, 21.

Thompson, "*Moses*'s Pharaoh presents Hurston's examination of the ideological content invested in the creation of the fascist state along the lines of the *Führerprinzip* (*Führer* principle, or principle of the male, charismatic, authoritarian guide or leader) at work in National Socialist Germany, and the role that ultranationalism plays as a religious faith in supporting fascist political power."[21]

Hurston's allusion to Nazi Germany in her 1939 novel is very specific. *Moses* opens with Pharaoh instituting a new political order in which "Hebrews were disarmed and prevented from becoming citizens."[22] As such, the Hebrews "found out that they were aliens, and from one decree to the next they sank lower and lower."[23] In 1939, when Hurston's novel was published, educated readers would certainly have been aware of the Nuremberg Laws, which were ratified on September 15, 1935 and enacted on January 1, 1936. According to these Laws, Jews could not marry citizens, which implies that Jews, by virtue of their alien blood, are not and could not be German citizens. This explains why the "Jews are forbidden to display the Reich and national flag or the national colors."[24] Denying Jews citizenship, and thereby rendering them "aliens," was merely the beginning of a downward spiral culminating in the *Kristallnacht* pogroms of November 9 and 10, 1938, exactly one year before the publication of *Moses* (I do not say that they culminated in the extermination camps because these had not yet been activated at the time of the publication of *Moses*).[25]

Based on Hurston's direct and not-so-subtle allusion to the Nuremberg Laws, readers could wrongly conclude that *Moses* is really about Nazi Germany. But this would be too reductive, because Hurston's work is in the tradition of Faulkner's *Light in August*, Wright's *The Outsider*, and Ellison's *Invisible Man* in that it details the way specific cultures formulate political justifications

---

[21]Thompson (2007), *Black Fascisms: African American Literature and Culture between the Wars*. Charlottesville and London: University of Virginia Press, 118.
[22]Hurston (1991), *Moses, Man of the Mountain*. New York: HarperPerennial, 2.
[23]Ibid.
[24]References to the Nuremberg Laws are taken from the Jewish Virtual Library online database. Here is the url: http://www.jewishvirtuallibrary.org/jsource/Holocaust/nurlawtoc.html
[25]For an insightful discussion of the way statelessness made Jews and other minorities vulnerable to human rights abuses, see Hannah Arendt (1976), *The Origins of Totalitarianism*. San Diego, New York, London: A Harvest Book, 275–90.

for racial oppression. For instance, later in the novel, Hurston strategically alludes to fascist Italy. After Moses takes charge of the military, Egypt begins the project of extending its power. As the narrator claims, the "might of Egypt was stretching across the world. Ethiopia was conquered."[26] That Hurston has Egypt start by invading Ethiopia is certainly no accident. In October of 1935, Italy invaded Ethiopia, which resulted in Italy's diplomatic isolation. Benito Mussolini was not fond of Hitler, but given his country's isolated situation, he could not refuse Germany's support. So Italy's invasion of Ethiopia is generally regarded as the beginning of the fascist alliance between Mussolini and Hitler.

Hurston, like Faulkner, Wright, and Ellison, creates a symbolic figure that could be used not so much to represent a specific political entity (Nazi Germany) but rather a particular political psychology (a racist political mentality), which could then be applied to multiple polities (Germany and Italy). While it is clear that Hurston is working within the same tradition as Faulkner, Wright, and Ellison, there are two things that make *Moses* separate and distinct: First, Hurston uses the biographical novel in order to formulate her critique. Second, she takes her biographical figure from a text that is generally regarded as sacred and inviolable. As I will now demonstrate, there was something in the nature of the way mid-twentieth-century political powers functioned that led Hurston to author a biblical biographical novel, which is the best aesthetic form for exposing the incoherent ideology underwriting the racist and totalitarian political agendas of the mid-twentieth century.

II

As I have suggested in Chapters 2 and 3, Hitler and many prominent Nazis frequently referenced and relied upon the authority of the Bible in order to justify their anti-Semitic political agenda. To illustrate how this Bible-based approach functioned in Nazi Germany, let me briefly discuss the person who is generally considered the primary disseminator of Nazi Germany's death-bringing anti-Semitism. Founder of *Der Stürmer*, Julius

---

[26]Hurston (1991), 57.

Streicher published from 1923 through 1945 articles and images in his newspaper that most clearly and crudely articulated the theological basis of the Nazis' Christian political agenda. This newspaper enjoyed enormous support among Germans, for as Streicher's biographer, Randall L. Bytwerk, claims: *Der Stürmer* "had been one of the most widely circulated papers in Germany, the one paper Hitler himself claimed to read from cover to cover."[27] According to the International Military Tribunal at Nuremberg, which concluded that Streicher's newspaper inspired everyday Germans to commit atrocities against Jews, *Der Stürmer* "reached a circulation of 600,000 in 1935."[28] Ann and John Tusa differ with the Tribunal's figure, claiming instead that *Der Stürmer* reached its peak in 1937 with "a circulation of 500,000." However, they claim that the "readership was higher" than its circulation, because "display cases for the paper were set up in public places."[29] Given the paper's success, Heinrich Himmler claimed that in the future "'it will be said that Julius Streicher and his weekly newspaper the *Stürmer* were responsible for a good part of the education about the enemy [the Jew] of mankind.'"[30] In *The Drowned and the Saved*, Primo Levi claims that "the great majority of Germans, young people in particular, hated Jews" because of "Streicher's propaganda."[31] Supporting this view, Rudolf Hoess claims in *Commandant of Auschwitz* that the guards at the Dachau concentration camp were heavily influenced "by *Der Stürmer*, which was on show everywhere in their barracks and the canteens." Indeed, Hoess stresses that the newspaper had a powerful and immediate impact: "When a display case containing *Der Stürmer* was put up in the protective custody camp, its effect on those prisoners who had hitherto been not at all anti-semitic was immediately apparent."[32] In *At*

---

[27]Bytwerk (1983), *Julius Streicher*. New York: Stein and Day, 1–2.
[28]All references from the Nuremberg Trials are taken from Yale's *The Avalon Project*, an online database with all the documents pertaining to the case. My citations will reference the URL: http://avalon.law.yale.edu/imt/judstrei.asp.
[29]Tusa (1986), *The Nuremberg Trial*. New York: Atheneum, 334.
[30]Quoted in Bytwerk (1983), 171.
[31]Levi (1989), *The Drowned and the Saved*. Translated by Raymond Rosenthal. New York: Vintage International, 154.
[32]Hoess (1959), *Commandant of Auschwitz: The Autobiography of Rudolf Hoess*. Translated by Constantine FitzGibbon. Cleveland and New York: The World

the Mind's Limits, Jean Améry expresses the matter best when he says that "the image from Streicher's *Stürmer*" was "burned" into the Jews' "skin."[33]

As a political leader of the Nazi Party (he was *Gauleiter* of Franconia, a region in Bavaria), Streicher wielded immense power. With regard to the concentration camps, he did not have a direct role in their making, but his newspaper certainly inspired the ideology of hate that allowed so many Germans to perform their duties in the death mills, which is why he was among the first group of Nazi leaders to be sentenced to death after his trial in Nuremberg. What separates him from others, however, is that there is no evidence that he killed a single Jew or that he ordered anyone to kill a Jew. Referring to him as "Jew-Baiter Number One," the Nuremberg Tribunal concluded that "he infected the German mind with the virus of anti-Semitism, and incited the German people to active persecution."[34] According to the Nuremberg Judgment, Streicher, more than anyone else, disseminated the version of anti-Semitism that had the most decisive impact in making the genocidal atrocities against the Jews possible.

One of the most consistent tenets running throughout the newspaper is that Christ's being necessitates the negation of the Jew. For instance, a 1933 Christmas issue titled "*Erlösergeburt*" (the birth of the Redeemer) pictures the holy mother holding the newborn Christ (see Figure 2). Rapt Germans surround the mother and child, and in the bottom corner is a Jew, who is retreating in fear, because he knows that Christ's birth will seal his doom. An accompanying caption, which is told from the perspective of the Jew, reads: "Their Lord does not abandon them. If one declares them lost, there's always one born who will lead them to the light."[35] In stark contrast to the Germans, the Jew is clad in black, and his terrified and guilty expression suggests that Christ's birth has exposed him, which is why he recoils from the scene. What enabled Streicher to suggest that the birth of Christ entails the negation of the Jew was his debt to Martin Luther (see Figure 3), who is

---

Publishing Company, 142.

[33]Améry (1980), *At the Mind's Limits: Contemplations by a Survivor on Auschwitz and Its Realities*. Bloomington and Indianapolis: Indiana University Press, 87.

[34]*The Avalon Project*, http://avalon.law.yale.edu/imt/judstrei.asp.

[35]*Der Stürmer*, December 1933, number 51. My translation.

FIGURE 2   Image entitled *The Birth of the Redeemer* (*Erlösergeburt*) in a 1933 Christmas issue of *Der Stürmer*.

described in a special issue as "one of the greatest antisemites in German history."[36] In particular, it was Luther's book *On the Jews and Their Lies* that made him one of the heroes of *Der Stürmer*, as is clear from an August 1935 issue (see Figure 4), which pictures a first edition of the 1543 work.[37] The visual effect of this image is extremely powerful. The suggestion is that Streicher's newspaper

---

[36] *Der Stürmer*, March 1937, Sondernummer 6. My translation.
[37] *Der Stürmer*, August 1935, number 31.

Dr. Martin Luther

Der Reformator und Kämpfer gegen den Judengeist in
der christlichen Kirche. Dr. Luther ist einer der größten
Antisemiten der deutschen Geschichte.

nicht allein die ganze Schrift mit ihren er-
logenen Glossen von Anfang bis noch da-
her ohn Aufhören verkehret und ver-

„Darum hüte dich
sie ihre Schulen hat
ist, denn ein Te-
ruhm, Hochmut. Lüg
Menschen schänden g-
und bitterste, wie die ?
ihnen!"

Am Schlusse schreib-
„Und Euch meine
Pfarrherren un-
ganz treulich Eu-
nert haben, daß
net vor ihrem e
daß sie sich vor-
meiden wo sie lö-

„Was wollen wir
wollen wir glauben, d
haftig sei, der von
men, sondern kreuzig
salb Schlangen g
der!..."

Und er schließt:
„Meines Dünkens
der Juden Lästerung
sen wir geschiede
rem Lande vertr
Dies ist der nächste
solchem Falle sichert."

Die Schrift „Vom
sich, wie die Schrift „
ebenfalls eine unerbit-
dische Volk.

Dr. Martin Luther
Immer schärfer wurde
gegen die Christusmör
Die Juden sahen
steigender Angst bedach

FIGURE 3 Image of Martin Luther featured in a 1937 special issue of
Der Stürmer.

and Luther's text share much common ground. But it also implies
that the ideals of Luther's book gave birth to or are being realized
in the pages of *Der Stürmer.* What influenced Streicher and his
newspaper most was Luther's suggestion "that *Christ* was one of
the greatest antisemites of all time."[38]

---

[38]*Der Stürmer*, March 1937, number 12. My translation.

Ehe mit einem Juden eine Schande und ein Verbrechen ist. Man sollte meinen, daß jede deutsche Frau selbst soviel gesundes Rassenbewußtsein hätte, dies zu fühlen und zu erkennen. In manchen Frauen ist die Stimme des deutschen Blutes erstickt. Bei ihnen fruchtet keine werden das Judenblut weiter in unser Volk hineintragen. Der Verbastardierung des deutschen Volkes muß endlich auf gesetzmäßigem Wege Einhalt geboten werden. Die Ehe zwischen Deutschen und Juden gehört verboten.

nicht durch ein gleiches Schreiben, sondern durch offenen Brief. Meine Ausführungen vom 18. Juni 1935 machte ich vor aller Oeffentlichkeit. Nicht der Beurteilung von Dogmatikern, von studierten Theologen und Schriftgelehrten wollte ich sie überlassen, sondern dem gesunden und ehrlichen Urteilsvermögen des Volkes. Der gleiche Grund veranlaßt zweier Persönlichkeiten, die für jeden protestantischen Christen in religiöser Hinsicht höchste Autorität sein müssen. Ich berufe mich auf Christus und auf Dr. Martin Luther.

Christus sagte zu den Juden:
„Ihr habt zum Vater den Teufel und dieses...

FIGURE 4 Image of the first edition of Martin Luther's *On the Jews and Their Lies* in a 1935 issue of *Der Stürmer*.

Throughout *On the Jews and Their Lies*, Luther claims that Jews "are like the devil,"[39] and, consequently, they have been "consigned by the wrath of God to the devil."[40] Indeed, Luther claims that the "devil with all his angels has taken possession of this people,"[41] which is why he refers to the "genuine Jew" as "'a

---

[39]Luther (1971), *On the Jews and Their Lies*, in *Luther's Works*, Vol. 47. Philadelphia: Fortress Press, 200.
[40]Luther (1971), 213.
[41]Luther (1971), 174.

devil incarnate'"[42] and issues the following warning: "Therefore, dear Christian, be advised and do not doubt that next to the devil, you have no more bitter, venomous, and vehement foe than a real Jew who earnestly seeks to be a Jew."[43] This link between the Jew and the devil becomes much weightier and more disturbing when we note how Luther strategically and consistently argues that it is Christ who most defined the Jews in this way. Early in the text, Luther notes that "Our Lord" refers to the Jews as "'a brood of vipers,'" and to underscore his point, he specifies the Gospel passage in which Christ demonizes the Jews: "In John 8 he states: 'If you were Abraham's children, you would do what Abraham did. . . . You are of your father the devil.'"[44] Having established that Christ considers the Jews a devilish people, Luther drives this point home by repeating it throughout the text: "We will believe that our Lord Jesus Christ is truthful when he declares of the Jews who did not accept but crucified him, 'You are a brood of vipers and children of the devil.'"[45] Of course, one could easily object: Luther is not talking about all Jews, for he specifies the Jews who crucified Christ. But later pronouncements ultimately condemn all Jews. For instance, after citing supposed crimes of Jews throughout the ages, which Luther acknowledges to be unverified, he ultimately argues that the Jews must certainly be guilty because the stories coincide "with the judgment of Christ which declares that they are venomous, bitter, vindictive, tricky serpents, assassins, and children of the devil."[46] In essence, it is the weight of Christ's judgment that convicts the Jews: "For Christ does not lie or deceive us when he adjudges them to be serpents and children of the devil."[47] Streicher's usage of Luther's work could only have a devastating impact on everyday Germans. Given Luther's stature as the founding father of the Lutheran faith and a leading interpreter of the Scriptures, the Bible's status as the inspired and infallible Word of God, and Christ's demonization of the Jew in the Gospels, *On the Jews and Their Lies* makes it seem like God himself has defined the Jews as

---

[42]Luther (1971), 214.
[43]Luther (1971), 217.
[44]Luther (1971), 141.
[45]Luther (1971), 277.
[46]Ibid.
[47]Luther (1971), 289.

evil. In other words, Luther and Streicher would have convinced many Christians to believe that to be truly Christian necessitates being an anti-Semite.

Given the depiction of the Jew as the opposite of Christ and inherently evil, Luther draws a conclusion that frighteningly anticipates Nazi Germany.[48] Since Jewish evil is infectious, he encourages political leaders to act like a physician, "who, when gangrene has set in, proceeds without mercy to cut, saw, and burn flesh, veins, bone, and marrow." In this instance, the Jews are gangrene, and when it comes to merciless action toward them, Luther is very specific and direct:

> Burn down their synagogues, . . . , force them to work, and deal harshly with them, as Moses did in the wilderness, slaying three thousand lest the whole people perish. They surely do not know what they are doing; moreover, as people possessed, they do not wish to know it, hear it, or learn it. Therefore it would be wrong to be merciful and confirm them in their conduct. If this does not help we must drive them out like mad dogs, so that we do not become partakers of their abominable blasphemy and all their other vices and thus merit god's wrath and be damned with them.[49]

As ominous as this passage is, it becomes even more so if one attends to Luther's not-so-subtle allusions to Deuteronomy 20, in which God does not just authorize but actually mandates genocide. As the author of Deuteronomy says:

---

[48]There has been much scholarship about the role Luther's writings played in making the Holocaust possible. I will discuss specific works later in this chapter, but let me mention just a few of the major ones. In *The Destruction of the European Jews*, Raul Hilberg begins with a chapter about the precedents of Nazi anti-Semitism, and he includes a section on Luther (8–10). In *The Cunning of History*, Richard L. Rubenstein notes that we can "see anticipations of Nazi antisemitism in Germany's greatest religious figure, Martin Luther," and he goes on to claim "that Luther's intolerance and hatred was thoroughly biblical in its rejection of those who do not maintain whatever is construed to be fidelity to the only true word of the Lord" (3). In *The War against the Jews*, Lucy S. Dawidowicz notes that there is a "line of anti-Semitic descent from Martin Luther to Adolf Hitler" (29). In *Kristallnacht*, Martin Gilbert suggests that "Hitler and his acolytes followed" Luther's advice from the "pastoral letter *On the Jews and Their Lies*," which "advised that the synagogues of the Jews 'should be set on fire'" (16–17). For one of the most insightful studies, see Robert Michael's chapter "The Germanies from Luther to Hitler" in his book *Holy Hatred*.

[49]Luther (1971), 292.

But in the cities of those nations which the Lord, your God, is giving you as your heritage, you shall not leave a single soul alive. You must doom them all—the Hittites, Amorites, Canaanites, Perizzites, Hivites and Jebusites—as the Lord, your God, has commanded you, lest they teach you to make any such abominable offerings as they make to their gods, and you thus sin against the Lord, your God.[50]

These two passages do not just suggest that genocidal action is acceptable. They actually say that failure to take extreme and decisive action would be a sin against God, because allowing infidels to live would lead true believers to become infidels as well.

Here we confront what can only be considered an inexplicable interpretive strategy that has had an enormously distorting impact on Holocaust studies. In its effort to use racial and political arguments to justify condemning Streicher to death, the Nuremberg Tribunal strategically silenced Streicher whenever he introduced religious justifications for his political agenda. For instance, in order to determine whether Streicher and his newspaper contributed to the making of the Holocaust, one of the attorneys asked if there were "any other publications in Germany which treated the Jewish question in an anti-Semitic way" comparable to *Der Stürmer*. Streicher's April 29, 1946, reply is telling. Instead of mentioning noted race theorists whose secular writings supposedly gave birth to the Nazis' political agenda, Streicher references Luther:

Anti-Semitic publications have existed in Germany for centuries. A book I had, written by Dr. Martin Luther, was, for instance, confiscated. Dr. Martin Luther would very probably sit in my place in the defendants' dock today, if this book had been taken into consideration by the Prosecution. In the book *The Jews and Their Lies*, Dr. Martin Luther writes that the Jews are a serpent's brood and one should burn down their synagogues and destroy them . . . .[51]

Angered by this response, the Tribunal did not let Streicher conclude his thought, and Mr. Justice Jackson objected, claiming

---

[50]All biblical references are taken from *Holy Bible: The New American Bible* (1971), Nashville, Camden, and New York: Thomas Nelson Publishers, Deuteronomy 20:15–18.

[51]*The Avalon Project*, 318, http://avalon.law.yale.edu/imt/04-29-46.asp.

that the remarks were "irrelevant": "It seems to me very improper that a witness should do anything but make a responsive answer to a question, so that we may keep these proceedings from getting into issues that have nothing to do with them."[52] Obviously for Jackson, the reference to Luther has nothing to do with the case.

Significantly, this was not the only time Streicher mentioned religion, and specifically Luther. During the Trial, an attorney expressed concern about two picture books that were put out by Streicher's publishing house and explicitly written for youngsters, and to establish culpability for their publication, the attorney confronted Streicher: "You know that two picture books were published, one with the title, *Trust No Fox in the Field*, and the other one with the title, *The Poisonous Toadstool*. Do you assume responsibility for these picture books?"[53] Totally confident about the rightness of his ideas and mission, Streicher assumed full responsibility and claimed to have published the books in order "to protect youth." What, in part, accounted for Streicher's confident response was his belief in the rightness of Luther. After the attorney asked Streicher to identify the authors, Streicher said: "The book *Trust No Fox in the Field and No Jew Under His Oath* was done and illustrated by a young woman artist, and she also wrote the text. The title which appears on the picture book is from Dr. Martin Luther."[54] That Streicher would know that the title of this book is taken from Luther makes perfect sense, for he concluded a March 1925 article in *Der Stürmer* with the very citation: "Meanwhile, consider Luther's saying: 'Trust no fox in the field and no Jew under his oath.'"[55] Given the attorney's line of questioning, it would seem that he would have gone on to ask Streicher about the content of the children's books. But after Streicher mentioned Luther, the attorney quickly shifted the conversation to another topic. Religion was clearly not a topic that the Tribunal wanted to address.

Ironically, the Tribunal's verdict is simply incomprehensible without taking Streicher's religiously inflected anti-Semitism into account. According to the Nuremberg transcript, Streicher convinced many Germans that Jews "must be destroyed in the

---

[52]Ibid.
[53]*The Avalon Project*, 335, http://avalon.law.yale.edu/imt/04-29-46.asp.
[54]Ibid.
[55]*Der Stürmer*, March 1925, number 10. My translation.

interest of mankind." This is obviously a version of Deuteronomy 20 and Luther's text, which hold that sawing off a gangrenous limb is a prerequisite for the spiritual health of the people and the nation. The most striking line in the Tribunal's final Judgment contains unwitting references to Christ. The transcript notes that Streicher "published on 25th December, 1941," an article that calls for "the extermination of that people whose father is the devil." The ironies here are multiple. The Tribunal mentions the date, but does not acknowledge that these words appear in the Christmas issue. More significantly, the Tribunal takes it as a given that readers will know that the "people whose father is the devil" are the Jews, but it does not acknowledge that the phrase is taken from the Gospel of John and that Christ is the originator of it. Put simply, it is impossible to understand the nature of Streicher's anti-Semitism, his call to exterminate the Jews, and the Tribunal's ruling without taking into account his Bible-based approach to Christianity, which he derived in large measure from Luther.[56]

III

Hurston was one of the first and only writers of her time (and this perhaps explains why so few were able to comprehend the magnitude of her achievement in *Moses*) to understand and appreciate the degree to which political leaders based their political agendas on the Bible. It is my contention that Hurston authored a biblical biographical novel because she considered it the most effective way of countering and disabling racist political regimes such as the one in Nazi Germany. Hitler and the Nazis used the Bible in order to claim that there is something logically necessary about their persecution of the Jews. The pressing question for Hurston was this: What aesthetic form could most effectively deconstruct a political agenda such as that of the Nazis'? The answer is the biblical biographical novel. If Hurston could show that the Bible

---

[56]For a detailed analysis of the Nuremberg Tribunal's reluctance to acknowledge the role Christianity played in the making of the Nazis' anti-Semitic political agenda and the way Luther and his work were used to justify the Nazis' death-bringing anti-Semitism, see my essay, "Conceptualizing Christianity and Christian Nazis after the Nuremberg Trials."

is profoundly untrustworthy and politically dangerous, then she would successfully undermine the Nazis' race-/racist-based political agenda, which is derived from the Bible.

We know that Hurston considered both the Old and New Testaments to be "biased"[57] and deadly, for she makes this clear in the bowdlerized chapter of *Dust Tracks*. As for her Moses novel, she begins with an "Author's Introduction" that casts "doubt" on "the Moses of the Christian concept."[58] To undermine the Bible's authority, Hurston consistently suggests that everything Moses says is his own invention rather than a revelation from God. For instance, in Exodus 7:3–5, God hardens Pharaoh's heart so that he will not free the Chosen People, thus justifying God's brutal treatment of Pharaoh and the Egyptians. But in Hurston's novel, it is Moses who strategically plans to keep Pharaoh from consenting to free the Hebrews: "What would be a better chance to show his [God's] powers than for Pharaoh to refuse and for me to beat him down with powers? That's what I aim to do."[59] More significantly, Hurston suggests that Moses invented the Ten Commandments rather than getting them from God. After leaving Egypt, Moses is in charge of "more than two million souls,"[60] and since people are constantly quibbling, he spends considerable time hearing petty cases. Jethro tells his son-in-law that this is a waste of his time, so he encourages Moses to find a better way to govern. To be expected, the next day "Moses went up on the mountain *as if* he had been called,"[61] and "that is how the people got laws and commandments from heaven."[62] Hurston is clearly calling the readers' attention to the fact that the Commandments have come from Moses (and indirectly from Jethro) rather than the Divine—he ascended the mountain as if he had been called. This interpretation will be reinforced later in the novel when the character Miriam tells Moses that she "thought God's voice in the tabernacle sounded mighty like yours."[63] If we see biblical edicts as coming from the Divine, then there is something

---

[57]Hurston (2006), 255.
[58]Hurston (1991), xxiii.
[59]Hurston (1991), 146–7.
[60]Hurston (1991), 222.
[61]Hurston (1991), 225. My emphasis.
[62]Hurston (1991), 228.
[63]Hurston (1991), 263.

logically necessary and valid about them, as Luther and the Nazis suggest. But if we see them as coming from a human such as Moses, then there is something totally arbitrary and contingent about them, as Hurston clearly suggests.

For Hurston, what makes Moses' behavior quite troubling is his treatment of the Hebrews when he comes down from the mountain to give them the Commandments. Hearing the Hebrews "'howling in idolatry,'" Moses lashes out at the people: "'If this is to be a great nation, it must be purged of such evil-doers, or all Israel must perish.'"[64] Given their blasphemy, Moses directs his soldiers to kill all offenders: "'You have your eager weapons, men. Spare not a soul who is guilty.'"[65] The language here is stunningly similar to Luther's admonition to slay three thousand lest the whole people perish, which strategically blends Exodus 32 and Deuteronomy 20. In Exodus 32:27, Moses directs the Levites to "'slay your own kinsmen, your friends and neighbors,'" and on "'that day there fell about three thousand of the people'" (32:28). Conspicuously absent from the Exodus passage is the language of spreadable evil, which could potentially bring the Chosen People to ruin. This spreadable evil discourse comes from Deuteronomy 20, which treats the non-Chosen People as evil beings who could potentially corrupt the Hebrews. Synthesizing Exodus 32 and Deuteronomy 20 makes mass slaughter seem more necessary and urgent, which is why God says that "you shall not leave a single soul alive" (Deut. 20:16). In Exodus 32, God, through Moses, is merely punishing those who committed idolatry. But in Deuteronomy 20, since the evil behavior of the offenders could spread, purging the nation of all evil-doers becomes more urgently necessary for the nation's future spiritual health ("or all Israel must perish"). This spreadable evil argument is central to Streicher's program to exterminate Jews for the good of humanity, and it is an argument that is central to Luther's *On the Jews and Their Lies*.

That Hurston was deeply troubled by Moses' slaughter of the Hebrews she makes clear in a letter to Carl Van Vechten. After mentioning how the Hebrews are frequently denounced "for not adhering to the Laws," Hurston says: "Nobody seems to consider

---

[64]Hurston (1991), 235.
[65]Hurston (1991), 239.

that the Hebrews did not value those laws, nor did they ask for that new religion that Moses forced on them by terror and death." What irritates Hurston most about Moses is his tyrannical brutality and violence: "Moses was responsible for the actual death of at least a half million of the people in his efforts to force his laws upon them. 3,000 were slaughtered right at Sinai in the very beginning. It went on and on."[66] For Hurston, Moses did not take his cue from God on behalf of the Chosen People. Rather, "Moses had worked out an idea for a theocratic government, and the Hebrews were just so the available laboratory material."[67] In this instance, a theocratic government is not one actually based on the dictates of a divine being; it is one that purports to be based on such injunctions. With regard to Hurston's Moses, since he invents the laws of the polity, he is actually a "dictator,"[68] as Hurston refers to him, rather than an empty vessel through which the Divine expresses itself. By exposing the Bible as a profoundly flawed and dangerous text, Hurston strategically invalidates any polity premised on its authority.

At this point, it would be worth contrasting Luther and Hurston. Luther references the Sinai slaughter in order to motivate "our rulers who have Jewish subjects"[69] to take decisive action against Jews, which is why many Nazi Christians believed that "'in the Nazi treatment of the Jews and its ideological stance, Luther's intentions, after centuries, are being fulfilled.'" Indeed, many German Christians saw Jesus "as prefiguring Hitler, who in turn was imagined as an avatar of Martin Luther."[70] By stark contrast, Hurston references the Sinai slaughter in order to expose Moses as a "dictator," who has constructed an extremely dangerous "theocratic government" that can justify barbaric atrocities against certain groups of people. By authoring a biographical novel about Moses, Hurston hoped to expose the Bible as a horribly dangerous text, thus undermining those theocratic governments, such as the one in Nazi Germany,

---

[66]Hurston (2003), *Zora Neale Hurston: A Life in Letters*. Edited by Carla Kaplan. New York: Anchor Books, 529.

[67]Ibid.

[68]Hurston (2003), 530.

[69]Luther (1971), 292.

[70]Susannah Heschel (2008), *The Aryan Jesus: Christian Theologians and the Bible in Nazi Germany*. Princeton and Oxford: Princeton University Press, 7, 283.

that appealed to the Bible in order to make their racist political agenda seem divinely necessary.

IV

The publication of *Moses* did not signal the end of Hurston's thinking about the theological conditions and structures that made massive political oppression possible, and nor was it the end of her work on the biographical novel. In fact, it was merely a beginning, for starting in the 1940s, Hurston began work on a biographical novel about the New Testament figure of Herod that would become a near obsession for the rest of her life. The Herod manuscript was never completed, and what we have of it has suffered both water and fire damage, especially the last thirty pages. Undamaged, however, are various introductions, which give us considerable insight into Hurston's thinking about the Herod manuscript and the biographical novel more generally. In what follows I do an analysis of Hurston's surviving introductions and prefaces to the Herod manuscript in order to clarify the nature of her political and aesthetic objectives in the biblical biographical novel.

There is a significant difference between Hurston's two biographical novels. In *Moses*, which was published before the Nazis erected their death camps, Hurston focuses mainly on political authority, specifically the way political leaders use the Bible to justify their oppressive agendas. After the magnitude of Nazi atrocities started to become apparent, Hurston shifted her focus from the Old to the New Testament, and it was at this point that she drew the startling conclusion: the content of the New Testament established the structures and conditions for the systematic violation of the twentieth century's culturally designated "inferiors." That Hurston was reflecting on the New Testament's role in the demonization of people we see most clearly in her first letter about the Herod project, which was written to Van Vechten in 1945. In this letter Hurston faults "the Christian world," which "reads the Bible with their [sic] prejudices, and not with their eyes."[71] This, she argues, is most clearly illustrated through the representation of the Jews.

---

[71]Hurston (2003), 529.

Instead of accepting the standard interpretation, which holds that Jews blindly accepted Moses' "new religion,"[72] Hurston claims that many Jews rebelled against Moses, an argument that she makes in a number of the introductions to *Herod*. Unfortunately, she continues, the stories of the rebel Jews were never heard, not simply because of the dictatorial tyranny of Moses and his disciples ("Arbitrarily, he [Moses] places his stooge, Aaron, his family and tribe over the people forever"[73]), but also because of the totalitarian hegemony of Christianity. For instance, after referencing the horrible suffering the Jews experienced, Hurston specifies the present situation. She criticizes what contemporary Gentiles are being "taught in Sunday Schools," for those lessons function to justify "our present-day prejudices" against Jews, but she also confesses that, like many Christians of her day, she had been "taught of the evil ways of the Jews." Indeed, "so evil" were the Jews, according to those lessons, "that God just had to do away with them. They are meant to be kicked around."[74]

This personal experience in the Sunday School Hurston considers more than just an isolated event. It reflects a mass movement among contemporary Christians to demonize Jews and to justify their suffering, which is why she claims in *Dust Tracks*: "To this day, the names of Pharisee and Sadducee are synonymous with hypocrite and crook to ninety-nine and a half percent of the Christian world."[75] After explaining to Van Vechten what she hopes to accomplish in her new book, which is to demonstrate that many post-Moses and pre-Christ Jews were "fighting for all those things which other people hold sacred and conducing to the rights and dignity of man,"[76] she notes the irony of the contemporary Christian representation of the Jews:

> We gloat over our own Reformation and freedom from the domination of the Catholic Church when it had and exercised temporal power, yet our Sunday School lessons teach us to regard the same instincts in the Jews as evil, thus justifying any evil & suffering that they have had and further that any imposed upon

---

[72]Ibid.
[73]Hurston (2003), 530.
[74]Hurston (2003), 532.
[75]Hurston (2006), 255.
[76]Hurston (2003), 530.

them at present or in the future as being what they have coming
to them for "disobedience to God."[77]

By doing a project of massive historical excavation, Hurston hopes
to set "forth the sufferings of the muted people."[78] But this leads her
to draw a clear line of connection between the sufferings of ancient
and twentieth-century Jews: "Was there ever a more helpless or
pathetic picture of terror and death before Hitler?"[79] she queries. In
essence, Hurston establishes parallels that explain not just why so
many early Jews suffered, but also why so many contemporary Jews
"at present or in the future" suffer.

Given this political reality, the aesthetic question for Hurston
was this: How could she best expose the conditions and structures
that made the systemic violation of culturally designated "inferiors"
such as the Jews possible? The answer was, through a biblical
biographical novel about Herod. As Hurston claims in the letter to
Van Vechten, her novel "the LIFE OF HEROD THE GREAT is not
really the story of a man, but of a movement which has ended up in
Christianity on one hand, and as the basis of Western civilization on
the other."[80] In other words, to understand the political situation of
the West in the mid-twentieth century, it is imperative that we take
a look at the story of Herod and Christ, for it is this story that gave
birth to a conception of God that set the stage for the oppressive
political systems of the twentieth century.

It was in the early 1940s that Hurston started to question the logic
of the Herod story (as articulated in Matthew two). For instance,
in the bowdlerized chapter from *Dust Tracks*, Hurston notes some
gaps and inconsistencies in the Herod story of the Bible. But instead
of working through the logic of those gaps and inconsistencies,
Hurston turns her attention to Christians, who she claims have
"slaughter[ed] more innocents in one night than" Herod's "soldiers
ever saw."[81] At this point, she specifically has Jewish victims in mind,
for as she claims in the next sentence: "Those Jews who would not
accept Christianity look very bad in the New Testament."[82] But this

---

[77]Hurston (2003), 530–1.
[78]Hurston (2003), 531.
[79]Ibid.
[80]Hurston (2003), 665
[81]Hurston (2006), 256.
[82]Ibid.

model of persecution, she continues, was not merely a thing of the past, for she then claims that "two thousand years have gone by and all the Western World [still] uses the sign of the Cross"[83] to enact its political agenda. After setting up this model, Hurston shifts her focus to the Germans, and specifically "Hitler's crime."[84] As readers, it is difficult to understand how Hurston can go from Herod to Christian anti-Semitism to Hitler. But Hurston's letters about and introductions to *Herod* clarify her logic.

After the Crucifixion, a number of people claimed that Christ's birth signified a complete rupture with Jews and Judaism. As Hurston says in a letter to William Bradford Huie: "It is ironical that immediately upon the death of Christ, His so-called followers, not understanding Him, went back to the primitive fears and demonology, and looked upon Herod as an enemy of religion, and concocted a bogeyman of him."[85] The most egregious example of this process of demonization can be found in Matthew two, where Herod is portrayed as a baby-murdering tyrant. No doubt, Hurston considers the New Testament representation of Herod to be a flagrant distortion, which falsifies Herod's character. As she claims in a letter by quoting an unspecified source: "'Scholars state that there is no historical basis for the legend of the slaughter of the innocents by Herod.'"[86] Indeed, given the surviving documents about Herod, Hurston claims that "there is NO historical background for the story in Matthew 2, that Herod butchered those children."[87] Hurston draws this conclusion because Herod, while a Roman, adopted an Essenes-based religious philosophy, which would have precluded such barbarous action: "So the doctrine of brotherly love, God the father of all mankind equally, and not just the Jews, gained ground in his [Herod's] reign."[88] In essence, the picture of Herod in Matthew two is in irreconcilable conflict with what we know about Herod's personal character and political reign.

If Hurston's depiction of Herod sounds similar to certain versions of Christ, this is not a mistake. Hurston actually considers Jesus to be the logical product of the Essenes' religious philosophy, and

---

[83]Ibid.
[84]Hurston (2006), 251.
[85]Hurston (2003), 710.
[86]Hurston (2003), 729.
[87]Hurston (2003), 737.
[88]Hurston (2003), 733.

this is the real scandal at the core of Hurston's work on Christian and political history. The traditional view holds that Christ emerged *sui generis* and, therefore, His being marks a decisive rupture with all previous cultural, religious, and philosophical traditions (the Nazis inherited this approach and view from Luther, Kant, and Chamberlain, as I have argued in Chapters 2 and 3). But for Hurston, the exact opposite was the case: A "new concept of God and His relationship to man which had been working like a yeast in Palestine for 300 years [was] emerging, formulated at last as what is now known as Christianity. It was a movement totally within the Jewish people, NOT A SUDDEN AND MIRACULOUS HAPPENING AS IS TOLD IN THE NEW TESTAMENT."[89] What really motivated Hurston to reject the *sui generis* Christ, and this is her primary motivation for debunking the New Testament, is that it institutes a type of representation that leads necessarily and inevitably to a racist politics that reached its apex in the twentieth century.

We see this form of representation most clearly in the way Christians portray the Jews. To make Christ and Christianity totally original, completely separate from Jews and Judaism, early Christians had to essentialize the Jews. Instead of noting the radical differences between Sadducees, Pharisees, and Essenes, early Christians lumped them all together as the Jews. In the introductions to *Herod*, Hurston differentiates the various Jewish sects of the day. Here is her depiction in Introduction A:

> Three Jewish philosophical sects—Pharisees, Sadducees and Essenes—were all in flourishing existence for at least two centuries before Herod was born. They came into being through the impact of Greek thought on Judea. Flavius Josephus, himself a Pharisee, the Pharisees were "kin" to the Stoics; the Sadducees were of the persuasion of the Greek pragmatists. These Sadducees, unlike the Pharisees and Essenes, denied that there was such a thing as arbitrary fate, but insisted that things came about through cause and effect. Therefore, men by their own attitudes and actions, controlled their own fate. Though Persian religious concepts influenced Jewish thought considerably during those seventy years, the Sadducees utterly rejected the Persian concept of life after death.[90]

---

[89]Hurston (2003), 737.
[90]Hurston: Introduction A, 5. Hurston wrote four introductions and three prefaces to her Herod manuscript. When I refer to the page number in a preface or an

Of the three sects, the Essenes were the ones to have the most decisive influence on Christ and Christianity. To quote Hurston: "Sublimated through Jewish monotheism, the contract-minded and avenging Jehovah emerges as the loving, understanding, tender Father of the Essenes and later, Christianity."[91] Given the logic of Hurston's depiction of the period, the *sui generis* argument about Christ only works if Christians totally reject the major influence the Essenes (and specifically Herod) had in determining Christ's character and theology.

The way early Christians were able to distance Christ and Christianity from the primary force that brought both into being was to subsume the various religious sects of the time under the single rubric of the Jews. In a passage that Hurston struggled in the various introductions to get exactly right, she says:

> That brings us to the observation that the Western world has for some reason, determined to make the Jews, God's "peculiar treasure," look more peculiar by omission. It is repeated that nowhere in the Sunday School literature are they presented as really human. Just as they were at Sinai when they received the Law from Moses, a child is left to conclude that they were the same when Jerusalem was destroyed by Titus in 70 A.D. Like a dried, pressed flower between the lids of the Bible. Something that just lives in the Bible, and has no other existence.[92]

In Introduction D, Hurston makes a few significant revisions:

> That brings up the observation of the strange and hard-to-explain attitude of the Christian world towards Jewish cultural development. It seems to be determined to make the Jews, "God's peculiar treasure," untruthfully and unnecessarily peculiar by omission. Nowhere in our Sunday School literature are the Jews presented as bound by the same natural laws of evolution of

---

introduction, I am using the page number that is at the top of Hurston's original typewritten manuscript housed in the University of Florida's Smathers Library. However, if I cite portions from Introductions C and D, I will cite the version I edited for the journal *Callaloo*. I would like to thank the staff at the Smathers Library for giving me access to Hurston's papers.

[91]Ibid.

[92]Hurston: Introduction C, 5.

social progress as compels others. No, just as the rude tribesmen appeared at Sinai receiving the Law, so Christian children are left to conceive of them in the First Century B.C. and even at the destruction of Jerusalem by Titus in 70 A.D. Not like a growing, changing living entity, but like a pressed flower between the leaves of the Bible. One has only to look at the Jews in one's own community to see that this is not, nor could ever have been, true.[93]

The Christian representation of the Jews ignores the "natural laws of evolution of social progress that compels others." Therefore, instead of acknowledging many different Jewish sects and traditions, early Christians claimed that there are only the Jews, and instead of acknowledging that Jews evolve from one age to the next, Christians represented them as eternally the same, crushed "like a pressed flower between the leaves of the Bible."[94] To underscore the absurdity of the Christian propensity to use the biblical representation of the Jews from the Sinai Theophany to understand contemporary Jews, Hurston asks her reader to reflect on the way present-day Nordics are represented: "Nobody now would assume that the present-day progressive Nordic was identical with his ancestors."[95]

For Hurston, the early Christian fabrication of the Herod story is important, because it established the model that would come to be used against minorities by the twentieth century's dominant political regimes. Hurston succinctly defines the twentieth-century incarnation of this model in her 1950 essay "What White Publishers Won't Print." For Hurston, there is an insidious dynamic between publishers and readers, which explains "the lack of literature about the higher emotions and love life of upper-class Negroes and the minorities in general."[96] "Publishing houses," Hurston rightly notes,

---

[93]Hurston (Winter 2011), "from HEROD THE GREAT." Edited by Michael Lackey. *Callaloo* 34(1): 124.

[94]In *Anti-Semite and Jew*, Jean-Paul Sartre examines the degree to which the Jew is defined in the West as a "metaphysical essence" (38), which prohibits Jews from growing and evolving. He, like Hurston, goes on to claim that "it is no exaggeration to say that it is the Christians who have *created* the Jew" (68).

[95]Hurston, Introduction D, 6.

[96]Hurston (1979), "What White Publishers Won't Print," in *I Love myself when I am laughing…And then again when I am looking mean and impressive: A Zora Neale*

"are in business to make money,"[97] but they are constrained by "the subconscious of the majority,"[98] which has been structured on the assumption "that all non-Anglo-Saxons are uncomplicated stereotypes."[99] Therefore, to ensure profit, American publishers only print books that portray minorities as "figures mounted" on a wall, composed "of bent wires without insides at all."[100] Given the publishing houses' tendency to print only books that ignore "the internal life of educated minorities,"[101] Hurston, with characteristic wit, offers a sophisticated interpretation of this behavior by referring to the situation in the United States as "THE AMERICAN MUSEUM OF UNNATURAL HISTORY."[102] According to the logic of this model, it is assumed that whites have an interior life, which is why they have a natural history, while it is generally assumed that minorities lack an interior life, which is why they only have an unnatural history.

For Hurston, what constitutes an interior life is a capacity for autonomy. (In Chapter 2, I discussed the development of this theory of autonomy from Kant through Chamberlain and Weininger to Wittgenstein, Hitler, and the Nazis.) To illustrate, she tells a story about an open-minded white master who educates his slave in order to demonstrate that blacks have the same capacities as whites. But then Hurston imagines how a white racist would respond to this slave's performance. He would say: "'Yes, he certainly knows his higher mathematics, and he can read Latin better than many white men I know, but I cannot bring myself to believe that he understands a thing that he is doing. It is all an aping of our culture. All on the outside.'"[103] For Hurston's hypothetical slave supporter, blacks are formed and shaped by external forces, such as their environment. In essence, they are like animals that can be trained. What they lack is that intangible something within humans that enables them to resist their environmental conditioning and thereby produce something

Hurston Reader. Editor Alice Walker. New York: The Feminist Press at the City University of New York, 170.
[97]Ibid.
[98]Hurston (1979), 172.
[99]Hurston (1979), 170.
[100]Ibid.
[101]Ibid.
[102]Ibid.
[103]Hurston (1979), 169–70.

uniquely their own. As a novelist with an exceptional capacity for identifying and defining the political psychology at work within racist political leaders, Hurston has perfectly pictured Hitler's view of minorities, which he clearly articulates in *Mein Kampf*. Hitler mocks contemporary newspapers that feature articles about a black who "has for the first time become a lawyer, teacher, even a pastor." Hitler believes that Jews are primarily responsible for these kinds of stories, because they use it in order to put forth a "theory about the *equality of men*." Hitler rejects this theory and conclusion, because he has another interpretation of the seeming education of blacks: "It is criminal lunacy to keep on drilling a born half-ape until people think they have made a lawyer out of him." For Hitler, what really occurs with blacks "is training exactly like that of the poodle, and not scientific 'education.'"[104] Blacks are shaped by external factors, which is basically training, but they cannot be educated, because they lack the internal faculty that would enable them to fight against or overcome the external factors that shape them. Put simply, they lack the capacity for autonomy.

We have no evidence that Hurston read *Mein Kampf*. And yet, she identifies and defines the ideology underwriting Hitler's racist views with stunning precision. How is this possible? My argument throughout this book is that the novelists' unique contribution to intellectual history is to create symbolic figures that can be used to illuminate the political psychology of people and events about which they are ignorant. They can do this because they have been able to define a dominant ideology that informs the behavior of prominent and ordinary people. For Hurston, the Herod story is the origin of what would become the Western concept of the autonomous interior and the nonautonomous minority. Note that I do not just say the Jew. Hurston believed that twentieth-century Christians used the concept of the Jew as a template for defining a wide range of people. For instance, in *Dust Tracks*, she claims that "two thousand years have gone by and all the Western World uses the sign of the Cross, and it is evident that the Jews are not the only ones who do not accept it."[105] Hurston's vagueness about the Jews not being "the only ones" who fail to accept Christianity should not be seen as intellectual

---

[104]Hitler (1971), 430.
[105]Hurston (2006), 256.

sloppiness on her part. She is suggesting that, in order to understand the demonization of various minorities in the twentieth century, we need to examine the originary source for this demonization, which is the Christian depiction of the Jew. Put differently, the model that early Christians developed in order to justify their violation of the Jews is the same one that twentieth-century Christians use to violate contemporary Jews and many others.

If it is true that the Herod story established the framework for justifying the demonization and violation of the Jews and many others, then the best way to deconstruct that model would be to give readers "the real, the historical Herod, instead of the deliberately folklore Herod"[106] of the New Testament. But Hurston feared doing that, for as she claims in a letter to Max Eastman, if her interpretation of Herod is right, then her novel would undermine Christ's uniqueness, underscore Christ's Jewishness, and ultimately be "destructive of the divinity of Christ."[107] Why would Hurston want to undermine the idea of Christ's divinity? And how would this function to disable the racist political agenda of a dominant power like National Socialism? The logic of Hurston's biographical novel goes something like this: demonstrating that Jesus derived many of his teachings from the Essenes, thus inextricably linking Jesus with this Jewish sect, would effectively deconstruct the view that Jesus was "A SUDDEN AND MIRACULOUS HAPPENING AS IS TOLD IN THE NEW TESTAMENT." In essence, it would render Jesus less original by demonstrating how he naturally evolved from the Essene tradition, thus exposing the Bible as a deeply flawed and untrustworthy text. Moreover, it would effectively debunk the demonized view of the Jews by giving the Jewish sect of the Essenes considerable credit for the production of Jesus. To be very specific, Hurston's biblical biographical novel would effectively counter the representation of Jesus found in the writings of Luther, Kant, Chamberlain, Weininger, Rosenberg, Goebbels, Streicher, Hitler, and the Nazis, which hold that the birth of Jesus represents a decisive rupture with and a total overcoming of the Jew and all things Jewish. For Hurston, Christ and Christians are no more capable of transcending their environment than Jews or anyone else, because all humans are equally subject to the "natural laws of evolution

---

[106]Hurston, Preface B, 1.
[107]Hurston (2003), 737.

of social progress." But for people to finally understand and accept this, they need to reject the fantastical beliefs that led New Testament writers to forge an unrealistic theory of the autonomous interior in terms of *sui generis* transcendence and to crush non-Christians between the leaves of the Bible. Since it can be shown that the story of Herod is based on strategic distortions and willful misrepresentations of Christ and the Jews, Hurston suggests that those people who take their political cue from the New Testament's *sui generis* Christ and its unnatural history of the Jew would be steeped in dangerous political error. By authoring a book that would expose the absurdities and excesses of the Bible's implicit conception of autonomy and transcendence as well as the depiction of the nonautonomous Jew, Hurston would be able to take away the white West's most effective instrument for demonizing and subsequently violating "Jews and many others."

V

The task at this point is to clarify how Hurston's biblical biographical novels expose Bible-based polities as fatally flawed and socially unjust. When reading *Moses, Man of the Mountain* in relation to Nazi Germany, it would be a mistake to suggest that Hurston invites readers to place Hitler in the position of Moses as a figure who supposedly receives his commands directly from the Divine, which he subsequently promulgates to the people. Hitler's anti-Semitic source of authority was not based on a direct line of communication with God. Rather, it was founded on the authority of the Bible. We see this most clearly in an April 12, 1922 speech in which Hitler discusses the best way to legislate in relation to the Jews. Responding to Count Lerchenfeld, who claimed before the German Landtag that his faith as a Christian prevented him from being an anti-Semite, Hitler says: "My feeling as a Christian points me to the man who once in loneliness, surrounded only by a few followers, recognized these Jews for what they were and summoned men to the fight against them and who, God's truth! was greatest not as sufferer but as fighter."[108] To legitimize this claim,

---

[108]Hitler (1969), "Speech of 12 April 1922," in *The Speeches of Adolf Hitler: April 1922–August 1939*. Translated by Norman H. Baynes. Vol. I. New York: Howard Fertig, 19.

Hitler clarifies how he arrived at his view through his reading of the Bible: "In boundless love as a Christian and as a man I read through the passage which tells us how the Lord at last rose in His might and seized the scourge to drive out of the Temple the brood of vipers and of adders."[109] Given this treatment of the Jew in the Gospels, Hitler then applies the biblical lesson to the contemporary political situation in Germany. After mentioning Christ's "fight for the world against the Jewish poison," Hitler says: "Today, after two thousand years, with deepest emotion I recognize more profoundly than ever before in the fact that it was for this that He had to shed His blood upon the Cross."[110] Christian action is mandatory, for the Bible has provided him with a blueprint for specific action against the Jews in the present, which is why Hitler concludes:

> As a Christian I have no duty to allow myself to be cheated, but I have the duty to be a fighter for truth and justice. And as a man I have the duty to see to it that human society does not suffer the same catastrophic collapse as did the civilization of the ancient world some two thousand years ago—a civilization which was driven to its ruin through this same Jewish people.[111]

This is the Bible-based approach that informed the Nazis' party program and that would become deadly for Jews after Hitler and the Nazis came to power.

And, significantly, it is exactly this kind of Bible-based approach to the political that Hurston sought to expose and counter in her writings. She makes this point clearly in her bowdlerized chapter when discussing the desire for social justice. Hurston considers it foolhardy to seek absolute justice anywhere. To illustrate, she challenges readers to consult "the Book of Books," for if they did, they would discover that such justice "is not even there."[112] This is the case because "it is foolish to expect any justice untwisted by the selfish hand."[113] To support her critique of the Bible, Hurston briefly discusses the Ancient Hebrews' demonization of the Canaanites,

---

[109]Hitler (1969), 19–20.
[110]Hitler (1969), 20.
[111]Ibid.
[112]Hurston (2006), 254.
[113]Ibid.

which enabled the Hebrews to justify killing the Canaanites and then seizing their land. She then shifts to the New Testament, specifically the Christian demonization of the Jews. For Hurston, it is this biblical model of demonization and the subsequent violence that has determined the form and shape of the mid-twentieth-century Western polity. For Hurston, to understand how most mid-twentieth-century Western powers justified their brutal treatment of Jews and other minorities, it is crucial to understand how those governments took their cue from the "Book of Books," which functions to legitimize and glorify a power-hungry dictator such as Moses.

It is important to note, however, that this model does not apply exclusively to Nazi Germany. In the bowdlerized chapter, Hurston certainly uses this model to call her readers' attention to "Hitler's crime." But she also applies the model to the United States. For instance, she briefly discusses how the United States has justified its brutal treatment of "the Little Latin brother south of the border,"[114] and she faults President Roosevelt, "who could extend his four freedoms to some people right here in America before he takes it all abroad."[115] Hurston's reference to Roosevelt's Four Freedoms (freedom of speech and religion and freedom from want and fear), which were articulated in a January 6, 1941, speech, is particularly pertinent. At the beginning of *Moses*, Hurston clearly critiques Nazi Germany for enacting the Nuremberg Laws, which effectively divested Jews of citizenship and thereby made them vulnerable to vicious abuses that culminated in *Kristallnacht*. But Hurston's critique could be equally applied to the Jim Crow laws in the United States, which Hurston indicates in her essay "Crazy for this Democracy." After comically mocking the concept of democracy, and especially Roosevelt's democracy-inflected "Four Freedoms," Hurston notes the absurdity of a president preaching democratic freedom when his own country has "Jim Crow laws on the statute books of the nation."[116] In essence, there are deep-structure similarities between Hitler's Germany and Roosevelt's America, which is why the Moses novel could effectively illuminate both.

---

[114]Hurston (2006), 259.
[115]Hurston (2006), 261.
[116]Hurston (1979), "Crazy for this Democracy," 165, 167.

The primary similarity, and the one that most clarifies why Hurston authored a biblical biographical novel, is the source for the Nuremberg and the Jim Crow laws. After detailing how Jim Crow laws physically degrade blacks and psychologically elevate whites, Hurston alludes to Exodus 29:9, which instills within people "the conviction of First by Birth, eternal and irrevocable like the place assigned to the Levites by Moses over the other tribes of the Hebrews. Talent, capabilities, nothing has anything to do with the case. Just FIRST BY BIRTH."[117] More than anything else, what rankles Hurston is the way the Bible crushes people between its leaves, thus establishing a permanent hierarchy. Moses places the Levites above others in perpetuity ("by perpetual law"), which tacitly defines non-Levites as inferior for all time. Talent, qualifications, capacities, and motivation count for nothing. What matters is one's tribal heritage. Moses may have asserted this hierarchical doctrine, but the same idea was formalized in and through the New Testament's demonization of the Jews. For Hurston, the author of the Gospel of Matthew defines Jews as beings lacking an autonomous interior, thus justifying the Christian subjugation and violation of the Jews. Given the Bible's content, which has shaped and formed the Western polities of the mid-twentieth century, the divinely favored, like Germans and white Americans, must always be above God-appointed "inferiors," like Jews and black Americans, thus explaining the Nuremberg and Jim Crow laws.

This is the case, however, only on condition that the Bible is right and true. If it can be shown that the Bible is a profoundly untrustworthy and politically dangerous text, then those polities that have appealed to it in order to establish their agendas would be exposed as misguided and unjust. And it is exposing the Bible that Hurston does in and through her novels about Moses and Herod. To put the matter bluntly, Moses did not get his directive to slaughter 3,000 people from God, as Luther claims. That directive came from Moses the man, Moses the "dictator," who imposed his will on the people in order to establish his "theocratic government." Christ, as God, did not label the Jews "children of the devil" for all time, as Luther and Streicher insist. Rather, the early Gospel writers concocted that view of the Jews in order to demonize

---

[117]Hurston (1979), 168.

them, thereby distancing Christ from the environmental forces (the Jewish sect of the Essenes) that determined the content and form of his derivative teachings. By authoring biblical biographical novels, which expose the Bible's twisted, biased, and flawed origins, Hurston demonstrates the absurdity and dangers of premising a polity on biblical dictates. Using the biblical biographical novel to undermine the Bible's authority as a legitimate basis for legislating and governing would ultimately expose racist laws (Nuremberg and/or Jim Crow) as untenable and incoherent. For Hurston, the biblical biographical novel is the most effective aesthetic form for exposing the dangers of mid-twentieth-century racist polities.

5

Dual-temporal truths in the biographical novel

Biographical novelists and traditional historians/biographers have a difficult time talking to each other about a historical figure. This is the case because their conceptions of historical truth and their approaches to the subject matter are radically different. In an interview about the novel *Cloudsplitter*, which depicts the life of John Brown's son Owen, Russell Banks clarified the nature of the problem when he told me that a historian criticized him for picturing the Brown family in 1848 on a road alongside a chain of lakes in New York "because that road wasn't built until the 1870s."[1] When doing research for the novel, Banks had access to a map of the area from the time period, so he knew that the road was not there in 1848. But, as he goes on to claim, he included the road nonetheless, because he "wanted the image in the novel" so that he "could describe" the Brown family "as going along the blade of a scimitar and deploy the image as a prefiguration of the bloody swords that" the Browns "would use much later."[2] In this case, what differentiates traditional historians/biographers from biographical novelists is the kind of truth that they seek to access and represent. The historian's/biographer's objective is to epistemologically access and accurately represent the factual record of a given person, time, and/or place from the past, so strategically altering what actually occurred is not an option. By stark contrast, the biographical novelist's objective is to represent a symbolic truth. Therefore, if

---

[1] Banks (2014), 46.
[2] Banks (2014), 46–7.

strategically altering the historical record would enable an author to better articulate a symbolic truth, then that is what the creative writer will and must do.

This symbolic truth, which has a dual-temporal function, differentiates biographical novelists from traditional historians/ biographers. Again, Banks best articulates the nature of this idea. He notes that the historical Owen Brown died in 1889, but "by authorial fiat," he decided to have his fictional Owen tell his story in 1903. He explains his motivation:

> I let him live on into the twentieth century so that his story, John Brown's story, would lose some of the antique quality it might have had otherwise and would point toward the twentieth century, to our own time. Even to the twenty-first century, where it's [*Cloudsplitter*] now being read as a portrait of the terrorist that can be applied to our understanding of our present time.[3]

Banks' logic could be stated thus: understanding the psychology motivating John Brown to commit his crimes could illuminate the psychology at work in the contemporary terrorist mind. Within this framework, what makes a biographical novel successful and effective is the degree to which it accurately pictures the way a terrorist mind works in two separate time periods. Given this objective, there is empirical evidence to suggest that Banks succeeded in *Cloudsplitter*. After the publication of the novel he received a letter from a woman who had served twenty-four years in prison for committing a crime in the 1960s when she was a member of the Weather Underground. As Banks claims:

> She read the novel and wrote me the best fan letter I've ever gotten—a three-page, typed, single-spaced response to the novel—because she believed that Owen Brown's life and story were her life and her story. She is a late twentieth century person, Jewish, from New York, her father is a powerful and liberal lawyer. She was a radical person, but this was her story.[4]

---

[3]Banks (2014), 47–8.
[4]Banks (2014), 51.

The mark of a good biographer is his or her skillful and accurate representation of a historical person, but the mark of a good biographical novelist is his or her ability to convert a biographical figure into a cross-temporal symbol. Based on this distinction, Banks believes that the woman who wrote him would not have had a similar response "had she read a biography of John Brown instead,"[5] because the biography, fixated as it is on getting the past literally right, does not picture the cross-temporal dimension of the biographical subject.

In the following pages, I analyze three biographical novels that focus on racism and slavery: Arna Bontemps' *Black Thunder*, William Styron's *The Confessions of Nat Turner*, and Barbara Chase-Riboud's *Sally Hemings*. My goal is to assess the quality of these works as biographical novels, and my primary criteria are the effectiveness, suitability, and believability of the novel's cross-temporal symbolism. In the process, I intend to demonstrate the unique power of the biographical novel to expose and combat structures of oppression.

I

In *Gabriel's Rebellion*, an intelligent historical depiction of Gabriel Prosser's 1800 slave rebellion in Virginia, Douglas R. Egerton faults Bontemps' 1936 novel *Black Thunder*, because it gives readers a myth (here used in a pejorative sense) about Prosser, who is depicted "as a meek, apolitical bondman driven to revolt only by his master's cruel murder of an elderly slave."[6] The historical Prosser, Egerton claims, was very different from what we get in Bontemps' novel. The real Prosser was a "born rebel" who was ready and willing to be violent and who "was no apolitical servant but a literate artisan whose breadth of vision was truly international."[7] One certainly can understand Egerton's frustrations with Bontemps, for as a historian, he objects to those who tamper with agreed-upon facts. But if we understand that Bontemps, as a novelist, privileges very

---

[5]Ibid.
[6]Egerton (1993), *Gabriel's Rebellion: The Virginia Slave Conspiracies of 1800 & 1802*. Chapel Hill and London: The University of North Carolina Press, ix.
[7]Egerton (1993), x.

different types of "truths" and has radically different objectives than historians or biographers, then his decision to alter certain facts would make perfect sense.

In the introduction to the 1968 edition of *Black Thunder*, Bontemps gives readers a clear sense of his objective in the novel, which is not so much to accurately picture Prosser's life and rebellion as to use Prosser's story in order to construct a cross-temporal symbol. Bontemps opens the introduction with an important assertion: "Time is not a river. Time is a pendulum."[8] Instead of seeing time in terms of a linear narrative of progress, with each generation yielding separate and distinct issues and problems, Bontemps views it in terms of "intricate patterns of recurrence."[9] Within this cyclical framework, the oppressive conditions and structures of the past will recur in the present and/or future. Therefore, the biographical novelist's task is to find a symbolic way to picture the cross-temporal political conditions and structures.

There are numerous passages in the introduction that underscore Bontemps' cross-temporal approach. For instance, thinking about the situation of blacks in 1968, Bontemps draws a clear line of connection between Martin Luther King and Prosser: "If time is the pendulum I imagined, the snuffing of Martin Luther King, Jr.'s career may yet appear as a kind of repetition of Gabriel's shattered dream during the election year of 1800."[10] Bontemps' comment here is vague. Just as Gabriel's rebellion was squashed, so too was King's career. But in the following pages, Bontemps gets more specific. What motivated him to write the novel in the mid-thirties were the impoverished conditions of blacks. After losing jobs in New York and Alabama, Bontemps and his family moved to Watts in order to live with his parents, where he wrote *Black Thunder*. Here he specifies the nature of his situation while he was writing:

> Had the frustrations dormant in Watts at that date suddenly exploded in flame and anger, as they were eventually to do, I don't think they would have shaken my concentration; but

---

[8]Bontemps (2003), "Introduction to the 1968 Edition," *Black Thunder: Gabriel's Revolt: Virginia, 1800.* Boston: Beacon Press, xxi.
[9]Ibid. For an excellent discussion of the distinctions between the linear and the cyclical in Bontemps' novel, see Christine Levecq's "Philosophies of History in Arna Bontemps' *Black Thunder.*"
[10]Bontemps (2003), xxii.

I have a feeling that more readers might then have been in a mood to hear a tale of volcanic rumblings among angry blacks—and the end of patience.[11]

In a sense, Bontemps is explaining in this passage why his novel did not sell very well in 1936. The conditions were ripe for a societal eruption, like the 1965 Watts riots, and had such an explosion occurred, readers would have been better positioned to understand and appreciate the cross-temporal reality in *Black Thunder*. But since there was no such riot, Prosser's story could not resonate in 1936.

While it appears that Bontemps merely documents in the introduction what led him to author *Black Thunder*, his depiction actually outlines the cross-temporal conditions that lead to a societal eruption. Bontemps draws a link between the "volcanic rumblings" that led to Prosser's rebellion and the 1965 Watts riots. Before referencing the Watts riots, Bontemps briefly mentions his own challenges in gaining employment and then describes how his father struggled throughout his life to find meaningful work. After moving to Watts, Bontemps "began to explore Negro history"[12] in order to write his novel. In essence, Bontemps moves from his personal history to his family history and then to black history, and through this he discovers a pattern, a systemic problem of blacks being denied the opportunity to achieve autonomy and meaning through their own labor. Having exposed the basic forms of oppression, Bontemps is then in a position to clarify how the thwarted "will to freedom"[13] becomes a volcanic eruption of death and destruction.

My point here is this: Egerton and Bontemps focus on radically different truths. Egerton seeks to portray as literally and accurately as possible where Prosser lived, what he knew, how he behaved, and why he rebelled. Bontemps certainly considers many of these historical facts important, but as a novelist, he seeks to portray in general terms the cross-temporal conditions and structures that led Prosser and would subsequently lead others like him to stage a massive rebellion. In order to picture these cross-temporal conditions and structures, violating the literal historical record is necessary.

---

[11]Bontemps (2003), xxiii.
[12]Ibid.
[13]Bontemps (2003), xxvi.

This does not mean that Bontemps or biographical novelists dismiss the actual historical record as unimportant. It just means that they privilege different types of historical truth. Given their different truth-focuses, it is inappropriate for the historian Egerton to fault the biographical novelist Bontemps for changing some historical facts, just as it would be inappropriate for the biographical novelist Bontemps to fault a historian for not drawing parallels between, let us say, Prosser's situation and the Scottsboro boys.[14] If there is going to be a coherent conversation between biographical novelists and historians/biographers, they have to start by acknowledging that they foreground and privilege radically different figurations of truth in their works.

II

To bring into sharp focus the nature of Bontemps' achievement, I interpret *Black Thunder* in relation to Guy Endore's 1934 novel *Babouk*.[15] Frequently described as proletarian novels, these two works invite comparison because both focus on slave rebellions that occurred more than 100 years in the past, center their novels in the consciousness of black slaves, underscore the role race and class play in political oppression, expose the contradictions in Enlightenment philosophers, challenge official versions of the historical record, and deploy a dual-temporal model of critique. Most significant for my argument, however, is the one major difference between the two works. *Babouk* is not a biographical novel, because the main character is not named after or totally based on an actual historical figure. The character of Babouk is very loosely based on a person known as "Boukman, Boukmann, or Boukman Ditty,"[16] which is why David Barry Gaspar and Michel-

---

[14]For discussions of the link between Gabriel's situation and the trials of the Scottsboro boys, see Bontemps (xxiv); James A. Miller's *Remembering Scottsboro* (133–42); and Eric J. Sundquist's *The Hammers of Creation* (92–134).
[15]For works that either mention or analyze *Babouk* and *Black Thunder* in relation to each other, see Miller's *Remembering Scottsboro* (127–42), Cheryl Higashida's *Black Internationalist Feminism* (117–18), and Caren Irr's *The Suburb of Dissent* (114).
[16]Guy Endore (1991), "History, Fiction and the Slave Experience," in *Babouk*. Introduction by David B. Gaspar and Michel-Rolph Trouillot. New York: Monthly Review Press, 191.

Rolph Trouillot say that "Babouk is thus half-Boukman and half invented."[17] By contrast, the main character of *Black Thunder* is named after and actually based on the real person Gabriel Prosser. In terms of Bontemps' political objective, I want to specify the aesthetic benefit of naming his character after the actual historical person.

Endore aggressively, one could say too aggressively, exposes the degree to which racism leads to social injustice. Instead of letting the brutal slave story work its uncanny magic on his readers' inner lives, Endore frequently uses heavy-handed forms of irony and preachy discursive asides to hammer home his message. For instance, Endore's narrator briefly explains why it is dangerous for masters to be kind to their slaves. A kind master plans a trip to France, but the overseer who will replace him is not likely to be as kind, so a slave—perhaps—poisons scores of slaves or cattle, thus prohibiting the kind master from leaving. There is no conclusive evidence that a slave actually poisoned the slaves or animals. In fact, an "obscure epidemic"[18] could have been the cause of the tragedy. It is at this point that Endore's narrator interjects "that it would lead us astray into the whole subject of whether it's right or wrong to punish a Negro for a crime he did not commit, for example, to lynch a nigger who did or did not rape a certain girl."[19] For Endore, to sustain the horrific and unjust logic of subjugating a whole race of people, massive acts of unwarranted violence are politically and socially mandatory. Having established the cultural "logic" of unjust violence as an instrument of racial domination and social control, Endore's narrator can then suggest that the same "logic" is at work in twentieth-century America in the form of lynching a black man for supposedly raping a white girl. Endore concludes this chapter by having his narrator apologize to his reader for interjecting a contemporary reference into a novel that is set in the eighteenth century:

> I beg the reader's pardon. That was an anachronistic slip. This is a novel about the eighteenth century Negro. Today the black man is everywhere free and equal to the white.

---

[17] Ibid.
[18] Endore (1991), 53.
[19] Ibid.

For one reviewer, it is such "heavy irony" that "ruins the book as either literature or propaganda."[20]

The most searing and insightful criticism of the book comes from an unnamed reviewer of a *New York Times Book Review.* The reviewer begins by claiming that *Babouk* "is less a novel than a somewhat hysterical piece of special pleading."[21] For this author, what ultimately mars the book is the loss of the main character's individuality as he is transformed into a propagandistic symbol: "The first part of the book, depicting the terror and amazement of the blacks at their first encounter with the whites, is well done, but Babouk soon ceases to be clearly individualized, becoming a symbol rather than a person."[22] This was not the only review to identify such a flaw in the novel. In *The Saturday Review of Literature,* an unidentified reviewer says that "Babouk is always a symbol rather than an individual, there is little of the sensuous feel of the Haitian scene, and the author makes no bones of the fact that he is writing a work of propaganda—an indignant blast against the white man's treatment of the black, with an incidental leaning toward a vague sort of communism."[23] By changing the main character's name from Boukman to Babouk, Endore liberates himself from the actual figure's historical specificity, thus enabling him to make his protagonist a symbol representing his political ideology. But because Babouk becomes too heavily symbolic, he loses all his individual human qualities. Therefore, instead of inspiring compassion for Babouk and people in his situation, the work is dismissed by readers as "bad writing"[24] or mere "sensationalism."[25]

Based on this critique, it would be easy to say that the problem with *Babouk* is that Endore is a weak writer, and there is certainly some justification for making this claim on the basis of the 1934 novel. But I want to make a much different claim. Given developments in twentieth-century theories of knowledge, there was growing discontent with traditional forms of symbolism. From the late nineteenth century, as in the writings of Friedrich Nietzsche, until today, there has been an escalating sense of "incredulity

---

[20]Qtd. in Miller (2009), 132.
[21]"Negroes in Revolt," *The New York Times Book Review.* September 9, 1934, 7.
[22]Ibid.
[23]Review of *Babouk, The Saturday Review of Literature.* September 29, 1934, 148.
[24]Review of *Babouk* (November 1934), *The Nation.* 139(3618): 546.
[25]Martha Gruening, "Some Recent Fiction," *The New Republic.* October 17, 1934, 283.

toward metanarratives."[26] Applying this development to literature, symbolic figures, such as Babouk, function like a traditional metanarratological truth. But as people have become increasingly more suspicious of such overarching symbols, creative writers have had to update aesthetics accordingly. It is my contention that this epistemological development in part contributed to the rise of the biographical novel. More specifically, Bontemps had in the mid-thirties, as I will demonstrate shortly, a similar political agenda as Endore, but he needed to find a better aesthetic form to communicate that agenda, one that was more compelling and convincing than the one found in *Babouk* and less likely to alienate readers. That form was the biographical novel. By naming his protagonist after the actual historical figure, Bontemps could avoid to some degree the charge of conveniently concocting an arbitrary symbol (a metanarrative) that strategically and conveniently suits his ideological and political agenda.

III

Black Thunder opens by referencing the "Virginia Court records for September 15, 1800."[27] From the very beginning, Bontemps signals to his readers that this is a work rooted in and based on historical fact, officially recorded documents. It is as if Bontemps is saying: "Do not think that this story is my own invention, a symbolic phantom of one person's overheated imagination. Rather, it is something that has been verified by official authorities." If Endore made himself extremely vulnerable to critique by changing his main character's name and making him into a nonempirically based symbol of his political agenda, Bontemps decided that he was not going to make that same mistake, so he named his character after the original historical figure and flaunted the fact that he used official documents to build his narrative.

And yet, despite this seeming reverence for the historical record, Bontemps strategically alters some important facts. For instance,

---

[26]Jean-François Lyotard (1991), *The Postmodern Condition: A Report on Knowledge.* Translated by Geoff Bennington and Brian Massumi. Minneapolis: University of Minnesota Press, xxiv.
[27]Bontemps (2003), 9.

Egerton notes that Prosser was a privileged figure in his community for a number of reasons: "Status as a craft apprentice provided Gabriel with considerable standing in the slave community—as did his ability to read and write."[28] Since Prosser's literacy significantly contributed to his stature, why would Bontemps create him as a man "innocent of letters?"[29] The answer to this question gets to the heart of white racist justifications for subjugating blacks. From the eighteenth century, when Thomas Jefferson concludes that blacks are "in reason much inferior" to whites because he has never heard a black utter "a thought above the level of plain narration,"[30] until the early half of the twentieth century, when Hitler announces that blacks lack the capacity to engage in actual thinking (see Chapter 4 for an analysis of Hitler's views of blacks), the consistent assumption has been that blacks lack the capacity for intellectual autonomy. To put the matter simply, blacks can be trained to desire freedom and even to formulate arguments in favor of freedom, but they lack the intellectual capacity to know or experience freedom on their own. Therefore, blacks must always be guided, directed, and controlled by those (whites) who can actually understand and experience freedom.

If, like Endore, Bontemps wants to expose and debunk the racist ideology underwriting an oppressive political regime, the best way to do that would be to picture a black man engaging in an activity that is supposedly reserved exclusively for whites. This explains why Bontemps had to make Prosser illiterate. Just after Prosser is described as illiterate, he hears white men discussing the ideology that led to the French Revolution, which has an instant and enormous impact on him. On the surface, this scene might support the white racist argument that blacks must derive their views from whites. But Bontemps' strategic description of Prosser's experience refutes this view: "Here were words for things that had been in his mind, things that he didn't know had names. Liberty, equality, frater—it was a strange music, a strange music."[31] Had Bontemps' Prosser been literate, one could have said that he merely inherited

---

[28]Egerton (1993), 21.
[29]Bontemps (2003), 20.
[30]Jefferson (1955), *Notes on the State of Virginia*. Editor William Peden. Chapel Hill: The University of North Carolina Press, 140, 239.
[31]Bontemps (2003), 21.

his view of and desire for freedom from white-written texts. It is such a view that leads Hitler to say that blacks can only receive "training like that of the poodle, and not scientific 'education.'"[32] According to this view, blacks can inherit revolutionary ideas from whites, but they cannot originate such ideas on their own. But by underscoring that liberty and equality are Platonic-like ideals in Prosser's mind even before he encounters a formal discourse about them, Bontemps suggests that blacks and whites are the same—both equally have an innate notion of and capacity for freedom.

This is something that the whites in the novel could not accept, which explains why they insist that Prosser derived his views of freedom and rebellion from whites. For instance, after the revolt fails, whites blame whites for masterminding the insurrection. To illustrate the white consensus view, Bontemps has the black literate character Mingo hear a disembodied voice authoritatively dictating that no such rebellion could have originated with a black person:

> There were hands in this plot that haven't been suspected yet. . . . A surprise blow like this—you mark my word, such audacity and diabolical invention came from a trained mind, possibly a professional revolutionary. Search carefully for papers that might point to Callender, Duane, United Irishmen or to France by way of San Domingo. And by all means hold this Mingo; *he knows how to read*.[33]

In this case, reading functions to confirm an intellectual failing, which is why Bontemps italicizes the sentence. Blacks can read what whites have written about revolutions, but they could never have imagined or instigated one on their own.

To further expose the white racist assumption that blacks lack the intellectual capacity to understand the value of freedom as well as the ability to stage a successful rebellion, Bontemps creates the character of M. Creuzot, a French printer working in Richmond. When reflecting on a conversation about some undefined rumblings among local blacks, which one person interprets as evidence of an imminent rebellion, Creuzot wonders: "Actually, *could* it be? Could these tamed things imagine liberty, equality? Of course, he knew

---

[32]Hitler (1971), 430.
[33]Bontemps (2003), 149.

about San Domingo, many stories had filtered through, but whether or not the blacks themselves were capable of that divine discontent that turns the mill of destiny was not answered."[34] As a supporter of the French Revolution, it would seem that Creuzot would be eager to support the battle for black emancipation. But ultimately, Creuzot, like many Enlightenment thinkers, concludes that there is a difference between blacks and whites: "The blacks were not discontented: they couldn't be. They were without the necessary faculties."[35] Through Creuzot's racist musings, we get insight into the contradictory "logic" that allowed Americans to accord all people the right to life, liberty, and happiness but not to extend that right to blacks and that allowed the French to extend freedom to many in France during its revolution but to deny that same freedom to blacks in a French colony like Haiti.

In essence, there are two separate reasons why whites refused to acknowledge that blacks have a notion of and capacity for freedom. First, if it could be shown that blacks have a desire for freedom and the capacity for intellectual autonomy, then the arguments justifying black subjugation would be exposed as faulty and unjust. Since whites wanted and needed slaves, they refused to acknowledge blacks' yearning and ability for freedom. Second, if blacks have an innate desire for and experience of freedom, then they would have the motivation and capacity to stage an effective revolution. This is precisely what an article in the newspaper *Epitome*, which Bontemps cites in the novel, boldly announces: "The behavior of Gabriel under his misfortunes was such as might be expected from a mind capable of forming the daring project which he had conceived."[36] This passage reads as if it were a direct refutation of Creuzot's racist view of blacks. And, indeed, the idea expressed in this article is one of the most terrifying thoughts for the whites in the novel, which is why so few are willing to accept or admit it. To indicate what a frightening thought a black rebellion would be, Bontemps cites a letter from a Richmond resident, who acknowledges what the blacks almost accomplished: "'So well had they matured their plot, and so completely had they organized their system of operation, that nothing but a miraculous intervention of

---

[34]Bontemps (2003), 63.
[35]Ibid.
[36]Bontemps (2003), 197.

the arm of Providence was supposed to have been capable of saving the city from pillage and flames, and the inhabitants thereof from butchery.'"[37]

Put simply, Bontemps emphasizes the following points in his novel: contrary to what whites think, feel, and believe, blacks have a desire and capacity for freedom. Therefore, if white political leaders do not accord blacks what they believe is naturally theirs, then whites in America should expect blacks to respond just as Americans did to the British or the Haitians to the French, for there is a human and cultural law that applies to all people, black or white. The law goes something like this: people desire freedom, and if they are deprived of it, they will resort to violent means in order to secure it. Whites, of course, know this law, because it is what led to the American and French revolutions, but whites, like Creuzot, do not believe that this law applies to blacks, because they consider blacks a lesser species of being. But in *Black Thunder*, Bontemps pictures the interior life of an actual historical figure to illustrate that blacks do indeed possess the same desire and capacity as whites. So if whites, who have the economic and political power, do not create the possibility for blacks to experience life, liberty, and happiness, then a deadly rebellion is likely to erupt.

Moreover, like Banks and Endore, Bontemps suggests that this is not just a law applicable to people more than a hundred years in the past. It is a cross-temporal law. Therefore, Bontemps strategically uses anachronistic language to underscore the links between the situation for blacks in 1800 and the oppressed in the 1930s. For instance, in a conversation about "'*Slavery and the Rights of Man*,'" Creuzot responds with some indignation: "'More of that stuff intended to incite the proletariat.'"[38] The word proletariat certainly does not fit here, as it would not come into existence until the mid-nineteenth century and would become popular in the first half of the twentieth century. But this is certainly no mistake. Bontemps, like Banks and Endore, is drawing his reader's attention to the structural links between the two ages. That link is more clearly defined when Creuzot continues his thought: "'Trouble is the proletariat is innocent of letters.'"[39] His logic is that there is

---

[37]Bontemps (2003), 195.
[38]Bontemps (2003), 36.
[39]Ibid.

no reason to worry about the blacks or the proletariat, because, as illiterates, they lack the knowledge necessary for staging an effective revolution. But unlike Creuzot is Alexander Biddenhurst, who does not consider blacks or the proletariat as lacking the desire or capacity for freedom. As he muses later in the novel:

> The signs were hopeful, in one way of thinking. Biddenhurst thought; there was a definite foment among the masses in the state. The revolution of the American proletariat would soon be something more than an idle dream. Soon the poor, the despised of the earth, would join hands around the globe; there would be no more serfs, no more planters, no more classes, no more slaves, only men.[40]

The dual-temporal logic of this very modern-sounding passage should be clear: just as the oppressed and discontented blacks in 1800 are losing patience with the political system and beginning to organize a rebellion in order to improve their living conditions, so too is the oppressed and discontented proletariat in the 1930s losing its patience with the political system and beginning to organize a rebellion in order to improve its living conditions. And since the everyday workers in the 1930s, which includes blacks, have the desire and capacity for freedom, those in political power should be very worried.

The reviews of *Black Thunder* were extremely positive, and what made this so was Bontemps' skillful blending of history and fiction. In *The Saturday Review*, the reviewer praises Bontemps for giving readers in the character of "Gabriel no mere Negro with a sharpened scythe blade but a leader and a man."[41] In essence, by deftly attending to significant detail, Bontemps created a character that is both humanly individual and politically symbolic, which is why Martha Gruening says in her glowing review for *The New Republic* that "Mr. Bontemps' recreation of this historical incident is at once faithful and imaginative."[42] It is faithful in that it is historically specific, but it is imaginative in that it converts Gabriel into a cross-temporal symbol that can be used to illuminate the

---

[40]Bontemps (2003), 76.
[41]J. D., Review of *Black Thunder. The Saturday Review*. February 15, 1936, 27.
[42]Gruening, *The New Republic*. February 26, 1936, 86(1108): 91.

contemporary political situation. Thus, an unnamed reviewer in *The Literary Digest* says that the novel "has the curious effect of seeming contemporaneous, rather than almost 136 years buried in the dust of history,"[43] while Richard Wright says in his review for *The Partisan Review* that there is something in Prosser's character that "transcends the limits of immediate consciousness."[44] As Wright goes on to say, "Bontemps endows Gabriel with a myth-like and deathless quality."[45]

In particular, what the reviewers found most effective in the novel was its dual-temporal thematic. While the novel gives readers a vivid and compelling vision of the past, it does so in order to tell us something substantive and relevant about the present. As Lucy Tompkins intelligently says in her *New York Times* review, while incidents in the novel "are historically true," one should not see them in "any restricted sense," for "it would be ridiculous to say that 'Black Thunder' is limited in its meaning to its historic circumstances." To put the matter simply, Bontemps is less interested in a specific historical event than he is "primarily concerned with the spectacle of human dignity as manifest in the revolutionary spirit time out of mind."[46] This ability to convincingly picture that which applies to multiple times is what makes Bontemps' *Black Thunder* such a spectacular and still relevant novel.

It is also what separates the 1930s Endore from Bontemps. Even though the two writers have similar political sympathies and objectives, which explains why so many scholars mention and discuss *Babouk* and *Black Thunder* together, one novel fails while the other succeeds. Of course, one could account for this by simply acknowledging that Bontemps is a far superior writer to Endore, and there was certainly much justification for making this claim in the mid-thirties. But it is my contention that it is Bontemps' exceptional instinct as a novelist that led him to reject Endore's free-floating (nonempirical) symbolism and, instead, to experiment with the biographical novel. In essence, Bontemps understood the intellectual trajectory of the culture, an epistemological

---

[43]Review of *Black Thunder*, in *The Literary Digest*. February 1, 1936, 28.
[44]Wright (April 1936), "A Tale of Folk Courage," *The Partisan Review* 3(3): 31.
[45]Ibid.
[46]Tompkins (1936), "Slaves' Rebellions: BLACK THUNDER." *New York Times*. February 2, BR7.

trajectory that was in the process of rendering traditional literary symbols ideologically suspect and mandating a more empirically grounded symbolism, such as we see in the biographical novel. Since there was growing discontent with the metanarrative (the traditional symbol), Bontemps had to find a way to create a character that would function as a symbol of his politics, but he simultaneously had to avoid the charge of having manufactured a metanarratogoical symbol for his own ideological purpose. By grounding his fiction in historical documents and facts and naming his protagonist after the actual historical figure, Bontemps could avoid the criticisms that were leveled against Endore. But he could still preserve his aesthetic prerogative of offering a sociopolitical critique by converting his biographical character into a political symbol that functions to illuminate the cross-temporal conditions and structures of oppression. The biographical novel was not just an effective aesthetic medium for a writer like Bontemps to achieve his objectives as a writer; it was a logically necessary aesthetic form, one mandated by the culture and time, for refining our understanding of history and culture and advancing the cause of social justice.

IV

Understanding that biographers/historians and biographical novelists implicitly privilege radically different and sometimes contradictory "truths" explains a great deal about the famous controversy surrounding the publication of William Styron's *The Confessions of Nat Turner*. Scores of articles and books have been written about Styron's novel, but the one that has had the most decisive and enduring impact is *William Styron's Nat Turner: Ten Black Writers Respond*, which was published in 1968, only one year after the publication of Styron's novel. For those studying the nature and form of the biographical novel, what is striking is the fact that the writers fail to evaluate *The Confessions of Nat Turner* as fiction. For instance, in the introduction to the book, John Henrik Clarke begins with a brief discussion of the importance of history, which leads him to fault Styron for misrepresenting the historical facts: "Why did William Styron create *his* Nat Turner and ignore the most important historical facts relating to the real Nat Turner?"[47] Styron, of course, would agree with Clarke about the importance of history, but because the two focus on radically different types of historical "truth," they approach the subject from incompatible and sometimes contradictory perspectives. As a history professor, Clarke demands fidelity to the empirical facts. Therefore, changing details about Turner's life is not acceptable. But as a biographical novelist, Styron focuses on the dual-temporal conditions and structures of oppression. Here is how he states the matter in his essay "Nat Turner Revisited": "I'm sure that my early fascination with Nat Turner came from pondering the parallels between his time and my own society, whose genteel accommodations and endemic cruelties, large and small, were not really so different from the days of slavery."[48] Given this dual-temporal focus, Styron subordinates some historical facts to more important symbolic "truths." For instance, through his novel, Styron wants to expose and critique the exploitative nature of capitalism. In his estimation, the best way to do that would be to use the Southern plantation as a metaphor. But given the agricultural and political realities in Southampton County, where Turner was born and raised, it would be historically inaccurate to set the novel on a massive plantation. However, as Styron goes on to claim, he "had to create a plantation anyway." He explains his motivation:

> The plantation was an integral and characteristic part of Southern life in slave times; it was the very metaphor for the capitalist exploitation of human labor, and the plantation owners often represented the best and worst of those whom history had cast as masters in the peculiar institution, carrying within themselves all the moral frights and tensions which slavery engendered. I needed to dramatize this turmoil, and so I contrived to have Nat Turner grow up on a prosperous plantation which might

---

[47]Clarke (1968), "Introduction," *William Styron's Nat Turner: Ten Black Writers Respond.* Boston: Beacon Press, vii.

[48]Styron (1992), "Nat Turner Revisited," in *The Confessions of Nat Turner.* New York: Vintage International, 438–9. In his excellent biography of Styron, James L. W. West III articulates Styron's dual-temporal focus most succinctly: "What happened to Nat Turner in his novel had to be representative, in a larger sense, of what was happening in the present moment to the black man in America" (346).

have existed fifty years before far up the James River but could not have flourished in poverty-racked Southampton.[49]

Just as Banks changes historical fact by making Owen Brown live into the twentieth century and Bontemps changes historical fact by making Gabriel Prosser illiterate, so too does Styron change historical fact by setting his novel on a plantation that did not and could not exist at that particular time and place.

Ironically, this effective and important feature of the biographical novel is what led Styron to get into so much trouble with his critics. Clarke specifies the dominant critique of Styron's novel:

> The contributors to this book collectively maintain that the distortion of the true character of Nat Turner was deliberate. The motive for this distortion could be William Styron's reaction to the racial climate that has prevailed in the United States in the last fifteen years. Nat Turner, a nineteenth century figure, seems to have been used to make a comment on a twentieth century situation.[50]

What Clarke the historian identifies as one of Styron's major weaknesses is actually, from the perspective of a biographical novelist, one of the genre's greatest strengths. In essence, there can be no real or useful conversation between Clarke and Styron because the two privilege radically different "truths."

We get specific insight into the limitations and flaws of the approach taken in *Ten Black Writers Respond* if we note how the writers use Bontemps' *Black Thunder* in order to identify faults in Styron's novel. In "The Confessions of Willie Styron," John Oliver Killens claims: "If Styron really wanted to understand what went into the making of a Nat Turner, he might have gotten some valuable hints from Arna Bontemps' tremendous and perceptive novel, *Black Thunder*."[51] What irritates Killens most about Styron's novel is the fact that he takes "'poetic' liberties,"[52] thus giving readers a Nat

---

[49]Styron (1993), 442–3.
[50]Clarke (1968), viii.
[51]Clarke (1968), 37. It should be noted that Styron, who did his homework, read Bontemps' novel, as West claims in his biography of Styron (340).
[52]Clarke (1968), 40.

Turner in his novel that does not match the Nat Turner in history. But this is the exact critique that Egerton the historian levels against Bontemps the novelist, for Bontemps makes the historically literate Prosser into an illiterate fictional figure. It is my contention that if we understand how and why Bontemps the novelist converts the historical Prosser into a symbolic figure, then his decision to make this change makes perfect sense. In like manner, if it can be shown that Styron has a respectable purpose for converting the historical Turner into a literary symbol, then faulting him for doing what biographical novelists do would be inappropriate and unacceptable.

Another weakness in the *Ten Black Writers* approach is the writers' failure to understand how the dual-temporal rhetorical cues of the biographical novel function. For instance, John A. Williams critiques Styron for using anachronistic language, thus indicating that Styron failed to do adequate research for his novel: "Historical figures cannot move in a historical vacuum. Is the vacuum surrounding Styron's Nat Turner the result of the failure of the author to thoroughly research his material? A novelist embarked on a historical work becomes a historian in effect, and he must evaluate his character in terms of the time in which his character lived."[53] For Williams, a writer who focuses on a historical figure "is required to be *both* a novelist and a historian." To confirm his point, he references "Bontemps' novel, *Black Thunder*."[54] Ironically, when Williams specifies how Styron's novel fails, he focuses on anachronistic language, the same kind of language Bontemps uses when he puts the word "proletariat" into the mouth of a character in the year 1800, nearly a half-century before the word first came into existence. After noting that some characters swear in Styron's novel, Williams says: "I don't doubt that there *were* swear words, but not these. Like slang, swear words, certain kinds of them, have a vogue in time. Styron has transplanted the present back into the past."[55] Biographical novelists are fully aware of their usage of anachronistic language, but instead of signaling a weakness or flaw in their work, such language is actually one of the novel's greatest strengths, as it functions to underscore the dual-temporal focus of the novel.

---

[53]Clarke (1968), 46.
[54]Ibid.
[55]Clarke (1968), 49.

Perhaps the most glaring and uncomfortable flaw in the *Ten Back Writers* volume revolves around homosexuality. In Styron's novel, Turner has a homosexual experience with a fellow slave by the name of Willis, and of the ten black writers who critiqued Styron, five fault him for including the scene and some use disgraceful and inexcusable language to do so. Most significant, however, are the assumptions underwriting their critique, which is that homosexuals are subhuman, abnormal, anti-male, repulsive, grotesque, and—what they seem to consider the ultimate flaw—feminine.[56] For instance, Alvin F. Poussaint notes that Styron's Turner has an ambiguously "homosexual" experience "with another young black slave." Given this encounter, Poussaint rhetorically asks what this experience tells readers. Here is his answer: "Naturally, it implies that Nat Turner was not a man at all. It suggests that he was unconsciously really feminine."[57] For Poussaint, it is a given that homosexuality is synonymous with evils such as the feminine, "an emasculated and 'abnormal' character,"[58] which renders Turner illegitimate and ineffective. According to this framework, homosexuality totally undermines efforts to combat slavery and racism, for Poussaint concludes that "the depiction of the young rebel as a would-be deviant carries the implication that the whole revolt against slavery and racism was somehow illegitimate and 'abnormal.'"[59]

If this were the only instance of flagrant homophobia in the volume, one could dismiss it as a mere aberration. But these assumptions about homosexuality and this kind of analysis inform much of the work. For instance, after mentioning that "Nat has been engaged in homosexual mutual stimulation with a young black friend," Vincent Harding refers to a joint baptism scene with a white man. For Harding, what makes this scene so despicable,

---

[56]My focus in this chapter is on the black-separatist demonization of the homosexual. But it is worth noting that many black separatists also made horrible remarks about women. In "The Sexual Mountain," Calvin Hernton says:

> During the Black Power/Black Arts Movement of the 1960s, the unequal recognition and treatment of women writers was enunciated more bigotedly than perhaps ever before. "The only position in the revolution for women is the prone position!" "The women's place is seven feet behind the men!" Pronouncements like these were reflected again and again in the writings, and deeds, of the males of the period. (197)

[57]Clarke (1968), 21.
[58]Ibid.
[59]Clarke (1968), 22.

and a logical extension of Nat's homosexual experience with Willis, is that he is baptized with a homosexual. Like Poussaint, Harding assumes that there is a clear and unambiguous meaning in Styron's fictional representation of homosexuality: "Styron has used this event too, but in such a way as to continue the demeaning of Nat Turner."[60] We can agree, Harding is saying, that homosexuality is a universal symbol to discredit, delegitimize, and degrade a character.

Killens extends this view of homosexuality beyond Styron by referencing Sir Lawrence Olivier's movie version of *Othello*, which he considers profoundly flawed, because Olivier "reduced" Othello "to a shuffling stupid-cunning whining idiot, half man and half faggot."[61] In this register, the faggot signifies that which is neither fully human nor fully male (one gets the sense that to be fully human, for Killens, one must be a full-fledged heterosexual male), and Killens, like Poussaint and Harding, takes it as a given that his readers will accept this as a self-evident truth. So it should come as no surprise that Loyle Hairston casually refers to Turner's homosexual experience as "grotesque."[62] Given that so many writers in this volume are in agreement about the meaning of homosexuality, Charles V. Hamilton feels free to make a recommendation on behalf of the entire black community: "Styron's literary mind can wander [sic] about homosexuality and the like, and his vast readership can have their stereotypes strengthened by an image of a black preacher who is irrational and weak (unable to kill, excepting some white woman he loves) and uncertain. But black people should reject this; and white people should not delude themselves."[63] Hamilton is basically saying that black people should reject speculation about homosexuality, and white people should stop deluding themselves into thinking that prominent black males would have anything to do with homosexuality.

This, of course, is absurd, as the African American tradition can boast of having produced some of the finest, most complex, and most sympathetic portrayals of homosexuality. Here I am thinking of Wallace Thurman's *The Blacker the Berry . . .* and *Infants of the Spring*; J. Saunders Redding's *No Day of Triumph*; Ralph

---

[60]Clarke (1968), 27.
[61]Clarke (1968), 35.
[62]Clarke (1968), 71.
[63]Clarke (1968), 74.

Ellison's *Invisible Man*; and James Baldwin's *Giovanni's Room* and *Another Country*, works that were all published before 1968. But the work I want to briefly foreground in order to make a specific point is Richard Wright's *The Long Dream*, a 1958 novel that presciently articulates an argument that has come to dominate in the twenty-first century. The characters Tony, Sam, Zeke, and Fishbelly are going to play baseball, when they notice Aggie West, a young homosexual that all the other boys despise because of his homosexuality. After calling him a "pansy," "fairy," "Homo," and "sissy,"[64] Sam smashes a bat against Aggie's chest and the others beat him. In their subsequent conversation, Zeke, in a self-accusatory moment, uses an analogy to question what they have done to Aggie: "'We treat'im like the white folks treat us."[65] This leads the four to a fruitful conversation:

> "Why you reckon he acts like a girl?" Fishbelly asked.
> "Beats me," Tony said. "They say he can't help it."
> "He could if he really *tried*," Zeke said.
> "Mebbe he can't. . . . Mebbe it's like being black," Sam said.
> "Aw naw! It ain't the same thing," Zeke said.
> "But he ought to stay'way from us," Fishbelly said.
> "That's just what the white folks say about us," Sam told him.[66]

As beings that are ontologically different and inferior, gays, Fishbelly asserts, should be separate ("he ought to stay'way from us") from the "normal" people, heterosexuals in this case. But Sam and Tony rightly note that Fishbelly is deploying the same discursive strategies whites use against blacks ("That's just what the white folks say about us"). This link between racism and homophobia is a crucial theme in Styron's *Confessions*. But the question I want to answer through my analysis of *The Confessions* is this: Why were the four boys in Wright's 1958 novel able to critically reflect on and challenge assumptions about homosexuality while so many critics in the 1968 *Ten Black Writers* volume were not?

The answer has something to do with the dominant trajectory for establishing democratic justice in the United States. The unfortunate

---

[64]Wright (2000), *The Long Dream*. Northeastern University Press: Boston, 38–9.
[65]Wright (2000), 39.
[66]Wright (2000), 39–40.

assumption from the inception of the country through the late nineteenth century was that the United States is a white country. So dominant was this view that the prominent black writer Booker T. Washington tacitly concedes this point in his famous and now canonical "Atlanta Exposition Address" of 1895. When discussing the approach blacks should take to ameliorate their situation in the racist United States, Washington says: "To those of my race who depend on bettering their condition in a foreign land or who underestimate the importance of cultivating friendly relations with the Southern white man, who is their next-door neighbour, I would say: 'Cast down your bucket where you are.'"[67] For blacks, the United States is "a foreign land," because the country was founded by and belongs to whites. According to this logic, blacks cannot actually be legitimate Americans—they are aliens.

By the twentieth century, many prominent blacks and whites started to challenge and debunk the view that the United States is a white country. Underwriting the view that blacks cannot be legitimate Americans is the conviction that blacks and whites are ontologically separate and distinct. The logic of this model goes something like this: based on the color of their skin, whites have corresponding internal characteristics and abilities that make them superior to blacks and thus whites are capable of fulfilling the tacit mandates implicit within American democracy. Blacks, by contrast, lack these necessary characteristics and abilities, and are thus incapable of being American in the strict sense of the word. For those who sought to make the case for defining blacks as fully and legitimately American, they had to debunk the view that blacks are different from and inferior to whites. In other words, they sought to expose how blacks and whites are in essence the same, and consequently, equally worthy of constitutional rights and equally capable of fulfilling and advancing the promises of American democracy.

So in the early twentieth century, Franz Boas did important anthropological work, which would heavily influence Zora Neale Hurston, debunking essentialist models of blacks as intellectually inferior, while Robert Park did important sociological work, which would heavily influence Richard Wright, making the case for

---

[67]Washington (1996), *Up from Slavery*. Editor William L. Andrews. New York and London: W. W. Norton & Company, 99–100.

racial equality.[68] For Boas, Hurston, Park, and Wright, if it could be shown that there are no significant differences between blacks and whites, then it would only follow that both would have the same capacities, thus qualifying them all as equally and legitimately American. Those working within this integrationist tradition devoted themselves to the task of effacing difference, and what they shared in common was the view that race is a human and political invention. As Hurston claims:

> Light came to me when I realized that I did not have to consider any racial group as a whole. God made them duck by duck and that was the only way I could see them. I learned that skins were no measure of what was inside people. So none of the Race clichés meant anything anymore. I began to laugh at both white and black who claimed special blessings on the basis of race. Therefore I saw no curse in being black, nor no extra flavor by being white.[69]

Here is how Baldwin puts the matter in his book *The Fire Next Time*: "Color is not a human or a personal reality; it is a political reality."[70] In my estimation, Redding, who was one of the most famous and accomplished African American academics of the mid-twentieth century, best articulates the view in his book *On Being Negro in America*:

> What I wanted . . . was to loose and shake off the confining coils of race and the racial experience so that the integration—my personal integration and commitment—can be made to something bigger than race, and more enduring, and truer. For race is a myth: it is artificial; and it is, I hope, at last a dying concept.[71]

---

[68]For an excellent work examining the role Boas and Park had in debunking essentialist representations of blacks, see Christopher Douglas' *A Genealogy of Multiculturalism*.
[69]Hurston (2006), *Dust Tracks on a Road*. New York, London, Toronto, Sydney: HarperPerennial, 190–1.
[70]Baldwin (1993), *The Fire Next Time*. New York: Vintage International, 104.
[71]Redding (1962), *On Being Negro in America*. Indianapolis and New York: Charter Books, 152.

What makes many of these writers' works so moving and totally relevant today is the fact that their integrationist agenda extended far beyond racial loyalty. Ellison's insightful and sympathetic portrayal of the white stripper in the "Battle Royal" chapter and his poignant representation of a white homosexual ("one of the unspeakables"[72]) in *Invisible Man*, Baldwin's heart-wrenching depiction of two white gay men in Europe in *Giovanni's Room*, and Redding's devastating experience of a white woman's senseless death in *On Being Negro in America* are indications of the degree to which their integrationist agenda made them sensitive to the sufferings of all people, irrespective of sexual orientation and race. But I specifically mention Ellison, Baldwin, and Redding for a particular reason. These three writers played a crucial role in the making of Styron's novel—Redding supplied Styron with materials for doing research about Turner[73]; Ellison was a friend of Styron's, though that friendship cooled after "The Uses of History in Fiction" forum (I discuss this forum in Chapters 1 and 2); and Baldwin lived with the Styrons and encouraged Styron to access and represent a black person's interiority, which emboldened Styron to write about Turner.[74] I want to underscore how these three contributed to and advanced the integrationist ethos, which they believed would do the most to establish and advance democratic justice in the United States.

For the three black writers, the separatist ideology on which this country was premised—one that defines people in terms of a superior/inferior binary, subtly or overtly encourages the hatred or demonization of the culturally designated inferior, and uses this binary as a basis for denying marginalized others access to public goods and equal rights—is the primary evil plaguing the United States. Having reflected on this social evil and devised an integrationist strategy that they hoped would combat and ultimately defeat anti-black racism, they started to realize that the separatist ideology victimized other marginalized groups, such as homosexuals. Consequently, they drew parallels between the

---

[72]Ellison (1995), *Invisible Man*. New York: Vintage International, 188.
[73]For a discussion of Redding's role in the research for the novel, see West's biography of Styron (221).
[74]West contends in his biography of Styron that Turner is based to some degree on Baldwin, and Baldwin admitted as much in an interview about the novel (336).

situation of blacks and gays in order to advance the cause of both groups, as we see in Wright's *The Long Dream*.

Redding's effort to draw such a link can be found in his 1942 book, *No Day of Triumph*, which consists of brief biographical sketches about blacks in the United States. One story is about Rosalie Hatton. Before narrating it, Redding makes an ominous declaration: Rosalie's story is like "the hearse of an American dream."[75] For Redding, this is not just a tragic story about one person. It represents the failure and perhaps the death of America's promise of democratic access to life, liberty, and the pursuit of happiness. Daughter of a prosperous and doting father, who is a well-regarded physician, Rosalie descends into alcoholism and despair. On the surface, it appears that it was Rosalie's dark skin that causes her psychological deterioration, for it is made clear throughout the narrative that "Rosalie did have nice, even features and fairly straight hair, but she wasn't light, and that can make a world of difference for a girl."[76] There is additional evidence for the race-based approach to Rosalie's situation when Redding mentions her brother, Tom, who is passing for white. The suggestion is that, in order to access the public good in the United States, one must deny one's non-white racial heritage and don the appearance of whites.

Ironically, Redding strategically indicates that passing for white, instead of humanizing, actually transforms Tom into a machine-like being: "He was a small, slender fellow, who looked as if he had been turned out by a machine. His features were sharp and immobile, like the profile drawings of ancient Egyptian statuary, and his skin and hair were as smooth as aluminum."[77] Contrary to expectations, appropriating America's normative ideal of whiteness does not make a person more human; it dehumanizes. The problem here is a normative ideal underwriting what is considered a legitimate American identity. Race is merely a symptom of a much deeper problem. When the American is defined in terms of a tacit normative ideal, when a content-specific norm underwrites the American dream, the average American will chisel his or her

---

[75]Redding (1942), *No Day of Triumph*. New York and London: Harper & Brothers Publishers, 215.
[76]Redding (1942), 223.
[77]Redding (1942), 236.

body into conformity with the statuesque ideal. In other words, the norm establishes an immutable ideal for identity, and within this framework, a person can become truly American only insofar as he or she conforms to the preestablished ideal.

But this normative model does not just operate according to a racial logic, thus maiming blacks; it also operates according to a sexual logic, thus maiming homosexuals. Redding gets the story of Rosalie from her mother, and she indicates from the outset that Rosalie has lesbian inclinations. In high school, Rosalie "got a crush on one of her teachers, Maudestine Chambers."[78] Pancho Savery claims that, for Redding, "Rosalie 'becomes' a lesbian"[79] because of her dark skin. But there is no evidence in the text suggesting a clear cause and effect relationship between Rosalie's blackness and her lesbian desires. Instead of using the Rosalie story to critique Rosalie and/or lesbianism, Redding actually critiques the American system, which sometimes subtly and sometimes overtly coerces people into a specific identity. For instance, after noting that Rosalie became a teacher, her mother mentions that "'there was a law in the city that married girls can't teach, and that left quite a few girls unmarried.'"[80] Note the logic. This is not saying that women desperate to get married were unmarried teachers. It is saying that female professionals committed to their jobs were not getting married, because they preferred their profession to marriage. The problem, however, is that the law coerces women into a specific role, that of a homemaker. In essence, women have to make a choice: be professionals or be wives. Given the way women are implicitly defined, which the legal system simultaneously presupposes and dictates, this is their only choice.

What Redding is actually doing in the Rosalie section is examining the degree to which psychological and legal coercion in the United States functions to straightjacket people into a specific identity, and for Redding, this is the logical consequence of the white, male, heterosexual normative ideal underwriting the American dream. We see this clearly through his characterization of Tom. Tom is in pursuit of the American dream, which leads him to pass for white.

---

[78]Redding (1942), 220.
[79]Savery (1990), "'Git a Stool. Let Me Tell You Something': Call and Response in *No Day of Triumph*," *Black American Literature Forum* 24(2): 292.
[80]Redding (1942), 226.

On the surface, what compels him to distance himself from his family is his desire to become truly American, which he believes means becoming white. But in a conversation with Redding, when he lashes out at Rosalie, we get more insight into his thinking. "'She's a common drunk and a pervert,'" he tells Redding. So maddened is Tom by this state of affairs, he repeats himself: "'Rosalie is a drunken woman-lover.'"[81] Instead of challenging the white heterosexual ideal underwriting American identity and the American dream, Tom, like Fishbelly, wants Rosalie either to simply stop acting like "a pervert" or to keep her distance from him. In becoming a true American by passing for white, Tom has internalized the separatist sickness infecting the country, which is why Redding began the section by claiming that Rosalie's story is "the hearse of an American dream." Incapable of critically interrogating and ultimately rejecting the ideology underwriting American identity and the American dream, Tom forces himself to fit America's white, heterosexual normative ideal, and in the process, he distances himself from and condemns people like his sister, who are the antithesis of that ideal. For Redding, it is this ideal, which defines people as separate and distinct, that is maiming blacks, women, and lesbians in the United States and thereby converting the American dream into a funeral march for so many. For Redding and many integrationists like him, race, while a problem in the United States, is symptomatic of a much deeper issue, which is the separatist ideology underwriting the country's political documents. Non-whites, gays, women—in one way or another, all of these groups were marginalized on the basis of their seemingly ontological distinctness and inferiority. To combat the problem, debunking racism, homophobia, and sexism may be important. But the most urgent task is to expose and debunk the separatist philosophy undergirding the political system, for it is this separatist philosophy that makes sexism, racism, and homophobia possible.

When Ellison publishes *Invisible Man* in 1952, Wright publishes *The Long Dream* in 1958, and Baldwin publishes *Another Country* in 1962, three works that include sympathetic portrayals of homosexuals and draw a clear connection between racism and homophobia, they are working within the same tradition as Redding by expanding, deepening, and strengthening the integrationist

---

[81]Redding (1942), 236.

critique of America's separatist sickness, thereby contributing to the making of a polity that would recognize all people, irrespective of race, sex, and sexual orientation, as legitimately American and therefore worthy of the promises contained in the Constitution and the Declaration of Independence. *The Confessions of Nat Turner* is Styron's literary attempt to contribute to this integrationist critique of the pernicious separatist ideology underwriting American identity and politics. With regard to the novel's dual-temporal structure, Styron exposes how white oppression ironically leads prominent blacks in both the 1830s and the 1960s not to a wholesale rejection but to an ultimate adoption of the separatist ideology that has undergirded American identity and politics since its inception.

V

The novel intelligently charts Turner's transformation into a full-blown separatist who develops "an almost unbearable hatred for white people."[82] Throughout the novel, Styron strategically illustrates how this separatist ideology infects all slaveholding whites, whether they are kind liberals (Samuel Turner), indifferent functionaries (Thomas Moore), twisted outcasts (Reverend Eppes), or monstrous racists (Nathaniel Francis). To bring into sharp focus the nature of the separatist ideology underwriting slavery, Styron gives considerable fictional dimension to the character of Thomas Gray, the lawyer who took Turner's confession. Styron's Gray is an obtuse character, an arrogant know-it-all who has glaring blind spots. In his discussion with Styron's Turner, he wants to get to the root cause of the insurrection, but he never entertains the possibility that enslaving people is sufficient or even compelling reason for a people to take violent action. This, in part, is because he, like Bontemps' Creuzot, subscribes to a separatist philosophy which holds that blacks are ontologically distinct from whites, and as such, they lack the capacity for morally and politically responsible behavior. If democracy mandates that its citizens be capable of informed and autonomous action, then blacks could never fulfill their democratic obligation, as "the qualities of

---

[82]Styron (1993), *The Confessions of Nat Turner*. New York: Vintage International, 286.

irresolution, instability, spiritual backwardness, and plain habits of docility are so deeply embedded in the Negro nature."[83] Therefore, Styron's Gray concludes, the black person inhabits a space within the great chain of being between the animal and the human: "All these characteristics fully and conclusively demonstrate that the Negro occupies at best but a middling position amongst all the species, possessing a relationship which is not cousin-german to the other human races but one which is far closer to the skulking baboon of that dark continent from which he springs."[84] To put the matter starkly, blacks are ontologically separate and distinct from whites, and as such, they cannot fulfill the duties of a citizen in a democracy. Consequently, there must be a separate and distinct space for them within the sociopolitical order. Hence the refrain of Styron's Gray: "Justice! That's how come nigger slavery's going to last a thousand years."[85]

One slave owner seems different. Samuel Turner is the novel's white liberal who champions the cause of black emancipation. Samuel believes "'that the more religiously enlightened a Negro is made, the better for himself, his master, and the commonweal.'"[86] Therefore, Samuel educates Nat. But it is not just that Samuel has faith in some blacks. He actually opposes slavery. As he says in a conversation with his brother and some ministers: "'I have long and do still steadfastly believe that slavery is the great cause of all the chief evils of our land. It is a cancer eating at our bowels, the source of all our misery, individual, political, and economic.'"[87] Based on these comments, it might seem that Styron wholeheartedly supports the novel's primary white liberal. But actually, Styron indicates how Samuel's approach contains provisos that strategically delay emancipation: "'It is evil to keep these people in bondage, yet they cannot be freed.'"[88]

Note the language Samuel uses in order to justify his position: "'They must be educated! To free these people without education and with the prejudice that presently exists against them would be

---

[83]Styron (1993), 88.
[84]Styron (1993), 93.
[85]Styron (1993), 25.
[86]Styron (1993), 124.
[87]Styron (1993), 159.
[88]Styron (1993), 160.

a ghastly crime.'"[89] Styron presents Samuel as a character that is deeply flawed on two separate levels. Philosophically, he has devised clever arguments to extend slavery into the ever receding future, but interpersonally, he fails to see blacks, and especially Nat. Styron's Nat is intellectually exceptional. Given his ability to cite scripture and his grasp of biblical history, he would be an ideal seminarian. In his white-liberal way, Samuel acknowledges Nat's extraordinary gifts, so he surprises Nat by telling him that he plans to educate him. But instead of providing an education uniquely suited to Nat's interests and abilities, he secures him training as a manual laborer. Styron's depiction of Nat's response is poignant:

Grand plans indeed. The beginning of an apprenticeship in carpentry, which, as it turned out for long years, was of as little use to me or anyone as so much rotting sawdust clogging a millwheel. But I could not have known that then. I flung myself into this new fresh field of learning with all the delight and anticipation and hungry high spirits of a white boy setting off for the College of William & Mary and an education in the mysteries of law.[90]

When doing research for *The Confessions*, Styron says that he read everything he could get his hands on,[91] and for those aware of Malcolm X's *Autobiography*, this passage is simply too similar to Malcolm's experience to be just coincidence.

After Malcolm's mother has a mental breakdown, the young boy is sent to a "detention home" run by "good people."[92] Malcolm genuinely likes these people, but he notices that, even though they seem to be supportive of a black person like himself, they still harbor prejudices. For instance, they frequently use the word "nigger" in

---

[89]Ibid.
[90]Styron (1993), 171.
[91]In an interview with Gavin Cologne-Brookes, when asked about the research he did for the novel, Styron said: "I had read all those people, Du Bois and so on. Even fanatics like Marcus Garvey. There's hardly anyone I hadn't read." Styron (1995), "Extracts from Conversations with William Styron," in *The Novels of William Styron: From Harmony to History*. Baton Rouge: Louisiana State University, 219.
[92]Malcolm X (1993), *The Autobiography of Malcolm X*. New York: Ballantine Books, 27.

his presence and "one of their favorite parlor topics was 'niggers.'"[93]
Based on this experience, Malcolm issues the following warning to
his readers: "This is the sort of kindly condescension which I try
to clarify today, to these integration-hungry Negroes, about their
'liberal' white friends, these so-called 'good white people.'"[94] One of
the turning points in Malcolm's life comes around this time when
he detects this same kind of racism in his English teacher, who is
supposedly an enlightened white liberal. The teacher asks Malcolm
what he would like to be when he grows up. Although Malcolm has
not given this much thought, he suggests that he would like to be a
lawyer. The teacher's response parallels exactly Samuel's treatment
of Nat:

> Malcolm, one of life's first needs is for us to be realistic. Don't
> misunderstand me, now. We all here like you, you know that. But
> you've got to be realistic about being a nigger. A lawyer—that's
> no realistic goal for a nigger. You need to think about something
> you *can* be. You're good with your hands—making things.
> Everybody admires your carpentry shop work. Why don't you
> plan on carpentry?

A liberal enlightened supporter of equal rights who favors education
interacts with an exceptionally intelligent black, but, instead of
encouraging the young black to pursue studies suited to his interests
and abilities, he encourages him to become a carpenter. This sentence
could describe either the interaction between Samuel and Nat in the
early half of the nineteenth century or Malcolm and his teacher in
the middle of the twentieth century. And to punctuate the parallel,
Styron strategically mentions a white student going to college to
study law, Malcolm's hypothetical profession of choice. What is
more significant, however, is the parallel response to this situation.
Both Styron's Nat and Malcolm begin the process of turning on all
whites, defining all whites as evil, and rejecting integration after this
experience.

Also important for understanding Nat's turn against Samuel is
the slave's homosexual encounter with Willis. This is significant,
because if Styron were solely interested in the issue of race, the

---

[93]Malcolm X (1993), 28.
[94]Ibid.

inclusion of the Willis scene would be unnecessary and distracting. But as I have been trying to argue throughout this chapter, race is only a symptom of a much deeper problem that Styron and other integrationists seek to expose, and it is shortly after Nat's homosexual encounter that Styron indicates that a separatist ideology is the primary problem with the country and that integration is the best way to expose and combat the oppressive philosophy underwriting American identity and politics.

When Nat first meets Willis, he is immediately drawn to him. He describes Willis as "a slim, beautiful boy with fine-boned features, very gentle and wistful in repose, and the light glistened like oil on his smooth black skin."[95] This sensuous description prepares the reader for their sexual experience, which is depicted through an emancipatory political discourse:

> We somehow fell on each other, very close, soft and comfortable in a sprawl like babies; beneath my exploring fingers his hot skin throbbed and pulsed like the throat of a pigeon, and I heard him sigh in a faraway voice, and then for a long moment as if set free into another land we did with our hands together what, before, I had done alone. Never had I known that human flesh could be so sweet.[96]

The idea of being "set free into another land" is crucial. The land Nat currently inhabits is the separatist United States, which defines people as black or white, male or female, and heterosexual or homosexual, binaries that are generally registered in superior/ inferior or normal/abnormal terms. The homosexual encounter psychologically transports Nat and Willis out of the separatist United States and into another land, an integrationist land of freedom in which binaries and divisions make no sense. For Styron, this psychological space of freedom is the precondition for a real democracy.

Immediately after their sexual encounter, Willis and Nat are baptized together. To underscore the integrationist significance of their experience, Nat cites the following Bible passage: "'*For by one Spirit are we all baptized into one body,*' I said, '*whether we be Jews*

---

[95]Styron (1993), 202.
[96]Styron (1993), 204.

or Gentiles, whether we be bond or free, and have been all made to drink into one Spirit . . .'"[97] Updating the passage and making it relevant for a democracy, we could rephrase the text as saying: there is neither black or white, nor heterosexual or homosexual, for we are all one as Americans, and therefore equally worthy of the rights of life, liberty, and the pursuit of happiness. This integrationist approach is the novel's democratic ideal, and when Nat and Willis transcend the specific division (the taboo against homosexuality) and the separatist philosophy on which American identity and politics has been premised, they are momentarily "set free into another land," a land premised on the integrationist ideals of democratic freedom for all.

Significantly, what ultimately dooms this integrationist agenda and experience and leads Nat to adopt the pernicious separatist ideology underwriting American identity and politics is the white liberal Samuel Turner. Shortly after Nat's homosexual experience, Samuel sells Willis. If we accept the view that Willis is Nat's lover, which is supported through Nat's fantasies about the two of them together in the future as freemen "dedicated to spreading God's word among the black people,"[98] then in selling Willis Samuel has broken up a black family. And his motivation for doing this is money. Given the destruction of the Tidewater farmland, Samuel incurs considerable debt, which forces him to sell everything, including many of his slaves. So the liberal white man opposes slavery and believes that blacks should have equal rights, but only on condition that those beliefs do not inconvenience him. And if he is inconvenienced by the belief in black people's inalienable rights and freedoms, then those rights and freedoms could become alienable again.

Ironically, Samuel's perfidy leads Nat not to condemn the separatist ideology that allows the white liberal to sell people with legal, emotional, and psychological impunity, but to adopt that same ideology. As Nat tells his followers, *"to draw the blood of white men is holy in God's eyes."*[99] In a sense, Nat has adopted the same separatist approach as Gray, who essentializes blacks by referring to "the biological and spiritual inferiority of the Negro

---

[97]Styron (1993), 206.
[98]Styron (1993), 207.
[99]Styron (1993), 410.

character."[100] Therefore, Gray holds that all blacks should be denied access to America's inalienable rights. Nat essentializes whites by referring to "the white man's wiles, his duplicity, his greediness, and his ultimate depravity."[101]

The most effective narrative device for depicting Nat's psychological transformation revolves around the white woman Margaret Whitehead. Many of the ten black writers were particularly incensed by Styron's decision to have Nat entertain sexual fantasies about a white woman, and they had two main critiques: Styron ignores the fact that Nat was married to a black woman and Styron wrongly assumes that black men have an obsession with white women. But both of these critiques miss Styron's point. Styron, who knew that it was possible that Turner was married,[102] made the right decision to make him unmarried, for in picturing the dual-temporal structures and conditions that lead to violent insurrections in the past and the present, Styron had to create the kind of scene he did with Whitehead, as I intend to argue. The question is this: How do Nat's sexual fantasies about a white woman contribute to our understanding of the novel's dual-temporal themes?

In his essay about the novel, Poussaint says that "Styron presents a Caucasian stereotype of the black man's innermost desires, which is to sexually possess a white woman."[103] To indicate that this stereotype is inaccurate, Poussaint notes that Turner "was married to a black slave girl."[104] Poussaint's interpretation, however, overlooks the nuance and complexity of Styron's portrayal of Turner. Readers get some specific insight into Turner's view of white women through his sexual fantasy when masturbating. At this point in the novel, Turner retreats into a forest in order to mentally prepare himself for the insurrection, so he is already in a violent state of mind and committed to the project of killing whites. After fasting and praying, Turner is beset with sexual visions and desires. Initially, Turner fantasizes about having sex with a black woman he "had seen often in the streets of Jerusalem,"[105] but midway through

[100]Styron (1993), 95.
[101]Styron (1993), 257.
[102]In his biography about Styron, West says that he found evidence to indicate that Styron had considered the possibility that Turner was married (338).
[103]Clarke (1968), 20.
[104]Ibid.
[105]Styron (1993), 346.

the experience, he shifts his fantasy to an abstract white woman. To signal the shift, Styron does not use a word generally expressive of a desire for sexual intimacy. Rather, he uses a word signifying violence and anger: "The rage I had at that moment to penetrate a woman's flesh—a young white woman now."[106] For the black woman, Turner has a standard sex fantasy. But when he shifts his focus to the white woman, the normal sex fantasy becomes an imagined rape scene. To accentuate the degree to which Turner's masturbatory fantasy reflects violence and rage, Styron uses a discourse of illness: the rage he experiences "was like a sudden racking spasm or an illness so shattering to the senses that it imposed wonder, and disbelief."[107] There is nothing in this passage to suggest that Turner yearns to "possess" a white woman. This scene is about "rage," a sexual violation stemming from "an illness."

Given Turner's rage against all white people, it makes sense that his sex fantasy about an abstract white woman, instead of reflecting a desire for union, should be overcharged with violence and hate. Not surprisingly, shortly after this experience, Turner transfers his feelings of rage to a specific white woman, Margaret Whitehead. Whitehead is a young, idealistic woman, who rejects the idea that blacks are inferior, opposes slavery, and exposes the hypocrisy of proslavery Christians. Tasked with taking Whitehead to a friend's house, Turner finds himself afflicted with an overwhelming desire to rape the young white woman. The description of his rape fantasy is telling:

Suddenly, despite myself, the godless thought came: I could stop now and here, right here by the road in this meadow, do with her anything I wished. There's not a soul for miles. I could throw her down and spread her young white legs and stick myself in her until belly met belly and shoot inside her in warm milky spurts of desecration. And let her scream until the empty pinewoods echoed to her cries and no one would be the wiser, not even the buzzards or the crows.[108]

What makes this scene so surprising and poignant is the fact that Styron's Turner nearly abandoned the whole idea of an insurrection

---

[106]Styron (1993), 347.
[107]Ibid.
[108]Styron (1993), 367.

precisely because of his profound objections to rape. The character of Will is driven by an anti-white "mania," an "unfocused hatred and madness."[109] Turner fears that this mania will determine Will's behavior during the rebellion, and he suspects it will manifest itself in the form "of raping white women," which is something that Turner "could not abide."[110] Understanding that Styron makes Turner into a would-be rapist of a white woman simultaneously poses a major challenge to Poussaint's interpretation, which suggests that Styron's Turner desires white women, and answers one of the critic's most pointed questions. Given all the changes Styron makes to Turner's character and story, especially with regard to white women, Poussaint asks: "Why does Styron in his tale go so far in distorting the actual historical facts?"[111] This is an important question to answer, as it gets to the heart of Styron's objectives as a biographical novelist.

Styron realizes that there is a perverse and twisted "logic" (one could call it a law of sorts) to massive racial oppression, which is most clearly expressed in Eldridge Cleaver's *Soul on Ice*. The subjugation, violation, and emasculation of black males in a racially oppressive country like the United States lead some to develop a sick desire to wreak revenge on white women. As Cleaver says, "it was of paramount importance for me to have an antagonistic, ruthless attitude toward white women."[112] For Cleaver, this ruthless attitude manifests itself as an act of sexual violence, which Cleaver considers a meaningful political symbol: "Rape was an insurrectionary act. It delighted me that I was defying and trampling upon the white man's law, upon his system of values, and that I was defiling his women."[113] Politically, this act sends a direct and specific message to the white community: "From the site of the act of rape, consternation spreads outwardly in concentric circles. I wanted to send waves of consternation throughout the white race."[114] It might seem that this is merely an aberrant experience of a sick man, and Cleaver confesses that he is perhaps "sicker than most."[115] But

[109]Styron (1993), 362.
[110]Ibid.
[111]Clarke (1968), 20.
[112]Cleaver (1968), *Soul on Ice*. New York: Dell Publishing Co., Inc., 25.
[113]Cleaver (1968), 26.
[114]Ibid.
[115]Cleaver (1968), 27.

after describing his inner experience, he cites Amiri Baraka's (LeRoi Jones') poem "Black Dada Nihilismus," which reads: "Come up, black dada nihilismus. Rape the white girls."[116] After claiming that he has lived what Baraka expresses in his poem, Cleaver submits that this experience is no anomaly. "There are, of course, many young blacks out there right now who are slitting white throats and raping the white girl."[117] But Cleaver cautions readers not to think that blacks are doing this "because they read LeRoi Jones' poetry."[118] Rather, readers should understand that Jones accurately expresses in his poetry some of the "funky facts of life."[119] In other words, there is a cultural and psychological law that Cleaver and Jones are trying to communicate to the larger community of oppressors, which goes something like this: extreme forms of racial oppression can lead some of the oppressed to respond by brutally and sexually violating females from the oppressor class.[120]

By picturing Turner at the mercy of a cultural and psychological law, which transforms a would-be minister of a gospel of unity into a potential rapist and an actual murderer, Styron is clearly working within the same tradition as Baraka and Cleaver. In short, we could say that Styron alters many "historical facts" about Turner in his effort to picture some important dual-temporal truths about the political psychology that leads to violent eruptions within the culture. Styron's dual-temporal logic could be stated thus: the political conditions and societal structures of oppression in the 1830s led Turner to commit his atrocities against whites, and similar conditions and structures obtain in the 1960s, which could lead to a similar type of insurrection. Let me be more specific. Like Styron's Turner, Malcolm X turns against all white people because

---

[116]Cleaver (1968), 26.

[117]Ibid.

[118]Cleaver (1968), 27.

[119]Ibid.

[120]Blacks are not the only ones to indicate that oppressed males entertain rape as a logical response to their oppression. In the Yiddish version of his memoir *Night*, Elie Wiesel explains how some of his fellow Holocaust survivors resolved "to rape German girls" after their liberation. However, Wiesel says that these survivors did not follow through with their plan. For an excellent discussion of this passage, see Naomi Seidman's essay "Elie Wiesel and the Scandal of Jewish Rage." For an extensive discussion of the way Styron uses this tradition to construct the character of Nathan in *Sophie's Choice*, see my forthcoming essay, "The Scandal of Jewish Rage in William Styron's *Sophie's Choice*."

of America's oppressive political structure. After his conversion to Islam and his study of American racial oppression, Malcolm condemns all white people. He accepts the view of his brother and Elijah Muhammad that the "white man is the devil."[121] At first, Malcolm questions this view, because he can think of a decent white person. But his brother presses the point by stipulating that there are no exceptions. Malcolm eventually accepts this view, so if a white person were to offer assistance to the cause of black uplift, he would reject him or her. And, in fact, this happens. After lecturing at a New England college, a blonde co-ed (Styron's Margaret Whitehead?) approached Malcolm, asking what she could do to help the cause. Malcolm's response is harsh and insensitive: "'What can I *do?*' she exclaimed. I told her, 'Nothing.' She burst out crying, and ran out and up Lenox Avenue and caught a taxi."[122] Throughout the autobiography, Malcolm details the conditions and structures of oppression that lead so many blacks to adopt this unnuanced view of whites.

But late in the autobiography, Malcolm admits that he made a mistake in applying this false universal to all whites. After his break with Elijah Muhammad and the Nation of Islam, he visits Mecca, where he meets Muslims from many countries and of many races. This leads Malcolm to renounce his "sweeping indictments of *all* white people," because he now realizes "that some white people *are* truly sincere, that some truly are capable of being brotherly toward a black man."[123] Given this new view, Malcolm rues his treatment of the white co-ed. As he claims: "I regret I told her that. I wish that now I knew her name, or where I could telephone her, or write to her, and tell her what I tell white people now when they present themselves as being sincere."[124]

Styron's Turner has the same response. Just before his hanging, he experiences regret for having murdered Margaret. To signify that Turner has undergone a transformation, Styron pictures him fantasizing about a white woman, presumably Margaret. This time, however, the fantasy is driven, not by a sick desire ("an illness") for violation and revenge, but for a healthy experience of union

---

[121]Malcolm X (1993), 162.
[122]Malcolm X (1993), 292.
[123]Malcolm X (1993), 369.
[124]Malcolm X (1993), 383.

and reconciliation. While he yearns for Margaret "with a rage," his climactic experience symbolizes intimacy: "With tender stroking motions I pour out my love within her; pulsing flood; she arches against me, cries out, and the twain—black and white—are one."[125] Given all the parallels between Malcolm's autobiography and Styron's novel (both Styron's Turner and Malcolm desire to be educated, but are encouraged by a white liberal to be a carpenter; both have religious conversions; both are discriminated against on the basis of their race, which leads them to adopt America's separatist ideology; both use sweeping generalizations to condemn a whole race of people; both justify brutal treatment of a specific white woman on the basis of a false universal; and both ultimately reject that essentialist philosophy and thus come to regret their treatment of the white woman they wronged), it is hard not to draw the conclusion that Styron patterned his protagonist's development on Malcolm's life. But the larger point I want to make is this: for Styron, the solution to the problem of racism in the United States is not to counter the white separatist sickness with a black separatist sickness. Rather, a real solution would be to overcome the ontologically separate and distinct ideology altogether, and this explains why Styron had to include the homosexual scene with Willis.

At stake for writers in the integrationist tradition is not so much race but the separate and distinct philosophy that has been used to define, demonize, and subjugate a wide array of peoples such as blacks, women, and homosexuals. White separatists/supremacists could not see that they were violating blacks by subjugating them, because they considered blacks ontologically different and inferior. Therefore, they believed that there should be a separate and distinct place for blacks within the culture, one best suited for their "inferior" nature. Unfortunately, many black separatists, when fighting for black rights, adopted a similar separatist ideology, and it is my contention that their focus on a superficial thing like race blinded them to the deeper problem plaguing America. Like Wright's Fishbelly, many of the black separatists considered gays a lesser species of being, who should be separated from "normal" society. Consequently, instead of interpreting the sex scene between

---

[125]Styron (1993), 426.

Nat and Willis as an instance of genuine intimacy and love, which psychologically sets them "free into another land," they saw it as something perverse, unnatural, and abnormal. In essence, the very separatist sickness that led white racists to criminalize, demonize, and pathologize the black body is the same sickness that led black separatists to criminalize, demonize, and pathologize the gay body. By including the gay scene in the novel, Styron is not saying to his readers: let's wage war on the twin evils of racism and homophobia; rather, he is doing something much more fundamental. He is saying: let's wage war on the separatist ideology that undergirds the country's racist and homophobic agenda.

To put the matter simply, Styron clearly understood and accepted the intellectual trajectory of the integrationist tradition, and he contributed to it by updating and expanding its logic through his inclusion of the gay scene. By stark contrast, the black separatists sought to overturn the intellectual trajectory of integration and they in part made this happen, thus setting back not just the move toward a less racist culture but also one toward a less sexist and homophobic one. Let me bring into sharp focus the differences between the two traditions and approaches by looking at the works of one prominent black separatist and one prominent black integrationist.

Killens, one of the ten black writers to respond to Styron's novel, also contributed an essay to Addison Gayle's volume *The Black Aesthetic*, which uses a black separatist model to systematize American literary history. According to Gayle, for blacks to flourish in the United States, they need to "build a literature of heroes, myths, and legends."[126] To initiate the process, Killens refers to the "lives of Harriet Tubman, Frederick Douglass, Nat Turner, [and] Sojourner Truth," whose stories "are as formidable as George Washington's, and are based on a much more substantial reality."[127] Significantly, Killens tells his black readers that "slavemasters Washington and Jefferson do not belong to *our* children."[128]

Black integrationists reject the call for strictly demarcating American history and culture along racial lines because they

---

[126]Killens (1971), "The Black Writer vis-à-vis His Country," in *The Black Aesthetic*. Garden City, New York: Doubleday & Company, 390.
[127]Killens (1971), 390–1.
[128]Killens (1971), 391.

consider the project untenable and incoherent. Ellison clarifies why this is the case in a 1970 article. The subtle brilliance of this article is that Ellison addresses two audiences simultaneously. Separatists, black and white, have adopted an approach to American history and culture that is based on nothing more than an irrational fantasy, because it is impossible to understand America without taking into account the presence of blacks. For the black separatist agenda to work, its supporters have to demonstrate that America is primarily and perhaps exclusively a white country, which forces them to say that blacks were never allowed to and never did contribute anything of significance to the making of the nation and its identity. Hence their claim that America is a white country. But for black integrationists, the black separatist position is historically uninformed and ultimately false. As Ellison claims, "materially, psychologically, and culturally, part of the nation's heritage is Negro American, and whatever it becomes will be shaped in part by the Negro's presence."[129] For Ellison, black separatists are wrong to suggest that the United States is a white country, because black people have played "a complex and confounding role in the creation of American history and culture,"[130] while white separatists are equally wrong, because they fail to understand or acknowledge the degree to which blacks have significantly contributed to the making of America's cultural and political identity. Given how much blacks have contributed to the making of the United States, Ellison draws the surprising but inescapable conclusion "that most American whites are culturally part Negro American without even realizing it."[131] The problem in the United States is not that blacks, in becoming American, have lost their blackness or become white, as the black separatists assert. Rather, the problem is that American whites do not "know who and what they really are"[132] because they have failed to realize or acknowledge the degree to which blacks have contributed to the making of the United States and its people's identity.

   To put the matter succinctly, integration is a necessary condition of being. As Ellison claims in another essay: "As a writer who tries

---

[129]Ellison (1995), "What America Would Be Like without Blacks," in *Going to the Territory*. New York: Vintage Books, 111.
[130]Ellison (1995), 107.
[131]Ellison (1995), 108.
[132]Ibid.

to reduce the flux and flow of life to meaningful artistic forms I am stuck with integration, because the very process of the imagination as it goes about bringing together a multiplicity of scenes, images, characters and emotions and reducing them to significance is nothing if not integrative."[133] Given Ellison's racially blended, integrationist approach to American history, culture, and identity, he would reject Killens's position, which suggests that blacks must embrace Douglass and Tubman and disown Washington and Jefferson as part of their history. What Ellison would say is that Douglass and Tubman are as central to the realization of America's national identity and democratic ideals as Washington and Jefferson. Therefore, instead of urging blacks to disavow racist white Americans as part of their cultural-national heritage, Ellison challenges whites to fully acknowledge and own their actual American heritage, which includes Douglass and Tubman, and he issues this challenge not because it is something that whites should do, but because it is a sociological, political, cultural, and historical fact of being American. Ellison's racially integrated approach is brilliant, because it effectively exposes the incoherence of the separatist positions of both whites and blacks.

Based on this integrationist approach, it would only be a matter of time before its logic would be extended to other marginalized groups. In essence, Styron uses the story of Nat Turner in order to project his vision of the implicit logic of democracy, which is something America has yet to realize. There is neither white nor black, neither male nor female, neither heterosexual nor homosexual, for we are all one as Americans. Therefore, we should all have equal access to the polity's public goods. In other words, Styron wants to take us out of the separatist American land of the 1830s and 1960s and transport us to the integrationist one of the future, where democracy for all would really and actually be born.

To conclude this section, let me briefly address Baldwin's famous remarks about Styron's novel. Shortly before *The Confessions* was published, an interviewer discussed the novel with Baldwin, who read the galley proofs. In the interview, the black writer acknowledged that he sees some of himself in Styron's Turner,

---

[133]Ellison (2013), "Statement," in *The Haverford Discussions: A Black Integrationist Manifesto for Racial Justice*. Editor Michael Lackey. Charlottesville and London: University of Virginia Press, 111.

which is why he says that Styron "has begun the common history—
ours."[134] Based on this comment, West says: "The remark can be
read as a tribute to Styron for his nerve in attempting, as a white
man, to re-create black history."[135] Ross takes this same approach
when he uses Baldwin's dictum to claim that Styron's novel is an
attempt "to recognize that freedom is a common dream for people
of all colors."[136] While there is certainly much truth in West's and
Ross's interpretations (I have deep admiration and respect for their
work), what makes Baldwin's comment more resonant, prescient,
and substantive is that the richly ambiguous "ours" could imply our
integrated black (Baldwin) and white (Styron) American history and
identity or our integrated homosexual (Baldwin) and heterosexual
(Styron) American history and identity. My point is this: to read
the "ours" solely along racial lines misses the broadly conceived
integrationism of the novel.[137] And it is this more broadly conceived
integrationist agenda that could set many Americans (and perhaps
America) free into another land, one in which two black men
(Turner and Willis) could enjoy the same rights and liberties as a
heterosexual couple and one in which a black northern homosexual
and a white southern heterosexual could live together in harmony.

VI

In a 1997 review of Conor Cruise O'Brien's book *The Long
Affair: Thomas Jefferson and the French Revolution, 1785–1800*,
the historian Gordon S. Wood made a dismissive remark about
Chase-Riboud's biographical novel *Sally Hemings*. What prompted
the comment was O'Brien's theory about Jefferson's behavior in
Europe. Jefferson's youngest daughter (eight or nine at the time)
took a ship to Europe. She landed in London, but Paris, where her
father was living and working, was the ultimate destination. She
was attended by the slave Sally Hemings. The two girls arrived
in London in 1787 and were greeted by Jefferson's friends, John

---

[134]Qtd. in West (1998), 336.
[135]West (1998), 336–7.
[136]Ross (2012), "William Styron, James Baldwin, and *The Confessions of Nat Turner*:
The Dream of a Common History" *CEA Critic* 74(2–3): 97.
[137]My approach is similar to that of Cologne-Brookes, who reads the novel "without
the emphasis on race at the forefront" (124).

and Abigail Adams. But why didn't Jefferson meet his daughter in London? O'Brien speculates that Jefferson did not go because he "did not want to face questions from Abigail Adams about Sally Hemings."[138] At this time, Hemings was fourteen, and while she and Jefferson had not yet begun their sexual relationship, Hemings was the half-sister of Jefferson's deceased wife Martha—the two supposedly looked strikingly similar. New Englanders were aware of such relations between slaves and masters in the South, and according to O'Brien, "Abigail Adams, a strong-minded New England woman, detested such arrangements, as degrading to women in general, white as well as black."[139] What distresses Wood about O'Brien's theory is not so much the claim as the source for the claim, which "is the questionable account in the novel *Sally Hemings* by Barbara Chase-Riboud."[140] Angered by his dismissive treatment, Chase-Riboud penned a spirited defense. In response, Wood tried to justify his remark. He started by citing the passage he considered objectionable in O'Brien's book: "'In her entertaining novel *Sally Hemings*, Barbara Chase-Riboud has a brief and lifelike dialogue between John and Abigail Adams about Sally, their puzzling guest in London in June 1787.'"[141] Wood believes that, in quoting this passage, he has delivered a fatal blow to the works of both O'Brien and Chase-Riboud, because, as he counters, "Chase-Riboud's dialogue may be brief, but it is not lifelike, meaning that it is not entirely historically accurate, which is why I said in the review that it was 'questionable.'"[142] Specifically, what renders *Sally Hemings* unlifelike are Chase-Riboud's errors about Abigail Adams. According to Wood, Chase-Riboud says that Hemings was the first slave Adams had ever seen. But Wood notes that "Abigail knew slavery very intimately: not only had slavery been an everyday reality in pre-revolutionary Massachusetts, but Abigail's father himself had owned two slaves."[143] Moreover, Adams "was not the flaming abolitionist the novel depicts."[144]

---

[138]O'Brien (1996), *The Long Affair: Thomas Jefferson and the French Revolution, 1785–1800*. Chicago and London: The University of Chicago Press, 24.
[139]Ibid.
[140]Wood (February 1997), "Liberty's Wild Man," *The New York Review of Books* 44(3): 24.
[141]Wood (Summer 2009), "Gordon S. Wood replies," *Callaloo* 32(3): 823.
[142]Wood (2009), 824.
[143]Ibid.
[144]Ibid.

There are two points in Wood's response that are worth addressing. First, as I have been arguing throughout this chapter, biographical novelists and traditional historians privilege radically different "truths," which has made it frequently difficult and sometimes impossible for novelists and historians to engage in meaningful or intelligible conversations. As a case in point, while Wood seems to think that he has scored a victory over Chase-Riboud by exposing her seeming errors about Abigail Adams, the reality is that he has merely replicated the same kind of mistake that plagues the works of most historians who discuss biographical novels. For instance, Chase-Rioboud does not say that Hemings was the first slave that Adams had seen. Hemings makes that point, so it is a reflection of her mind, and not necessarily Chase-Riboud's. But even so, Chase-Riboud uses the scene in order to introduce a searing critique of Jefferson that she will develop throughout the novel. In other words, Chase-Riboud, like nearly all biographical novelists, alters less significant "truths" in order to picture more substantial ones.

Second, and much more important, Wood badly misinterprets the dual-temporal dimension of Chase-Riboud's novel. According to Wood, "Chase-Riboud has taken biographer Fawn Brodie's concoction that Jefferson and Sally Hemings engaged in a thirty-eight-year-long passionate and secret love affair and run with it."[145] Politically and racially, Wood actually sides with Chase-Riboud's seeming decision to picture the long-term, loving relationship, as "it symbolizes what many of us believe is the ultimate solution to our race problem."[146] There is something very perceptive in this remark. Wood realizes that, while Chase-Riboud's novel dramatizes the lives of major figures from the late eighteenth and the early nineteenth centuries, the work's dual-temporal focus actually shapes the way we experience the world in the present. And he specifically credits Chase-Riboud with bringing about a transformation in the cultural ethos:

> Thirty or forty years ago the slightest suggestion of miscegenation between Jefferson and his slave was objectionable to many Americans; indeed, as late as 1966, nineteen states still forbade interracial marriages. But since then, especially with Brodie's biography of 1974 and Chase-Riboud's novel of 1979, . . . it has

---

[145]Ibid.
[146]Wood (2009), 825.

become widely accepted that a thirty-eight-year-long liaison of love took place.[147]

With regard to the dual-temporal function of the biographical novel, Wood is exactly right, as Chase-Riboud has, with others, significantly altered cultural conceptions about the plausibility of interracial relationships, such as the one Jefferson and Hemings had.

But with regard to the specific content and objectives of Chase-Riboud's novel, Wood is totally wrong. To clarify why Wood's claim that the Jefferson-Hemings relationship symbolizes a solution to the race problem makes no sense, let me state just a few textual facts: Hemings wants Jefferson to love their sons, but she comes to realize that "the master had no sons," because his black sons "would never count as real sons."[148] Jefferson vows never to bring a white woman to Monticello, thus making Hemings the de facto mistress of the estate, but Jefferson breaks his promise by installing his white daughter as mistress, which leads Hemings to draw the following conclusion about Jefferson: "Beneath the suave manners, the glacial serenity, the almost deferential politeness, remained that special Virginian brutality that came from the habit of despotism and privilege, of never being crossed, of handling blooded horses, controlling ambitious men, ruling your own small kingdom, and contemplating your own place in history."[149] Based on Jefferson's dismissive treatment of blacks, Hemings realizes that there is a difference between the way the two relate to each other: "She owned him just as surely as he owned her, the only difference being that her possession of him was a gift while his was a theft."[150] And after Hemings attends Nat Turner's trial, she realizes that the black slave, in staging an insurrection, was fighting "for her,"[151] while Jefferson would only liberate her, her children, and blacks on condition that it would not inconvenience him. It is this discovery that ultimately breaks her spirit. How Wood can suggest that the Hemings-Jefferson relationship in Chase-Riboud's novel symbolizes a solution to the race problem is totally baffling.

---

[147]Ibid.
[148]Chase-Riboud (1994), *Sally Hemings*. New York: Ballantine Books, 276.
[149]Chase-Riboud (1994), 293.
[150]Chase-Riboud (1994), 298–9.
[151]Chase-Riboud (1994), 57.

In relation to the novel's dual-temporal thematic, it would be more accurate to say that the Jefferson-Hemings relationship symbolizes the monstrous "logic" and epistemological blindness that have been tacitly scripted into the Declaration of Independence and that have undermined American democracy from its inception until the present. That Chase-Riboud has a critical view of the Declaration is clear from the slave representation of the document. Late in *Sally Hemings*, a couple of slaves comment on Jefferson's amazing inventions. They specifically mention his creation of an indoor toilet, which makes use of "a system of ropes and pulleys and wheels" to transport a chamber pot "from the house to an opening in the ground about twenty-five feet away."[152] This invention makes life much more pleasant for Jefferson and his white family, but it makes life for the slave decidedly more humiliating, for as one slave says of the chamber pot: "Once this thing gets out there, there is still got to be a slave standing here ready to catch it, and empty it! Typical that Thomas Jefferson can't invent nothing that don't have a slave on the receiving end of it . . . ."[153] Given the unpleasant consequences of Jefferson's invention, his slaves give the chamber pot humorous names, such as "'ultimatums,' 'levees,' and 'Indian Treaties.'"[154] But the most uncharitable description comes from Jefferson's black son Beverly who names it the Declaration of Independence. For the son of the former president of the United States, the Declaration of Independence, like Jefferson's chamber pot, is full of shit, because its contents are so offensive.

How can we account for such a scathing representation of one of America's most revered documents? And is there any justification for Chase-Riboud to have one of her characters make such a scurrilous remark? At first glance, the Declaration seems to secure the rights of life, liberty, and the pursuit of happiness for all, but in reality, it is an anti-democratic blueprint that presupposes social death and thereby establishes selective justice. Jefferson claims "that all men are created equal, that they are endowed by their Creator with certain unalienable Rights, that among these are Life, Liberty

---

[152]Chase-Riboud (1994), 294.
[153]Chase-Riboud (1994), 295.
[154]Chase-Riboud (1994), 294.

and the pursuit of Happiness."[155] For Jefferson, governments are instituted in order "to secure these rights," and "whenever any Form of Government becomes destructive of these ends, it is the Right of the People to alter or abolish it, and to institute new Government, laying its foundation on such principles and organizing its powers in such form, as to them shall seem most likely to effect their Safety and Happiness." Given the document's logic, if it can be shown that certain people were systemically denied access to what is by nature theirs, then they would have the right to alter or abolish the government. That would be the case, however, only on condition that Jefferson's "all men" included all people. But as Gore Vidal's Aaron Burr rightly notes in the biographical novel *Burr*, "the unalienable rights of man" did not include "slaves, Indians, women and those entirely without property."[156] This novel, published six years before *Sally Hemings*, is as likely a source and inspiration for Chase-Riboud as Brodie's biography of Jefferson, as both works take it as a given that Jefferson fathered multiple children with Hemings.

In essence, what made the Declaration of Independence and the reality of slavery (as well as other human rights abuses) possible was Orlando Patterson's concept of social death. Within this framework, the socially dead individual is characterized "as the permanent enemy on the inside," a figure that "did not and could not belong" to the official political order "because he was the product of a hostile, alien culture."[157] As such, this person lives in a perpetual condition of "unborn being."[158] In other words, this socially dead person has never been welcomed as an official member into the political community, which explains why he or she could be denied the right to life, liberty, and the pursuit of happiness with political, legal, and psychological impunity. My claim here is not that we can use Patterson's idea of social death in order to make sense of the contradiction between Jefferson's document and human rights violations. The claim is much stronger: read the Declaration of

---

[155]References to the Declaration are taken from the National Archives online website: http://www.archives.gov/exhibits/charters/declaration_transcript.html
[156]Vidal (1973), *Burr*. New York: Ballantine Books, 209.
[157]Patterson (1982), *Slavery and Social Death: A Comparative Study*. Cambridge and London: Harvard University Press, 39.
[158]Patterson (1982), 38.

Independence without taking into account the idea of social death, and it would be impossible to explain the contradiction between the document's claim for natural rights and the systemic violation of targeted groups in the United States by people like Jefferson and others.

To underscore the way powerful figures strategically conceal the contradictory reality of Jefferson, the Declaration, and America, Chase-Riboud invents scenes with John Trumbull, the famous painter whose *Declaration of Independence* is on display in the Rotunda of the United States Capitol. This glorious painting gives viewers a stately image of noble American leaders submitting a draft of the Declaration to the Congress. In the novel, Trumbull visits Paris in 1787 in order to do a portrait of Jefferson "commemorating the Declaration of Independence."[159] While there, he meets Hemings and makes "several sketches"[160] of her. Chase-Riboud's portrayal of Trumbull is extremely significant. He is a perceptive character. For instance, there are signs of danger and discontent in the Paris of 1787, but Jefferson and Sally's brother, James, are so totally enamored by the discourses of "'freedom' and 'revolution' and 'liberty'"[161] that they fail to see the political dangers. As an artist, Trumbull is different from Jefferson and James: "Only the painter Trumbull, with his great black eyes, seemed to have a sense of what was happening."[162] Trumbull can see so much more than Jefferson, James, and so many others, and as an artist, he can, if he chooses, represent what he sees with precision and accuracy.

But, like many white American males in positions of power, Trumbull chooses to represent the sublime and the beautiful rather than the gritty and the real. We see this most clearly when the narrator, Nathan Langdon, visits Trumbull, not to discuss the famous painting about the Declaration, but because he wants a painting of Hemings, Jefferson's secret and outcast slave wife. By the time Langdon meets the American painter, Trumbull has become totally devoted to Jefferson and America, so he refuses to give Langdon any such painting. Most significant is his "motive" for his decision, which "is the wish to commemorate the great events

---

[159]Chase-Riboud (1994), 96.
[160]Ibid.
[161]Chase-Riboud (1994), 100.
[162]Ibid.

of our country's Revolution, to preserve and diffuse the memory of the noblest series of actions which have ever presented themselves in the history of man."[163] Given this objective, he cannot betray the former president. As he says of Jefferson: "The history of private passions has no place in public history."[164] The problem, of course, is that the Declaration is a document about the private passions of everyday citizens. As a blueprint for social relations, it defines the natural rights we have as citizens of the United States of America. Since Jefferson authored the document, his private life gives us considerable insight into the overt and tacit logic scripted into the document. So if his private passions involve a slave concubine and their slave children, individuals who are explicitly denied the rights promised in the Declaration, then that relationship would emblematize the document's content. According to this reading, by strategically ignoring Jefferson's "private passions," which is a direct reference to Hemings, Trumbull merely replicates the racist and anti-democratic logic tacitly scripted into the Declaration, which simultaneously affirms the rights of all and yet strategically negates the existence of targeted groups, thus rendering them socially dead and therefore negligible. Put differently, Trumbull records the official public reality of Jefferson, as represented in and through the Declaration of Independence, but he refuses to picture the president's private life, which gives the lie to the noble document.

In essence, this scene with Trumbull illuminates the psycho-epistemological orientation that makes physical manifestations of the Declaration's contradictory logic possible. Take, for instance, Jefferson's treatment of Sally's brother James, Jefferson's de facto brother-in-law. Living in France, James is legally free, because the country does not recognize slavery. But James refuses to use this legal loophole to secure his freedom, because he "wanted his master to acknowledge his existence and his debt, instead of simply allowing him to 'stroll' away."[165] But Jefferson uses all his skills as a diplomat and a rhetorician to outmaneuver the young black man. So "tongue-tied" and "abject" had James become during this exchange that "he had practically thanked Thomas Jefferson when he said that he, James, would be freed by his grace as soon as he had

---

[163]Chase-Riboud (1994), 174.
[164]Ibid.
[165]Chase-Riboud (1994), 126.

trained another cook at Monticello to take his place."[166] James has a major breakdown immediately after the making of this concession, and his rage escalates from this point forward until his suicide. What makes this scene so powerful is the dramatic irony regarding equality and freedom.

In the Declaration, Jefferson condemns King George III for his "absolute Despotism." For Jefferson, since "the Laws of Nature and Nature's God" dictate that people are born with the inalienable right of freedom, the people have a right and even a duty to overthrow the unjust rule of a tyrant who would deprive them of their natural right. Jefferson's claim is not that a person can work for a period of time in order to earn or buy his inalienable right of freedom. It is that a person is born with this right, which is why Jefferson considers it unacceptable for a government to violate or abolish a person's natural right to freedom. When Jefferson tells James that he will grant the slave his freedom after a multiyear stint of slave service, he is behaving just like King George III by refusing to "assent to Laws, the most wholesome and necessary for the public good."

Jefferson's contradictions are central to the novel, which is why Hemings refers to Jefferson as a man "full of contradictions and secrets"[167] and John Qunicy Adams mentions Jefferson's "power of self-deception."[168] We see this contradiction in a conversation with Hemings. After Prosser's 1800 insurrection, Hemings and Jefferson have a conversation about the consequences. Jefferson says that "'an insurrection is easily quelled in its first effects, but far from being local, it will become general and whenever it does, it will rise, more formidable after every defeat until one will be forced after dreadful scenes and sufferings to release them in their own way . . . .'"[169] Jefferson follows this train of logic to its horrific conclusion: "If something is not done, and done soon, we shall be the murderers of our own children."[170] After making this comment, Jefferson notices that Hemings is cold, so he asks her if he should have the slave "Jupiter to come and light a fire for" her.[171] Based on

---

[166]Chase-Riboud (1994), 147.
[167]Chase-Riboud (1994), 144.
[168]Chase-Riboud (1994), 158.
[169]Chase-Riboud (1994), 230.
[170]Ibid.
[171]Ibid.

the logic of their conversation, Hemings can only look at him with shocking incomprehension: "He could speak of murder and his children, and then his slave Jupiter. . . ."[172] By this point, Jefferson's mind has become totally habituated into the mental contradiction on which the Declaration is premised.

To understand the insidious nature of this mental contradiction, it is important to note that Jefferson undergoes a major transformation. As Annette Gordon-Reed indicates in her excellent study *The Hemingses of Monticello*, Jefferson developed the language of natural rights in 1770 when he was a pro bono lawyer for Samuel Howell, a black man whose grandfather was black and grandmother was white. Jefferson worked diligently to secure Howell's freedom, but Gordon-Reed finds the case more significant and important because it contains Jefferson's "first known public comment on the natural rights of man."[173] Thus, when Jefferson wrote the Declaration in 1776, it is likely that he believed that natural rights applied to blacks as well as whites, for he incorporated language from the Howells case into the Declaration, which suggests that the natural-rights clause applies to blacks as well as whites. As Chase-Riboud's Jefferson tells Hemings, slavery was abolished in his original version of the Declaration of Independence, but "the clause reprobating the enslaving of the inhabitants of Africa was struck out in complaisance to South Carolina and Georgia,"[174] two states that would not ratify the document if it contained the clause "reprobating slavery." But something happened between 1770 and 1790 that led Jefferson to change his view of slavery. That this transformation is of central importance to Chase-Riboud is clear from an inner monologue of Quincy Adams, who wonders: "Why had Thomas Jefferson, a staunch abolitionist up until 1790, suddenly lost all fastidiousness about slavery?"[175] For Chase-Riboud, the answer is multifarious and complex, but the most salient relates to the contorted political psychology inherent within the Declaration. Eliminating the clause "reprobating slavery" was tragic because it made slavery possible in the newly born United

---

[172]Ibid.
[173]Gordon-Reed (2008), *The Hemingses of Monticello: An American Family*. New York and London: W.W. Norton & Company, 100.
[174]Chase-Riboud (1994), 194.
[175]Chase-Riboud (1994), 156.

States, but it was even more catastrophic because it intensified and expanded the social-death dictum that was already tacitly scripted into the document. Women, Native Americans, and the property-less were already excluded from the political realm of natural rights, but by removing the clause "reprobating slavery," which came to be linked exclusively with blackness, the document mentally habituated Americans into a contradiction that ensured that natural rights would not apply to blacks and many others for the indefinite future. This idea of being mentally habituated into the Declaration's contradiction explains Jefferson's transformation from 1770, when he used the natural-rights clause to defend a black man's right for freedom, to 1800, when he fails to see how his treatment of one of his slaves could inspire him to revolt. In essence, Jefferson has become so mentally habituated into the Declaration's contorted political psychology that he can no longer see blatantly obvious contradictions around him.

That Jefferson authored a document predicated upon social death is bad enough, but what makes matters worse is that he, via the Declaration, did more to shape American politics and identity than any other person. Chase-Riboud underscores this point in her afterword when discussing her objectives in the novel: "I had wanted to illuminate our overweening and irrational obsession with race and color in this country. I would do it through the man who almost single-handedly invented our national identity—and through the woman who was the emblematic incarnation of the forbidden, the outcast; who was the rejection of that identity."[176] Through the Declaration, Jefferson did a considerable amount to shape American identity, which explains why Chase-Riboud's Burr refers to Jefferson as "'the image-maker, the definer of America, the nation's most articulate voice.'"[177] It is important to note, however, that when we answer the question, in what sense Jefferson has shaped American identity, the answer is not that he bequeathed to Americans a natural right to life, liberty, and the pursuit of happiness. Rather, he bequeathed to them a contorted political psychology based on the contradiction between the natural right to life, liberty, and the pursuit of happiness for all and the concomitant social death of targeted groups.

---

[176]Chase-Riboud (1994), 345.
[177]Chase-Riboud (1994), 166.

I say targeted groups rather than African Americans because Chase-Riboud strategically explores how the Declaration's inherent contradiction functions to exclude others. Note, for instance, how Hemings reflects on Jefferson's treatment of Native Americans:

> In the past four years, my master, as president, by fair means and foul, had transferred fifty million acres of Indian land from their sovereignty to the United States, paying a total of one hundred and forty-two thousand dollars; one-tenth of a penny an acre, or as he said, the equivalence of one hundred and forty-three prime male Negro slaves.[178]

Clearly, the right to life, liberty, and the pursuit of happiness does not apply to Native Americans. What makes such violations of natural rights possible is a subtle qualification within words. Chase-Riboud clearly brings this idea into sharp focus when Hemings gets into a conversation with the feminist, Frances Wright, who realizes how provisos are tacitly scripted into words. As she says to Hemings, "truths" do not necessarily apply to all people. But they should, because "truth is the same for all humankind; there are not truths for the rich and truths for the poor, truths for men and truths for women, truths for blacks and truths for whites, there are simply TRUTHS."[179] Wright understands the way language functions to simultaneously affirm and negate—Jefferson's natural-rights clause affirms the rights of all but simultaneously negates those same rights for others.

As I argued in Chapter 2, fictional truth is central for biographical novelists like Chase-Riboud, as it enables them to use their biographical subjects in order to illuminate something in the present, even if it is something that the author does not know. To conclude this section, I want to illustrate how the critique of the Declaration in *Sally Hemings* could be used to illuminate two things that Chase-Riboud could not have known. At long last, Harper Lee's second novel has been published. But, to the horror of many, the Atticus Finch of *Go Set a Watchman* is not the noble antiracist hero readers got in *To Kill a Mockingbird*. Instead of championing the cause of blacks, as he did in the 1960 novel, the Atticus of 2015

---

[178]Chase Riboud (1994), 259.
[179]Chase-Riboud (1994), 324.

is a racist, who uses Jefferson's writings in order to justify denying blacks full citizenship.

After the twenty-six-year-old Jean-Louise discovers a rabidly racist pamphlet in her father's home, she decides to secretly attend a citizens' council meeting—Atticus is on the board of directors. With shock and dismay, she realizes that her father, in reaction to the Brown versus Board of Education ruling, supports a racist political agenda. It is when Jean-Louise confronts Atticus directly that he discloses the basis for his political philosophy. Atticus tells his daughter that he is "a sort of Jeffersonian Democrat," by which he means that "full citizenship was a privilege to be earned by each man, that it was not something given lightly nor to be taken lightly." Within this framework, people are not born with the natural right for full citizenship and its attendant promises. They must earn it, for as Atticus says: "A man couldn't vote simply because he was a man, in Jefferson's eyes."[180]

What makes Atticus' political philosophy so troubling is the racism undergirding it. For Atticus, "white is white and black's black," and so far, he had "not yet heard an argument that has convinced" him "otherwise."[181] For Atticus, blacks are a primitive species of being, which is why he does not want white children to be forced to attend the same schools as blacks. Doing so would drag down white children in order "to accommodate Negro children."[182] To put the matter bluntly, Atticus will only accept blacks as full citizens if they become white. Readers see this most clearly when Atticus discusses the progress that blacks have made in this country: "They've made terrific progress in adapting themselves to white ways, but they're far from it yet."[183] With just a little more whiteness, blacks will finally become full-fledged humans, thus making them worthy of the right to full citizenship. In essence, Atticus' Jeffersonian approach leads him to draw the conclusion that blacks are not, strictly speaking, human. Jean-Louise specifically references the fact that with regard to blacks there has been a "systematic denial that they're human."[184] Lee

---

[180]Lee (2015), *Go Set a Watchman.* New York: Harper, 244.
[181]Lee (2015), 246.
[182]Ibid.
[183]Lee (2015), 246–7.
[184]Lee (2015), 252.

underscores how this view functions in relation to the Declaration when Jean-Louise is in a conversation with racists who think like Atticus. After listening to others denounce the Communists who defend blacks, Jean-Louise thinks to herself: "When in the course of human events it becomes necessary for one people to dissolve the political bands which have connected them with another they are Communists."[185] Immediately after silently reciting this revised version of the Declaration, a woman says to Jean-Louise that the blacks "always want to marry a shade lighter than themselves, they want to mongrelize the race."[186] It is at this point that Jean-Louise begins to challenge her interlocutor. Important for my argument, however, is this: it is the subtle qualification within words that makes it possible to deny groups of people their natural right, which is why Jean-Louise parodies the Declaration. She realizes how the subtle qualification is already tacitly scripted within the document, thus justifying the denial of full citizenship for blacks.

It is important to keep in mind that the 2015 Atticus, while a racist, would certainly not perpetrate a crime against blacks, nor would he condone such behavior. However, the real problem and danger is that Atticus' nuanced approach to the Declaration makes possible criminal violations of human rights in the name of American democracy from less informed and more uncivilized types of people. To see how this functions, let me briefly discuss Dylann Roof's racist manifesto, which explains why he believes that he needed to slaughter nine blacks in a famous South Carolina church. For Roof, being an American is of crucial importance. However, he believes that America is in decline and losing its true identity: "As an American we are taught to accept living in the melting pot, and black and other minorities have just as much right to be here as we do, since we are all immigrants."[187] But this is incorrect, because, as Roof claims, the immigrants who first came to America were from Europe, and "Europe is the homeland of White people." According to this logic, America is a white country, so only whites have a legitimate "right" to this land.

---

[185]Lee (2015), 176.

[186]Ibid.

[187]Immediately after Roof's shooting rampage, I googled his name. I found his racist manifesto online, which I downloaded, but it was removed from the internet shortly thereafter. So I do not have a web address for the document.

Undergirding this view is the belief that blacks and whites are ontologically distinct. As Roof asserts: "Anyone who thinks that White and black people look as different as we do on the outside, but are somehow magically the same on the inside, is delusional. How could our faces, skin, hair, and body structure all be different, but our brains be exactly the same?" The answer for Roof is that they are not. To be specific, "Negroes have lower Iqs, lower impulse control, and higher testosterone levels in generals. (sic) These three things alone are a recipe for violent behavior." Since blacks and whites are so radically separate and distinct, integration would be a political and cultural disaster, which is why Roof seeks to return to an earlier political model:

> Segregation was not a bad thing. It was a defensive measure. Segregation did not exist to hold back negroes. It existed to protect us from them. And I mean that in multiple ways. Not only did it protect us from having to interact with them, and from being physically harmed by them, but it protected us from being brought down to their level. Integration has done nothing but bring Whites down to the level of brute animals.

The political goal is segregation, which should be based on the ontological differences between blacks and whites. Within this framework, if the United States does not re-establish a properly segregated racial order, then whites will become as animalistic as he thinks blacks are. Therefore, he believes that he has no political choice but to take violent action in order to recover and restore the noble principles and ideals of American democracy: "I have no choice. I am not in the position to, alone, go into the ghetto and fight. I chose Charleston because it is [the] most historic city in my state, and at one time had the highest ratio of blacks to White in the country." Roof has clearly internalized the Declaration's contorted and contradictory political psychology, which leads him to believe not just that he has a right but also that he has a moral and political obligation to violate the rights of blacks in the name of American democracy.

As I write this, today is June 26, 2015, and Clementa Pinckney, the South Carolinian legislator and pastor, is being buried. This is very distant in time from July 4, 1776, when the Declaration of Independence was adopted by the Continental Congress, or 1979, when Chase-Riboud's novel was published. And yet, what unifies these three seemingly disparate events is a contorted and contradictory political psychology inherent within one of the most important and sacred American documents. Through the Declaration of Independence, Jefferson and his compatriots officially instituted in America and formally installed within Americans a devastating political psychology that has made possible a wide range of human rights abuses that persist even today. It is my contention that no genre of fiction is better suited to identify and define this political psychology than the biographical novel, which is why Chase-Riboud's *Sally Hemings* is just as valuable today as it was when it was first published.

But this work is vital not just because it identifies the monstrously anti-democratic "logic" tacitly scripted into the Declaration. It is also important because Chase-Riboud concludes the novel with a radical suggestion: if we actually believe in democracy and we want to make that a reality in the United States, then we need to revise and correct the Declaration of Independence. The epigraph of the concluding chapter is the excised passage "reprobating slavery" from the sacred document. Chase-Riboud is basically saying: we can start the process of overcoming the criminality of American democracy, which presupposes social death and leads to selective justice, by revising and correcting the Declaration of Independence, by acknowledging and confronting what has been literally and tacitly excised from the document. Doing this would be a necessary step in destroying the psycho-epistemological structure that the Declaration of Independence both presupposes and brings into being. For Chase-Riboud, in the name of social justice for the actual democratic all, it is time to bring about political healing by updating the slavery-justifying, life-destroying, and anti-democratic document that has made us and continues to make us what we are.

VII

In his book about some of the finest and most famous African American novels, Addison Gayle argues that readers should think of the "writer as combatant" and of "literature as a weapon in the struggle for human freedom."[188] John Ernest would certainly

---

[188]Gayle (1975), *The Way of the New World: The Black Novel in America*. Garden City, NY: Anchor Press, xi.

agree with Gayle, but he would underscore the role of history in the project of exposing the structures and conditions of oppression and imagining potential pathways to future forms of emancipation and autonomy. Ernest usefully refers to this project as liberation historiography, which requires an author to "work from an understanding of the historical condition of oppression to a vision of historical agency."[189] Gayle and Ernest give us excellent lenses for understanding the literary projects of Bontemps, Styron, and Chase-Riboud as well as the biographical novel more generally. To conclude, I want to briefly clarify how these three writers contributed significantly to this liberationist aesthetic tradition by authoring biographical novels, which critique the political and imagine the future in unique and distinctive ways.

To get a clear sense of the nature of their contribution, it is important to see how the biographical novel represents an inversion and even a repudiation of the classical historical novel. The biographical novel totally inverts two central components of the classical historical novel. In *The Historical Novel*, Lukács claims that great representatives of an age can never be "central figures of the [novel's] action."[190] Actual historical figures can appear in the novel, but they must be on the periphery. In other words, the main characters must be fictional figures. Second, these figures have an important symbolic function, as they represent "historical-social types."[191] The aesthetic task of the historical novel, therefore, is "to portray the struggles and antagonisms of history by means of characters who, in their psychology and destiny, always represent social trends and historical forces."[192] Done well, the classical historical novel, Lukács argues, clarifies how the present is the logical product of the past and will thus enable us in the present to chart a path toward a more Marxist future.

It is my contention that the postmodernist incredulity toward metanarrative has simultaneously led to the decline of the classical historical novel and the concomitant rise and legitimization of

---

[189]Ernest (2004), *Liberation Historiography: African American Writers and the Challenge of History, 1794–1861*. Chapel Hill and London: The University of North Carolina Press, 18.
[190]Lukács (1983), 39.
[191]Lukács (1983), 35.
[192]Lukács (1983), 34.

the biographical novel. Contemporary readers have become more skeptical of and resistant to the traditional literary symbols (what Lukács refers to as historical-social types) of the classical historical novel, which explains to some degree why Endore's *Babouk* was such a failure. The problem for contemporary biographical novelists, however, is this: they want to use the traditional literary symbol, because it has been an excellent instrument for doing searing social and political critique, as we see in and through Joseph Conrad's Kurtz in *Heart of Darkness*, Virginia Woolf's Miss Kilman in *Mrs. Dalloway*, William Faulkner's Percy Grimm in *Light in August*, and Ralph Ellison's Brotherhood in *Invisible Man*. Contemporary biographical novelists, who understand the reality and power of ideology and have consequently become more skeptical about metanarratological truths, realize the dangers of inventing a free-floating literary symbol, but they also respect the value and power of the traditional symbol to critique the culture and to effect political change. Therefore, they make their protagonists actual historical figures, thus warding off the criticism of having concocted a literary symbol that suits their ideological agenda, but they then convert those figures into literary symbols, thus preserving their important role as social and cultural critics.

To bring into sharp focus the function of the historical figure as literary symbol, biographical novelists create characters. For instance, to illuminate the Enlightenment's inconsistent philosophy, which is best seen in the contradiction between the Declaration's equality clause and the country's enslavement of blacks, Bontemps creates the character of Creuzot, who cannot imagine that black people like Prosser possess the necessary faculties to desire freedom or to stage a rebellion. This invented character, however, is not always used merely to represent a psychological or political reality from the past. Sometimes it functions to signify a parallel situation in the present. So Styron creates Willis in order to illuminate how America's separatist philosophy destroys not just relationships between blacks and whites (1830s) but also gay men (1960s). In the best biographical novels, the invented character clarifies how the symbolic dimension of the historical figure's experience could be used to illuminate events yet to occur. Chase-Riboud creates the character of Langdon, whose discussions with Trumbull reveal how and why America's image-makers strategically conceal the link between the sublime surface rhetoric of America (the Declaration of Independence) and the country's gritty subsurface reality (the enslavement of Jefferson's slave wife and their black children). This model clarifies the logic that allows Atticus to deny blacks the right to vote and led Roof to massacre blacks.

What makes the biographical novel such an excellent and powerful instrument of sociopolitical critique and preferable to the classical historical novel is the historical specificity of its dual-temporal thematic. The traditional historical novel gives readers abstract fictional symbols, which could then be applied to specific figures in both the past and the present. The problem is that such an approach opens writers to the criticism of having concocted a symbol that suits their ideological agenda. But it also places a heavy burden on readers, which grows with each passing generation. For instance, we know that Robert Penn Warren's Willie Stark from *All the King's Men* is loosely based on Huey Long. It required an educated reader to make the conceptual link between Long and Stark back in the 1940s, when the novel was published. But today, one needs to be even better educated in history to understand the degree to which Stark is based on Long's life, because the history of populism in the early twentieth-century American South is not a regular part of most curriculums. By foregrounding a historically specific and real character, biographical novelists root their readers within an identifiable time and place. The passage of time does not lessen the power of the biographical novel as much as it does with the historical novel. Note that few people today read the novels of Sir Walter Scott, even though he is considered the master of the classical historical novel. The biographical novel enables general readers to connect with history in meaningful but less demanding ways. The connection is meaningful, because readers who understand how Jefferson could justify excluding his de facto wife and their children from the promises of the Declaration of Independence can also understand how that same psycho-epistemological orientation justifies human rights abuses in the late twentieth century, when *Sally Hemings* was published. But it is less demanding, because readers can see precisely how the present situation derives directly from actual historical events.

Given the liberationist dimension of their work, biographical novelists do not merely expose the major structures and conditions of oppression. They also imaginatively chart new ways forward. For instance, Bontemps suggests that establishing the conditions for all people to experience meaningful forms of labor and autonomy would effectively render cataclysmic insurrections incoherent. Styron suggests that rejecting the separatist ideology underwriting American democracy and adopting a massive integrationist political agenda would set Americans free into another land, one that is more truly democratic and socially just. And Chase-Riboud suggests that correcting the Declaration of Independence would enable Americans to eliminate the contorted form of thinking that leads to selective justice. In short, the biographical novel makes use of a powerful narrative technique (the dual-temporal truth) to critique the political and to advance social justice, and it is the historical specificity that makes this technique both easy to grasp and effective.

The biographical novel, however, is not without risk. By converting the historical figure into a literary symbol, biographical novelists could easily lead uncritical readers astray. When writers alter historical facts or invent characters and scenes in order to communicate their dual-temporal truth, there is the danger that the fictional representation could be reified into an empirical historical fact, which raises the question: Was the net result worth the strategic misrepresentation? This is a crucial question about the ethics of the biographical novel, and it is so important that it must be addressed in a separate chapter, to which I now turn.

6

The biographical novel:
A misappropriated life
or a truthful fiction?

The rise of the biographical novel raises a major ethical question: Given that authors use the life of an actual historical figure in order to project their own vision, what kind of liberties can writers ethically take with their subject? Willa Cather's *Death Comes for the Archbishop*, F. Scott Fitzgerald's *The Great Gatsby*, Aldous Huxley's *Point Counter Point*, Virginia Woolf's *Orlando*, Wallace Thurman's *Infants of the Spring*, and Robert Penn Warren's *All the King's Men* feature characters who are clearly based on actual historical figures, but because the authors change the characters' names, few if any object to the liberties these writers take with their representations of their protagonists. Biographical novels are significantly different, because the authors name their characters after actual historical figures. Given this fact, is it legitimate for Barbara Mujica in *Frida* to have her Frida Kahlo seduce a fifteen-year-old boy when she was in her late thirties, Jerome Charyn in *The Secret Life of Emily Dickinson* to make Emily Dickinson complicit in the mental breakdown of a servant, and Julia Alvarez in *In the Time of the Butterflies* to have Minerva Mirabal slap the dictator Trujillo, even though there is evidence to suggest that all of these are untrue? In this chapter, I provide some provisional frameworks for determining the kind of liberties biographical novelists should and should not take. My claim is that authors who make responsible and illuminating changes produce truthful fictions, while those who make irresponsible and confusing ones misappropriate a life (this is a form of identity theft).

I

Ironically, a writer who has formulated a solid framework for determining the ethics of representation in the biographical novel is one of the most flagrant offenders. Irvin D. Yalom is a professional psychiatrist, who specializes in a form of existential psychotherapy and who has authored three biographical novels, *When Nietzsche Wept*, *The Schopenhauer Cure*, and *The Spinoza Problem*. Given his background and training in psychiatry, Yalom's biographical novels focus on human interiors. And yet, Yalom insists that one of the central ideas in his creative work is the imaginative plausibility of human interiors within the context of an established historical frame. As he claims in his afterword to his novel *The Spinoza Problem*: "I've attempted to write a novel that *could* have happened. Remaining as close as possible to historical events, I've drawn on my professional background as a psychiatrist to imagine the inner worlds of my protagonists, Bento Spinoza and Alfred Rosenberg."[1] Faithful as he is to the established historical record, Yalom nonetheless invents characters and scenes in order to illuminate the human interior of his biographical subjects. These creative liberties are ethical for Yalom, because they do not conflict with or undermine the agreed-upon historical facts.

This framework of an imagined human interior in relation to the historical facts enables Yalom to answer a perplexing question: How could prominent Nazis, who are relatively well educated, adopt the view that Jews are intellectually inferior, when there is voluminous empirical evidence to the contrary? To bring into sharp focus the nature of this contradiction, Yalom imagines a scenario in which Rosenberg, a prominent Nazi leader and editor of the Nazis' official newspaper, was compelled as a high school student to read the philosophy of Spinoza, a brilliant Jew who is generally credited with formulating a philosophical system that would usher in the Enlightenment. After reading Spinoza's work, the young anti-Semitic Rosenberg is stunned, so much so that he develops a lifelong obsession with Spinoza's writings. As an anti-Semite, he cannot reconcile the fact that Spinoza, as a Jew, is so intelligent and that Goethe admired him. To expose Rosenberg's epistemological blind spots and cognitive

---

[1] Yalom (2012), *The Spinoza Problem: A Novel*. New York: Basic Books, 318.

dissonance, Yalom invents Friedrich Pfister, a psychiatrist who treats the Nazi for his depression. It is in the imagined sessions with Pfister that Yalom reveals one of the central truths about Rosenberg, a truth that is also supposed to illuminate the Nazis' motivation for waging their anti-Semitic war against the Jews.

Theoretically, the biographical novel is an ideal aesthetic form for Yalom to achieve his objective, because he can use Rosenberg's imagined obsession with Spinoza and his therapy sessions with Pfister in order to shed new and important light on the psycho-political ideology underwriting Nazi anti-Semitism. But what ultimately makes his novel unethical is his faulty understanding of the historical framework within which his "real" and imaginary characters function. Thus, instead of remaining relatively faithful to the historical record, as he purports to do, Yalom violates it in an egregious and irresponsible manner, as I intend to demonstrate.

The structure of *The Spinoza Problem* effectively communicates Yalom's agenda. The novel alternately features chapters about Spinoza and then Rosenberg. This narrative structure allows Yalom to underscore two facts, that the Nazis adopted a philosophy that Spinoza originated and that Spinoza's spectacular intellectual capacity refutes the Nazi view of Jewish inferiority. From early in the novel, when Rosenberg has his first conversation with Pfister, Yalom underscores the fact that Spinoza and Rosenberg subscribe to a similar philosophy, which is based on the Enlightenment's mechanistic worldview. Pfister initially describes the philosophy to Rosenberg in terms of the field of psychiatry: "'Sometimes I think our field really began with Spinoza, who believed that everything, every emotion and thought, has a cause that can be discovered with proper investigation.'"[2] In short, Spinoza is a materialist and a determinist, which, according to Yalom, is exactly the same philosophy that Rosenberg and the Nazis adopted.

To underscore the profound and substantive links between Spinoza and the Nazis, Yalom pictures Rosenberg's evolution from his early and very influential relationship with prominent Nazis like Dietrich Eckart and Hitler to his leading role as "the official party philosopher."[3] Each step of the way, Yalom's Rosenberg

---

[2] Yalom (2012), 86.
[3] Yalom (2012), 234.

discovers that the Nazis formulated a way of thinking that Spinoza originated. For instance, in the early years (1919–25), when the Nazis laid the foundation for the political party, Yalom's Rosenberg realizes that the Nazis' official views bear a striking resemblance to Spinoza's philosophy. To picture this link, Yalom clarifies how Rosenberg influenced Eckart, and it is through this relationship that Eckart comes to understand "the historical context not only for anti-Semitism," but also "for powerful anti-Christian sentiments as well."[4] According to this model, Eckart and Rosenberg, two of the most important early Nazis, are rationalists who oppose Judaism and Christianity as superstitious nonsense. To indicate that this view is nearly identical to Spinoza's, Yalom dramatizes Rosenberg's reaction to Spinoza's book *Theological-Political Treatise*:

> The very first page riveted Alfred's attention: "Fear breeds superstition," he read. And: "Weak and greedy people in adversity use prayers and womanish tears to implore help from God." How could a seventeenth-century Jew have written that? Those were the words of a twentieth-century German.[5]

What impresses Yalom's Rosenberg so much is Spinoza's rationalist contempt for religion, which is why he marvels when "Spinoza went on to speak of religion as 'a tissue of ridiculous mysteries' that attracts men 'who flatly despise reason.'"[6] Thus, Yalom's Rosenberg can only conclude: "There could be no denying the extraordinary intelligence of the author."[7]

To emphasize that Rosenberg's view of Spinoza accords with that of other Nazis, Yalom strategically portrays Hitler in a way that unmistakably aligns him with Spinoza. In one of Rosenberg's first meetings with the future Führer, Yalom's Hitler makes the case for "a rational anti-Semitism," because "rationality leads us to only one absolutely unshakeable conclusion: the elimination of Jews from Germany altogether."[8] As a staunch rationalist, Yalom's Hitler is as critical of religion as Spinoza, which is why the budding dictator

---

[4]Yalom (2012), 122.
[5]Yalom (2012), 134.
[6]Yalom (2012), 135.
[7]Ibid.
[8]Yalom (2012), 138.

says that the Jewish "religion is no worse than the others—they're all part of the same great religious swindle."[9] To indicate that Rosenberg shares this view, Yalom has Rosenberg say to himself "that Judaism and Christianity were two sides of the same coin,"[10] a thought that brings Hitler to Rosenberg's mind: "Alfred smiled as he recalled Hitler's apt phrase—that amazing man had such a way with words: 'Judaism, Catholicism, Protestantism—what difference does it make? *They are all part of the same religious swindle.*'"[11]

This paradox, that Nazi ideology bears a striking resemblance to and is perhaps indebted to the philosophy of a rationalist Jew, is the basis for the novel's title. Yalom clarifies the nature of this paradox when he has Rosenberg reflect on the fact that Spinoza is "both courageous and wise."[12] Given Spinoza's exceptional character and intellect, Yalom's Rosenberg wonders how Houston Stewart Chamberlain would "respond to the Spinoza problem."[13] Yalom's Hitler and Rosenberg consider Chamberlain one of their "primary intellectual mentors,"[14] so they visit him to find out—Chamberlain is generally considered the founding father of Nazi ideology, as I have already demonstrated in Chapter 2. Yalom's imaginative addition to the intellectual record consists of Rosenberg's obsession with the Spinoza problem, which is why Yalom has him ask Chamberlain "'how this Jew from Amsterdam could have written works so greatly revered by the greatest of German thinkers, including the immortal Goethe.'"[15] That Chamberlain is as perplexed and disturbed as Rosenberg by this fact is clear from his "agitated"[16] response. The implication is that the nature and quality of Spinoza's thought poses an insurmountable challenge to the Nazis' anti-Semitism, something that would have perplexed Chamberlain and his Nazi disciples.

We are now in a position to define the ethical framework in which Yalom places his Rosenberg. According to Yalom, there is only one piece of evidence linking Spinoza and Rosenberg, which

---

[9]Ibid.
[10]Yalom (2012), 154.
[11]Ibid.
[12]Yalom (2012), 153.
[13]Ibid.
[14]Yalom (2012), 214.
[15]Yalom (2012), 215.
[16]Ibid.

is a document written by one of the Nazi leader's subordinates. Rosenberg was tasked with confiscating millions of books throughout Europe, including the "libraries of the Societas Spinozana in Den Haag and of the Spinoza-House in Rijnsburg."[17] In a document describing the Spinoza collections, Rosenberg's subordinate claims that the books "contain extremely valuable early works of great importance *for the exploration of the Spinoza problem.*"[18] This is the basis for the whole novel, for as Yalom says, he "could find no other evidence linking Rosenberg and Spinoza."[19] Given the nature of "Rosenberg's character structure"[20] and Yalom's fidelity to "historical events,"[21] Yalom claims that his portrayal of Rosenberg's obsession with and response to Spinoza "*could* have happened."[22] What makes the novel ethical, therefore, is Yalom's ability to invent credible and legitimate scenes and characters within the context of an established characterological and historical framework. In other words, his biographical novel is historically useful, plausible, and responsible, because it gives readers a detailed picture of events that could have occurred.

The problem, however, is that *The Spinoza Problem* fails in terms of both characterological and historical representation, thus making it unethical by virtue of Yalom's own definition. To clarify why this is the case, let me start by noting one of Yalom's most flagrant oversights. Throughout *The Spinoza Problem*, Yalom refers to Rosenberg's *The Myth of the Twentieth Century*, a book that is described as "the ideological foundation of the Nazi party and offer[s] a justification for the destruction of European Jews."[23] Near the end of the novel, the book is described as profoundly similar in content to *Mein Kampf*, and it is the source of Rosenberg's greatest anxiety and considerable pride. In fact, the whole of chapter thirty of *The Spinoza Problem* revolves around Rosenberg's obsessive concerns about the book's reception.

These references to *The Myth* are crucial, for in the book, Rosenberg specifically mentions Spinoza's work in a way that

[17]Yalom (2012), 312.
[18]Ibid.
[19]Yalom (2012), 319.
[20]Ibid.
[21]Yalom (2012), 318.
[22]Yalom (2012), 319.
[23]Yalom (2012), 5.

functions to refute Yalom's portrayal of Rosenberg's hypothetical obsession with and response to Spinoza's work. In a section titled "Will and Instinct," Rosenberg condemns those philosophies that fail to take into account two separate dimensions of the human. Following Kant, who claims that humans belong simultaneously to the empirical and the intelligible worlds, Rosenberg holds that humans are determined by the material conditions of being, which means that humans, in an empirical sense, are not free, because they are subject to "the unalterable laws of cause and effect."[24] But as beings that also belong to the intelligible world, Rosenberg believes that there is a dimension to the human that "is groundless and mysterious."[25] This part of the human is the will, which "is completely different from all other phenomena"[26] in that it is "not subject to the principle of causation. It is groundless."[27]

For Rosenberg, one of the biggest threats to humanity's political well-being is a philosophy that fails to acknowledge the two separate dimensions of the human. To indicate that this is the case, Rosenberg uses an argument from authority. If there is only one dimension of the human (defined exclusively as either the empirical or the material), then moral action and human freedom would be impossible and incoherent, because we would all be biologically and/or environmentally determined. When it comes to defining both morality and freedom, Rosenberg's authoritative heroes are Christ and Kant. "Christ, Da Vinci, Kant, [and] Goethe"[28] recognize "the possibility of victory of the will"[29] over biological urges and environmental conditioning, and if it happens that human freedom, a prerequisite for morality, is but an illusion, then "moral prayers would be a source of laughter, and both Christ and Kant would seem to have been really stupid men."[30] The implication, of course, is that it is absurd to think that Christ and Kant are stupid men. Therefore, there must be a second dimension to the human, which would make moral freedom both possible and meaningful.

---

[24]Rosenberg (1982), *The Myth of the Twentieth Century: An Evaluation of the Spiritual-Intellectual Confrontations of Our Age.* Translated by Vivian Bird. Torrance, CA: The Noontide Press, 201.
[25]Rosenberg (1982), 203.
[26]Ibid.
[27]Rosenberg (1982), 200.
[28]Rosenberg (1982), 206.
[29]Rosenberg (1982), 205–6.
[30]Rosenberg (1982), 205.

Within this framework, Rosenberg identifies those philosophies that are ultimately inadequate or patently false, because they fail to take into account the two separate dimensions of the human. While he mainly targets Arthur Schopenhauer, he also has very critical words for Spinoza. Philosophies that treat the material world as a thing-in-itself and ignore the subjective lead to materialism, while philosophies that see "the subject as an absolute"[31] lead to idealism. Accordingly, "if one asserts that" the subject is solely a material being, thus rendering subject and object "one and the same," then "Spinozaism results."[32] This Spinozaoistic position, of course, is precisely one of the philosophies that Rosenberg rejects as faulty and misguided.

What is so stunning about this direct reference to Spinoza is that it undermines Yalom's claim that he could only find one tangential piece of evidence linking Spinoza and Rosenberg. There is no way to say with certainty what led to Yalom's failure to mention or even know about Rosenberg's reference to Spinoza in *The Myth*, but one can certainly speculate. The index of the English translation of *The Myth of the Twentieth Century* contains no reference to Spinoza, so if Yalom merely consulted the index rather than actually reading the work, he would have wrongly concluded that there are no references to Spinoza in the book. What makes it even more reasonable to assume that Yalom did not read Rosenberg's work carefully, if at all, is the degree to which his representation of Rosenberg's response to Spinoza is in egregious conflict with the Nazi's philosophy. In his conversations with the imagined character of Pfister, Yalom's Rosenberg is totally entranced. According to Pfister, Spinoza believes that a rigorous method of logic and science could ultimately explain everything about the material world, which is why religion will eventually become obsolete. Yalom's Rosenberg comes to understand this fully when he visits the Spinoza House, which is why he makes at this point an anti-religious comment that Spinoza would have approved: "Judaism and Christianity were two sides of the same coin."[33] Put simply, there is something inherently logical and necessary in Spinoza's rational and deterministic method, which explains why Yalom's Rosenberg

---

[31]Rosenberg (1982), 198.
[32]Ibid.
[33]Yalom (2012), 154.

is so overwhelmed in the 1936 session after Pfister defines Spinoza's philosophy: "'Everything is caused by something prior.'" Given this view, the logical task is to "'devote ourselves to the understanding of the causative network.'"[34] The reason why Yalom's Rosenberg is so thoroughly enthralled by this representation of Spinoza is that it is supposedly similar to the philosophy that Rosenberg and the Nazis adopted.

The problem, however, is that anyone with even a rudimentary knowledge of Rosenberg's philosophy would realize that (1) Rosenberg knows the cause-effect philosophy that Pfister defines and specifically attributes to Spinoza, (2) that Rosenberg rejects that philosophy because he considers it narrow, limited, Jewish, and anti-Aryan, and (3) that Rosenberg would dub Spinoza a typical Jew for espousing such a philosophy. To justify my claims, let me briefly discuss Rosenberg's most important book.

Central to Rosenberg's philosophy is not a rejection of religion, as Yalom would have his readers believe, but a correct understanding of its importance in relation to the two dimensions of the human. Rosenberg claims that "the Nordic spirit gained philosophical consciousness in Immanuel Kant, whose fundamental achievement lies in the separation he established between forces of religion and science. Religion is concerned with the kingdom of heaven within us, true science only with physics, chemistry, biology and mechanics."[35] Science concerns itself exclusively with the material dimension of human being, that which can be understood through the rigorous and logical method of cause and effect. But there is a dimension to the human that cannot be reductively defined in terms of cause and effect, which is why religion is of such crucial importance for someone like Rosenberg. He makes this point most forcefully in very typical Nazi fashion when he says: "If Christ acted against the 'generation of vipers,' if he took death upon himself for the sake of an idea, then this is the effect of a principle of freedom."[36] This reference to the "generation of vipers" comes from the Gospel of Matthew and is central to the Nazi project of establishing an oppositional and antagonistic relationship between Christ and the Jews. For the Nazis, Jews are materialists who not only fail

---

[34]Yalom (2012), 269.
[35]Rosenberg (1982), 74.
[36]Rosenberg (1982), 208.

to understand and appreciate Christ, but also stand in deadly opposition to Him, because they, as pure materialists, have no concept of or capacity for "freedom"—they define and experience the world only through the mechanistic laws of natural necessity. Within this framework, Spinoza is a typical Jew, for "Spinozaism" entails a denial of Christ and his "principle of freedom," that which is unconditioned and therefore impossible to define in terms of the mechanistic laws of natural necessity.

If this view of the Jewish philosopher were merely an idiosyncratic idea in Rosenberg's corpus, one would have to temper the critique of Yalom's representation of Rosenberg as a representative of Nazi ideology. But actually, Chamberlain, Eckart, and Hitler adopted exactly the same view, and both Chamberlain and Eckart explicitly use this Kantian model to define and condemn Spinoza as a typical Jew. In his study *Immanuel Kant*, which Yalom does not mention, Chamberlain discusses Spinoza, whom he describes as the quintessential materialist: "Spinoza recognizes no mysterium, he is astonished at nothing, saying expressly that no question rises above the human power of comprehension, and everything can be explained in the most convenient manner."[37] Given the nature of this philosophy, Chamberlain refers to Spinoza as "the dreamless man,"[38] a person who could never see or experience that which rises above the mechanistically determined universe.

For Chamberlain, what accounts for Spinoza's reductive approach to life and the world is his Jewishness. In other words, Spinoza predictably adopts a deterministic and mechanistic philosophy, because he is a Jew. Ironically, Chamberlain makes this point most clearly when he refers to Goethe's youthful (mis)appreciation of Spinoza. Chamberlain acknowledges "the attraction" that "Spinoza exercised over" Goethe "in his youthful days."[39] What appealed to the young poet is Spinoza's "mathematical method," which Chamberlain understands in ethnic terms as something "dear to the Jewish Thinker."[40] What differentiates Goethe from a Jew like Spinoza is his capacity to experience the unconditioned

---

[37]Chamberlain (1914), *Immanuel Kant*. Translated by Lord Redesdale. London: John Lane, I.382.
[38]Ibid.
[39]Chamberlain (1914), I.137.
[40]Ibid.

dimension of being, that which a Jew could never understand or appreciate. Distinguishing between the young and old Goethe is crucial for Chamberlain, for it enables him to say that it was a "misunderstanding which led to" the young Goethe's "fuss over Spinoza."[41]

Chamberlain's comments about Goethe's response to Spinoza are damning for Yalom's project for two separate reasons. First, Yalom's Rosenberg did not have to speculate as to Chamberlain's response to Spinoza. All he had to do was to read Chamberlain's book on Kant, which the actual Rosenberg clearly did as we see from his book *Houston Stewart Chamberlain als Verkünder und Begründer einer deutschen Zukunft* (Houston Stewart Chamberlain as Forerunner and Founder of a German Future).[42] Second, given the way the Nazis used Kant's empirical/intelligible distinction in order to pit Christ ("principle of freedom") and the Jews (materialists) in mortal opposition to one another, the Nazis would not have seen Spinoza's work as the basis for their ideology or as a challenge to their view of the Jew. In fact, quite the opposite is the case, which we see most clearly through the writings of Eckart.

Like Chamberlain and Rosenberg, Eckart takes his cue from Kant by making a distinction between the empirical and intelligible worlds—I discussed Eckart's Kantian-inflected version of Christianity in Chapter 2. Eckart defines this view most clearly in his essay "Das Judentum in und außer uns" (Jewishness in and outside us), which first appeared in his journal *Auf gut Deutsch* (in plain German). Yalom mentions this journal in the novel,[43] but he clearly did not understand the degree to which the distinction between the empirical and the intelligible is the basis for the Nazis' anti-Semitic political agenda. Even more significant is the fact that Eckart uses the empirical/intelligible distinction in order to define Spinoza as a typical Jew in his essay "Bolshevism from Moses to

---

[41]Chamberlain (1914), I.360.
[42]Rosenberg (1927), *Houston Stewart Chamberlain als Verkünder und Begründer einer deutschen Zukunft*. München: Hugo Brudmann, Verlag. Sprinkled throughout this work are references to Chamberlain's book on Kant, and there is a section devoted to Kant (29–35). The book concludes with what Rosenberg considers the best passages from Chamberlain's many publications, and many of them are taken from the Kant book (103–27). It is impossible for Rosenberg to have been ignorant of Chamberlain's critique of Spinoza.
[43]Yalom (2012), 105, 123.

Lenin." In a section about the Jewish worldview, Eckart mentions "Spinoza," whose "ethics would horrify a pig." To punctuate his point, the German ideologue sums up the Jewish philosopher's thought: "'In all things seek that which is advantageous' is the quintessence of his moral philosophy," which Eckart claims is "the genuine Jewish viewpoint." Germans can sacrifice self-interest in the name of a higher good. But since Jews are mere materialists, they can only formulate a philosophy that would justify narcissistic self-interest. Hence Spinoza's philosophy, which is the logical product of his Jewish heritage.

Hitler does not mention Spinoza in *Mein Kampf*, but he clearly adopts the same version of Christianity as Chamberlain, Rosenberg, and Eckart, which would have led him to categorize and denounce Yalom's Spinoza as a typical Jew. For Hitler, "the Jews are members of a *people* and not of a *'religion.'*"[44] If Yalom is to be believed, Hitler's claim would shed positive light on the German dictator, for both Yalom's Spinoza and Hitler consider religion an insidious swindle. But for the actual Hitler, religion is a good thing, and it is that which enables him to distinguish Jews from Christians. As he claims: "The Jew cannot possess a religious institution, if for no other reason because he lacks idealism in any form, and hence belief in a hereafter is absolutely foreign to him. And a religion in the Aryan sense cannot be imagined which lacks the conviction of survival after death in some form."[45] For Hitler, Jews live only for the material world; they are like animals who cannot sacrifice self-interest in pursuit of a higher good. Hence, they are incapable of experiencing or respecting anything that transcends the material dimension of being. Germans are different, because they are religious people who desire freedom, a freedom that enables them to sacrifice self-interest in pursuit of a higher and nobler moral good.

Given this clearly and consistently defined view, would Rosenberg have been startled by Spinoza's philosophy? Also, would Spinoza's philosophy have posed a major challenge to Rosenberg's and the Nazis' anti-Semitism? The answer to both questions is an emphatic no. The problem with Yalom's approach is that he fails to understand the Nazis' nuanced view of the Jews' intellectual capacity. Yalom

---

[44]Hitler (1971), *Mein Kampf*. Translated by Ralph Manheim. Boston: Houghton Mifflin, 306.
[45]Ibid.

thinks that the Nazis considered the Jews unintelligent. Therefore, when Yalom's Rosenberg reads Spinoza's work, he marvels that a Jew could be so smart. But here is what Hitler says about the Jews' intellectual capacity: the Jew "passes as 'smart,' and this in a certain sense he has been at all times."[46] The problem, however, is that the Jew has a certain and limited type of intellectual capacity, which is the ability to mimic what others have said, but never to originate a new system of thought. As Hitler says: The Jew's "intelligence is not the result of his own development, but of visual instruction through foreigners."[47] In other words, "the foundations" of the Jew's "intellectual work were always provided by others."[48] Hitler derived this view from Chamberlain's *The Foundations of the Nineteenth Century*,[49] which uses this model in order to characterize Spinoza's work. In a section titled "Christ and Kant," which draws a clear link between "the religious philosophy of Kant" and "the teaching of Christ,"[50] Chamberlain distinguishes Semitic from Teutonic ideas. For Chamberlain, Kant best represents the Teutonic way of thinking, which is a system of thought that he believes will "emancipate us from Judaism."[51] The Jew he specifically has in mind at this point is Spinoza. In short, Chamberlain considers Spinoza a typical Jew, which is why he says that the Jewish thinker "has not enriched with a single creative thought either mathematics, his special province, or science, his hobby."[52]

If it is true that Rosenberg nearly memorized Chamberlain's book,[53] as Yalom's narrator says, then the imagined scenario on which *The Spinoza Problem* is premised would be implausible and incoherent, because Rosenberg would have known that Chamberlain characterizes Spinoza as a typical Jew on the basis of his work and that Chamberlain would consider Spinoza's philosophy the logical

---

[46]Hitler (1971), 300.
[47]Ibid.
[48]Hitler (1971), 301.
[49]For a detailed analysis of Chamberlain's impact on Hitler's writing and thinking, see my book *The Modernist God State* (225–79).
[50]Chamberlain (1912), *The Foundations of the Nineteenth Century*. New York: John Lane Company, II.490.
[51]Chamberlain (1912), II.495.
[52]Chamberlain (1912), II.179.
[53]Yalom refers to Rosenberg's "near-memorization of Houston Stewart Chamberlain's book." Yalom (2012), 119.

product of his Jewish heritage. To put the matter bluntly, Yalom has a faulty and inaccurate grasp of the conceptual, historical, and characterological framework in which Rosenberg moves and has his being. Therefore, his imaginative addition to the intellectual record via his biographical novel is totally implausible. Moreover, the novel is completely irresponsible because it distorts our understanding of the actual political psychology that made the Nazi atrocities against the Jews possible. Hence, what we get in *The Spinoza Problem* is not a truthful fiction about Rosenberg or the Nazis. Rather, Yalom misappropriates the life of Rosenberg in order to put forth an implausible, misinformed, and uninformed theory about a Nazi leader and the Nazis more generally. As such, *The Spinoza Problem* is an unethical and irresponsible biographical novel.

II

In 2000, David Ebershoff published *The Danish Girl*, a biographical novel about the painter Einar Wegener, who was the first person to undergo a sexual reassignment surgery. Einar became Lili Elbe. With regard to the ethics of the biographical novel, the differences between the approaches of Ebershoff and Yalom are instructive and illuminating. Yalom claims to take creative liberties, but only within the context of an inviolable historical and characterological frame. By stark contrast, Ebershoff unapologetically alters and even violates historical facts in his attempt to project his own vision of life and the world. On the surface, this disregard for historical fact should render *The Danish Girl* an irresponsible and unethical work of literature. But as I intend to argue, it is precisely because of his flagrant reconstruction of the historical record that *The Danish Girl* is an exemplary model of an ethical and responsible biographical novel.

Let me mention some of the most egregious changes Ebershoff made to the historical and biographical record. The actual Einar was born in 1882, while Ebershoff's character was born in either 1890 or 1891. The actual Einar married in 1904 an artist named Gerda, who hailed from Fredericksberg, Denmark, and was the daughter of a clergyman. Ebershoff's Einar married after the First World War an artist named Greta, who hailed from Pasadena, California, and was the daughter of a wealthy American family. When the actual Einar met Gerda, he describes the experience as "love at first sight."[54] By stark contrast, when Ebershoff's Einar meets Greta, he is conflicted, distant, and reserved, and it takes Greta many years to finally win his affection. The actual Gerda had never been married before wedding Einar, while Ebershoff's Greta was a widow when she married Einar. After Lili's surgery, the actual Gerda became intimately involved with and eventually married an Italian man, while Ebershoff's Greta married Einar's childhood friend from Denmark. To put the matter bluntly, Ebershoff flagrantly violates the literal historical and/or biographical record, which is why he says that "the reader should not look to this novel for very many biographical details of Einar Wegener's life."[55] What motivated Ebershoff to dismiss and even alter the actual biographical and historical record? And how do his creative liberties enable us to better understand the nature and ethics of the biographical novel? To answer these questions, let me start by briefly discussing one of his primary sources, which is Niels Hoyer's *Man Into Woman*, a text that contains selections from Elbe's diaries and correspondence.

Given the title, it would seem that the main focus of the work would be on gender. But actually, throughout the work, Elbe foregrounds ambiguities in gender and ethnicity. For instance, Lili tells a story about her performance in a play in a small town in France before she had her sex change. She, as Einar, and the director went to the train station to pick up a performer who was supposed "to play a minor part, that of a typical Parisienne."[56] The woman did not arrive, so Einar replaced her as Lili. Her performance was so good that "not a soul in the hall suspected that Lili was not a genuine Parisienne."[57] What makes this story of ethnic passing so significant is the fact that it immediately follows a story of gender passing. While in Capri, Lili and her friends saw a Scotsman, who was always accompanied by a "very pretty boy."[58] However, the onlookers soon recognize that the pretty boy is actually "a very nice girl," which leads a Venetian-sculptor friend of Lili's to say: "I knew

---

[54]Elbe (2004), *Man Into Woman: An Authentic Record of A Change of Sex*. Edited by Niels Hoyer. London: Blue Boat Books, 64.
[55]Ebershoff (2000a), *The Danish Girl*. New York: Penguin Books, 271.
[56]Elbe (2004), 79.
[57]Elbe (2004), 80.
[58]Elbe (2004), 77.

it from the start! A girl cannot impersonate a man, neither can a man impersonate a girl. Those who have eyes to see can detect the deception immediately."[59] Gerda and Einar take this as a challenge, so the next day, Einar dresses as Lili and pretends to be a Parisian woman. The deception works. Einar successfully passes as both a woman and as a Parisian, thus deceiving the man who insisted that he could always spot an impersonator.

This idea of passing is merely a prelude to the book's focus on crossing. Passing is about appearance. Charles W. Chessnut's Waldens in *The House Behind the Cedars* (1900), James Weldon Johnson's unnamed narrator in *The Autobiography of an Ex-Colored Man* (1912), and Nella Larsen's Irene Redfield in *Passing* (1929) are so light-skinned that they can pass as white. But this ability to pass raises major ontological questions about the nature of human being. If, in the world of appearance, a person can pass for the seeming opposite of what one supposedly is, can the person, in the world of being, be the opposite of what one is perceived or supposed to be? Or, coming from a different angle, is it possible for a person to cross over from one type of being to its perceived opposite? Such are the ontological questions that obsessed Virginia Woolf in *Orlando* (1928), a book that was published only two years before Elbe's sex change and has a main character that crosses over from man to woman; and Zora Neale Hurston's *Moses, Man of the Mountain* (1939), a novel in which the main character crosses over from being an Egyptian to being a non-Egyptian. Elbe's text features examples of gender and ethnic passing, but these merely anticipate the more significant ontological transformation of crossing over from man into woman.

Issues of passing and crossing certainly take center stage in both *Man Into Woman* and *The Danish Girl*, but Elbe and Ebershoff draw radically different conclusions about both, and it is these differences that explain why Ebershoff does not include the scenes with Lili ethnically passing in his novel. While Ebershoff loosely bases his novel on the life of Einar/Lili, he states explicitly that he has profound disagreements with his actual biographical subject. As he says in a conversation about the novel: "In reality, Einar Wegener truly felt that he did a full switch from man into woman; that with

---

[59]Ibid.

the blade of a knife he went from male to female as efficiently as you or I turn on or off the light to a room."[60] Ebershoff rejects this view of sexual identity as "simplistic," for as he says: "My understanding of what happens in the transformation is different. I believe, and this is another reason I wrote this story as fiction, that Einar was both man and woman, not one or the other, and that living his life as either would never have been exactly correct."[61] By writing a novel instead of a biography, Ebershoff was not tethered to the facts of Lili's life and views. Rather, he could use his subject's life in order to project his own vision of life and the world, and as should be clear, his vision is in deep conflict with his biographical subject.

To be more specific, the actual Lili believes that her experience is so anomalous that she can only be characterized as a freak of nature. As she says: "Gradually it became clear to me that nothing which related to normal men and women could throw any light on my mysterious case."[62] Given this claim, *Man Into Woman* is a book about a total aberration, someone so unique that the lives of normal people could never be used to illuminate Einar's/Lili's experiences or his/her experiences could not be used to illuminate the lives of normal people. Ebershoff disagrees, for he believes that "there is universality to Einar's question of identity."[63] Therefore, *The Danish Girl* seeks to underscore the degree to which Einar/Lili is a figure who represents in an extreme what most people experience. Understanding this difference explains Ebershoff's decision not to include the scene of the Danish Einar passing as a French woman. To convert Einar/Lili into a representative literary symbol, Ebershoff created another character that could ethnically pass. That character is Greta, whom Ebershoff calls "the hero of the novel."[64] If *Man Into Woman* foregrounds how the Danish Einar could pass as a French person, *The Danish Girl* foregrounds how the American Greta could pass as a Danish girl—hence the clever ambiguity of the novel's title. Both works feature characters that ethnically pass. But in *Man Into Woman*, we only see Einar pass,

---

[60]Ebershoff (2000b), "A Conversation with David Ebershoff," in *The Danish Girl*. New York: Penguin Books, 9.
[61]Ibid.
[62]Elbe (2004), 100.
[63]Ebershoff (2000b), 8.
[64]Ibid.

whereas in *The Danish Girl*, Ebershoff normalizes the theme of identity transformation beyond Einar by having Greta ethnically pass, thus making the experience something more universal.

This focus on identity transformation as a more universal experience explains Ebershoff's decision to make Greta an American aristocrat. Greta rejects this identity, just as Einar will eventually reject his male identity. Born into the wealthy Waud family, "Greta's parents expected her to proceed as if she were one of them, . . ., as if she should become the young Californian woman she was born to be."[65] But Greta consciously seeks to shuffle off the confining coils of her familial identity. Note, for instance, how she tries to use language to reject one identity and to don another: "When she was a little girl, she used to write over and over in her penmanship notebook, 'Greta Greta Greta,' deliberately leaving off the 'Waud' as if to test what it would be like to be plain old Greta—something no one ever called her. She didn't want anyone to know who her family was."[66] In this case, the issue is the construction of identity in relation to her class status as a member of a wealthy family. But Greta also rejects her identity as an American. For a number of years, the Wauds lived in Denmark. But with growing instability in the First World War Europe, Greta's father decides to move his family back to California. Greta opposes the return to the United States, claiming that being American doesn't feel right to her. Greta's mother says that this is absurd, but Greta insists that "this was how she felt."[67] It is through her marriage to the nonaristocrat Teddy Cross that we most clearly see Greta's rejection of her inherited identity. Greta loves Teddy, but she cries for days after marrying him, "not because she was married to Teddy Cross but because she was now even farther from her beloved Denmark and the life she wanted to lead."[68] Marrying Teddy confines her to the United States, trapping her into the alienated identity of a wealthy American Waud.

To further underscore this idea of being alienated from one's inherited identity, Ebershoff creates the character of Hans, Einar's childhood friend and a man that Greta will eventually marry. Hans's father is a baron, and the family lives in a brick villa near

[65]Ebershoff (2000a), 33.
[66]Ebershoff (2000a), 13.
[67]Ebershoff (2000a), 34.
[68]Ebershoff (2000a), 41.

Einar's home in Bluetooth. Given the family's wealth and prestige, it would seem that Hans would eagerly embrace his privileged heritage. But such is not the case. After meeting Lili (at this point in the novel, he does not know that Lili is actually Einar dressed as a woman), Hans tells his disguised friend that "he hated the title" of Baron. Indeed, so much did he reject it that he abandoned his homeland: "'It's why I left Denmark,' he said. 'The aristocracy was dead.'"[69] Like Greta, Hans feels himself to be something other than what he was presumably born to be.

By starting the novel with examples of ethnic and class crossings and by having characters other than Einar have this experience, Ebershoff implicitly challenges and critiques Elbe's view in *Man Into Woman*, which is that Einar/Lili is totally abnormal. There are many types of crossing that function at different levels of intensity. Therefore, Einar's transformation from man into woman is just a more extreme example of what occurs to many people on a regular basis. In other words, if we understand that people are regularly born into family, class, and ethnic situations from which they feel alienated, then the idea of identity transformation would be quite normal and mundane. As such, Einar/Lili is neither abnormal nor alone.

What, in part, prompted Ebershoff to create characters that undergo transformations similar to Einar/Lili's is his attempt to foster understanding and respect for people in the transgender community. One gets this sense most clearly from an interview about Einar's experience in which Ebershoff claims that "even today transgendered people struggle to incorporate themselves into society, without much assistance from most of us."[70] While it might seem that Elbe's *Man Into Woman* would be the most obvious way to promote the health and cause of transgendered people, Ebershoff clearly thinks that the exact opposite is the case.

That Lili has successfully had a sex change is certainly a good thing, and there is no indication in the novel or in Ebershoff's writings that he faults Lili for doing so. However, the novel suggests that her subsequent definition of woman and her simplistic way of defining gender in strictly binary terms are extremely problematic.

---

[69]Ebershoff (2000a), 75.
[70]Ebershoff (2000b), 7.

Here is how Elbe defines woman in *Man Into Woman*. Women are not autonomous beings. They "need help and are helped."[71] Therefore, when thinking about and defining herself in relation to Einar, Elbe specifies how the sex change has led to a radical transformation in her character and personality:

> He [Einar] was ingenious, sagacious, and interested in everything—a reflective and thoughtful man. And I was quite superficial. Deliberately so, for I had to demonstrate every day that I was a different creature from him, that I was a woman. A thoughtless, flighty, very superficially-minded woman, fond of dress and fond of enjoyment, yes, I believe even childish. And I can say it calmly now: all this was certainly not merely farcical acting. It was my real character, untroubled, carefree, illogical, capricious, female.[72]

After the operation, Lili is truly a woman. This is not a being that lacks a penis and has a vagina, but one that is "superficial," "thoughtless," "flighty," "childish," and "illogical." To put the matter bluntly, she has all the defining features that seemingly characterize a woman as a woman. Not surprisingly, she decides that she must abandon her life as a painter after the surgery, since being a woman precludes being an artist: "For I do not want to be an artist, but a woman. Hence I must shut all artistic creation out of my life." She draws this conclusion because she "cannot continue the work of the virile artist."[73] Based on this logic, she can only become a more complete woman insofar as she eradicates the male from her life, and the male, in this instance, is a being with a capacity to be an artist.

To complete the transformation from man into woman, there is one last thing Lili must do, which is to have a child. On the surface, the ability to have a child functions to affirm Lili's female identity. But a careful reading of her views indicates that there is something else at stake in this act. In a letter, Lili asks a friend of hers to sympathize with her "desire for maternity," because she believes that through the act she can demonstrate that the male "has been completely

---

[71]Elbe (2004), 215.
[72]Elbe (2004), 222.
[73]Elbe (2004), 264.

obliterated in me—is dead."[74] Bearing a child, therefore, is as much about killing and extirpating every last trace of the male within her as it is about affirming and confirming the female within her.

Understanding this antagonistic dynamic, which ultimately leads to Lili's death, explains Ebershoff's decision to introduce fictional characters into the novel, as they function to expose and underscore the dangers implicit in the system of thought that Einar/Lili uncritically adopts and to offer a healthier and more life-producing alternative. By thinking of gender as either male or female, Lili believes that she must totally become one and completely reject the other. For instance, after the surgery, Lili tells Greta that "she felt she could play no greater role in this world than as a man's wife."[75] But being a legitimate and true wife means having a child, which is why Lili returns to Dresden to have a surgery that would enable her to get pregnant. As in *Man Into Woman*, birthing a child is not just a miraculous act affirming a woman's capacity to create life; it is also an act of violence, the death blow to the male monster within her. As she says to Greta, having a child will "prove to the world—no, not to the world but to herself—that indeed she was a woman, and that all her previous life, the little man known as Einar, was simply nature's gravest mishap, corrected once and for all."[76] Since she now is a female, her previous life as a male was a complete and total lie, a grave mishap that must be obliterated and forgotten.

To suggest that this is a mistaken and even a psychologically unhealthy way to think about her situation, Ebershoff intelligently juxtaposes the responses of Lili and Greta. While Lili and Greta are cleaning out their apartment, Greta asks Lili what they should do with Einar's paintings. Lili says she does not want them. At this point, the narrator interjects: "Something in Lili knew she was making a mistake."[77] That Lili makes a mistake is clear. But why? Ebershoff answers the question through Greta's response.

To universalize the theme of identity transformation, Ebershoff has Greta and Einar go through parallel experiences. As Lili grows increasingly alienated from her inherited identity, she strategically rejects her heritage as a male. In like manner, as Greta grows

[74]Elbe (2004), 260.
[75]Elbe (2004), 241.
[76]Elbe (2004), 243.
[77]Elbe (2004), 253.

increasingly alienated from her inherited identity, she strategically rejects her heritage as a wealthy American Waud. Both are in danger of establishing a destructive dynamic within themselves— the more Lili becomes a woman, the more does she believe that she must destroy the male inside her, while the more Greta becomes an ordinary Dane, the more does she believe that she must destroy the wealthy American Waud inside her. But herein lies the difference. By the end of the novel, Greta recognizes that it is not only unrealistic but also dangerous to establish a psychological dynamic of rejecting one's previous identities. Notice how Eberhoff brings these two separate responses into sharp focus when Lili insists that she must have children:

> "I've made up my mind," Lili said. "Greta, can't you understand? I want to have children with my husband."
> The sun was now reflecting off the Royal Theatre's dome. Lili Elbe and Greta Waud, as she had begun calling herself again, alone in the apartment.[78]

For Lili, having children is the best way to shuffle off every last coil of her previous male self. But by the end of the novel, Greta rejects Lili's antagonistic approach to her previous self. Instead of obliterating her inherited identity, she decides to accept and embrace it by calling herself "Greta Waud" again. For Greta, becoming an ordinary Danish girl does not mean that she must extirpate her former self as a wealthy American Waud. In fact, pretending to overcome her previous identity is just a self-destructive lie.

Therefore, Greta decides to accept and embrace her previous identity. We see this most clearly when Greta and Hans decide to go back to California and to "marry in the garden of the Waud house."[79] Early in the novel, Greta says that she does not feel at home in America. But now that she has rejected the antagonistic either/or approach to human identity, she feels comfortable calling America home: "'Homeward bound,' she would say. 'I never thought I wanted to go home.'"[80] Now that she is heading back to her home in America, is she a wealthy American Waud or an ordinary Danish

[78]Elbe (2004), 248.
[79]Elbe (2004), 261.
[80]Ibid.

girl? The answer is both. One does not preclude the other, as it does with Lili. Rather, it is possible to be all these things simultaneously. So just as Ebershoff claims that "Einar was both man and woman, not one or the other," so Greta is both a wealthy American and an ordinary Dane, not one or the other. This is something that Lili could neither understand nor accept, and she paid for this failure in imagination with her life.

III

My goal in this chapter has not been so much to illuminate Yalom's *The Spinoza Problem* or Ebershoff's *The Danish Girl* as it has been to use these two biographical novels in order to make some observations about the ethics of the genre. Both authors take significant liberties with their biographical subjects. If they were writing traditional or fictional biographies, in which accurate representation of a life or a dimension of a life is the primary objective, then the liberties that they take would be inexcusable and unethical. However, since they author novels rather than biographies, they are free to take considerable liberties with their subjects. But how many and what types of liberties are ethically justifiable?

Russell Banks gives us a useful framework for answering this question. For Banks, authors make a tacit contract with their readers. If a work is called a novel, then that implies one type of contract, while if a work is "called a memoir, [then] it has a different contract."[81] Within this framework, readers need to specify the nature of the implied contract, and failure to do so could lead to serious forms of misinterpretation. For instance, in Chapter 5, I explain how historians/biographers have very different truth contracts with their readers compared with fiction writers. For biographers and historians, it is not acceptable for an author to alter a fact about a person's life, such as the year of the subject's death. But for Banks, such a change is permissible for novelists, because it enables them to communicate a more important symbolic

---

[81]Banks (2014), "The Truth Contract in the Biographical Novel," in *Truthful Fictions: Conversations with American Biographical Novelists.* Editor and Interviewer Michael Lackey. New York and London: Bloomsbury, 50.

truth. As an author, Banks feels free to take this kind of liberty and, given that his work is called a novel, he expects his readers to know that he takes such a liberty. To illustrate the importance of taking into account the implied contract of a given genre, imagine for a moment that every word in Banks' novel was the same, but that he titled it *Cloudsplitter: A Biography of Owen Brown*. That single change would have rendered his work unethical, because it would have tacitly bound him to a different truth contract. And based on that contract, Banks would certainly understand why readers would be outraged by some of the changes he made to his subject's life.

There are, of course, detailed and specific kinds of ethical questions one can raise about the biographical novel. For instance, to capture the essence of Frida Kahlo's mind-distorting desperation, Barbara Mujica has the Mexican artist seduce a fifteen-year-old late in her life, and the boy she seduces is named after an actual historical person. However, in the "Author's Note" to *Frida*, Mujica acknowledges that there is no evidence that Kahlo "seduced a fifteen-year-old Esmeralda student (or any other minor)."[82] Given the slanderous nature of this fictional representation and the fact that Mujica names the boy after an actual historical figure, critics would certainly be within their right to raise some ethical objections to Mujica's novel.

But my focus is on the ethics of the aesthetic form rather than the specific content or details of any particular biographical novel. At a metalevel, biographical novelists expect readers to know that, because a work is called a novel, authors have the freedom to invent scenes and characters in order to communicate their particular vision of life and the world. So it should not surprise readers that Gore Vidal's *Burr* features the fictional character of Charlie Schuyler, that Madison Smartt Bell's *All Souls' Rising* (Toussaint Louverture) features the fictional character of Riau, and that Jerome Charyn's *The Secret Life of Emily Dickinson* features the fictional character of Zilpah Marsh. Yalom clearly subscribes to the view that authors can invent scenes and characters, but he qualifies that liberty by saying that they can do so only within the context of an established and inviolable historical and characterological frame. Ebershoff adopts a totally different approach, because he believes

---

[82]Mujica (2012), *Frida: A Novel of Frida Kahlo*. New York: The Overlook Press, 365.

that biographical novelists can flagrantly alter the biographical and/or historical frame in order to communicate their own vision. So which author's approach is ethical and which is not? Given that I have offered a scorching criticism of *The Spinoza Problem*, it might seem that I consider Yalom's approach unethical. But this is not the case. I actually think that Yalom has given us a useful paradigm for understanding the truth contract underwriting his biographical novel, but I think he fails to fulfill the mandates of his implied truth contract. Kate Moses authored *Wintering: A Novel of Sylvia Plath*, which is based on the same implied truth contract as Yalom's. But her novel, I would argue, is much more effective and ethical than Yalom's, because she succeeds to a much greater degree in understanding, respecting, and representing the biographical and historical frame in which her character moves and has her being. In essence, there can be no single truth contract on which a biographical novel should be premised. The question, rather, should be this: To what degree does the biographical novel succeed in fulfilling the mandates of the implied truth contract on which it is based? Once readers define the contract, they can begin the process of determining whether the writer has produced a responsible or ethical work.

   With regard to Yalom, I say that *The Spinoza Problem* is an instance of misappropriating a life because, instead of accurately representing a significant dimension of Rosenberg's life in order to illuminate the Nazis more generally, he manufactures a character that bears very little resemblance to the actual person (identity theft) in order to advance his own uninformed and misinformed view of Nazi anti-Semitism. The difference between Duffy's *The World As I Found It* and Yalom's *The Spinoza Problem* is instructive. After living in Wittgenstein's works for many years (it took seven years to write *The World As I Found It*), Duffy built a narrative that brought into sharp focus a deadly self-negating ideology within Wittgenstein. Duffy's novel is successful, effective, and ethical (it is a truthful fiction), because his representation of the crucial psychological conflict within Wittgenstein is piercing and believable and it is useful in illuminating the deadly racist structure at work in both early twentieth-century Europe and late twentieth-century America. To be more specific, *The World As I Found It* is truthful in that it accurately and intelligently represents a vital dimension of Wittgenstein's person and thought. However, it is important to keep in mind that Duffy gives readers a fictional rather than a biographical truth. Biographical truth is temporally bound to the established facts about the subject's life. But Duffy changes many facts, as I have demonstrated in Chapter 2, in order to picture what is most important, which is the central conflict within Wittgenstein. Moreover, Duffy, via the character of Max, converts Wittgenstein into a literary symbol that functions to illuminate more than just Wittgenstein's life, which is why *The World As I Found It* qualifies as a truthful fiction.

Ironically, Ebershoff unapologetically violates the historical and biographical record in the most flagrant manner imaginable. And yet, *The Danish Girl* would qualify as a truthful fiction just as much as Duffy's *The World As I Found It*. The novel is truthful in the sense that it incisively and accurately pictures a deadly psychological dynamic at work within the actual Einar/Lili, but it is a fictional rather than a biographical truth, because Ebershoff alters many historical and biographical facts and subsequently converts his protagonist into a literary symbol that can be used to illuminate a deadly structure pervasive in both the early twentieth century and the early twenty-first century. In essence, both models (Yalom's and Ebershoff's) can be the basis for an ethical biographical novel. The question is this: Have they done the necessary work and do they have ability to fulfill the mandates of their implicit truth contract?

My objective in this study has not been to do an exhaustive analysis of the American biographical novel. Rather, I have tried to provide a provisional framework for the biographical novel and to analyze some crucial biographical novels in order to clarify my approach and to initiate a new line of aesthetic inquiry. For those interested in historical representation and political critique in literary texts, the emergence of literary forms, and the American novel, we have a lot of work ahead of us. But there has never been a better time to do this work, as there have been so many brilliant biographical novels published over the last fifty years. Now it is time to start making sense of what only this rich aesthetic form is suited to do.

BIBLIOGRAPHY

Alvarez, Julia (1994 [2010]), *In the Time of the Butterflies*. Chapel Hill: Algonquin Books.

Alvarez, Julia (2014), "Fixed Facts and Creative Freedom in the Biographical Novel," in *Truthful Fictions: Conversations with American Biographical Novelists*. Editor and Interviewer Michael Lackey. New York and London: Bloomsbury, pp. 26–41.

Améry, Jean (1980), *At the Mind's Limits: Contemplations by a Survivor on Auschwitz and Its Realities*. Bloomington and Indianapolis: Indiana University Press.

Arendt, Hannah (1963 [2006]), *Eichmann in Jerusalem: A Report on the Banality of Evil*. New York: Penguin Books.

Arendt, Hannah (1968 [1976]), *The Origins of Totalitarianism*. San Diego, New York, and London: A Harvest Book.

Atwood, Margaret (1996), *Alias Grace*. Toronto: McClelland & Stewart.

Austriacus (1997), "The Case of Professor Schlick in Vienna—A Reminder to Search Our Conscience," in *The Vienna Circle: Studies in the Origins, Development, and Influence of Logical Empiricism*. Ed. Friedrich Stadler. Vienna and New York: Springer, pp. 871–7.

The Avalon Project, http://avalon.law.yale.edu/imt/judstrei.asp.

Baldwin, James (1963 [1993]), *The Fire Next Time*. New York: Vintage International.

Banks, Russell (1998), *Cloudsplitter*. New York: HarperPerennial.

Banks, Russell (2014), "The Truth Contract in the Biographical Novel," in *Truthful Fictions: Conversations with American Biographical Novelists*. Editor and Interviewer Michael Lackey. New York and London: Bloomsbury, pp. 43–56.

Barrett, William E. (1938), *Woman on Horseback: The Biography of Francisco Lopez and Eliza Lynch*. New York: F.A. Stokes.

Bell, Madison Smartt (1995 [2004]), *All Souls' Rising*. New York: Vintage Books.

Benjamin, Walter (1968), "Theses on the Philosophy of History," in *Illuminations: Essays and Reflections*. Trans. Harry Zohn. New York: Schocken Books, pp. 253–64.

Benjamin, Walter (1978), "Surrealism," in *Reflections: Essays, Aphorisms, Autobiographical Writings*. Trans. Edmund Jephcott. New York: Schocken Books, pp. 177–92.

Bergen, Doris L. (1996), *The Twisted Cross: The German Christian Movement in the Third Reich*. Chapel Hill and London: The University of North Carolina Press.

Bird, Stephanie (1998), *Recasting Historical Women: Female Identity in German Biographical Fiction*. Oxford: Berg.

Bode, Carl (1955), "The Buxom Biographies," *College English* 16(5) (February): 265–9.

Bontemps, Arna (1936 [1992]), *Black Thunder: Gabriel's Revolt: Virginia, 1800*. Boston: Beacon Press.

Breton, André (1969 [1972]), "Manifesto of Surrealism," in *Manifestoes of Surrealism*. Trans. Richard Seaver and Helen R. Lane. Ann Arbor: The University of Michigan Press.

Buechner, Fredrick (1993 [1994]), *Son of Laughter*. New York: Harper One.

Buisine, Alain (1991), "Biofictions," *Revue des Sciences Humaines* 224: 7–13.

Bytwerk, Randall L. (1983), *Julius Streicher*. New York: Stein and Day.

Capote, Truman (1965), *In Cold Blood: A True Account of a Multiple Murder and Its Consequences*. New York: Random House.

Carnes, Mark C. (2001), *Novel History: Historians and Novelists Confront America's Past (and Each Other)*. New York: Simon & Schuster.

Césaire, Aimé (1972 [2000]), *Discourse on Colonialism*. New York: Monthly Review Press.

Chakrabarty, Dipesh (2000), *Provincializing Europe: Postcolonial Thought and Historical Difference*. Princeton and Oxford: Princeton University Press.

Chamberlain, Houston Stewart (1912), *The Foundations of the Nineteenth Century*. New York: John Lane Company.

Chamberlain, Houston Stewart (1914), *Immanuel Kant*. New York: John Lane Company.

Charyn, Jerome (2010), *The Secret Life of Emily Dickinson*. New York: Norton.

Chase-Riboud, Barbara (1979), *Sally Hemings: A Novel*. New York: St. Martin's Press.

Clarke, John Henrik (1968), "Introduction," *William Styron's Nat Turner: Ten Black Writers Respond*. Boston: Beacon Press.

Cleaver, Eldridge (1968), *Soul on Ice*. New York: Dell Publishing Co., Inc.

Coetzee, J. M. (1994), *The Master of Petersburg*. New York: Viking.

Cologne-Brookes, Gavin (2014), *Rereading William Styron*. Baton Rouge: Louisiana State University Press.

Cooley, Elizabeth (1990), "Revolutionizing Biography: 'Orlando', 'Roger Fry', and the Tradition," *South Atlantic Review* 55(2)(May): 71–83.

Cunningham, M. Allen (2007), *Lost Son: A Novel*. Denver: Unbridled Books.

Cunningham, Michael (1998), *The Hours: A Novel*. New York: Picador.

Cunningham, Michael (2014), "The Biographical Novel and the Complexity of Postmodern Interiors," in *Truthful Fictions: Conversations with American Biographical Novels*. Editor and Interviewer Michael Lackey. New York and London: Bloomsbury, pp. 89–100.

Dahms, Hans-Joachim (1995), "The Emigration of the Vienna Circle," in *Vertreibung der Vernunft: The Cultural Exodus from Austria*. Wien and New York: Springer-Verlag, pp. 57–79.

Dawidowicz, Lucy S. (1975), *The War against the Jews: 1933-1945*. New York: Bantam Books.

The Declaration of Independence. The National Archives website: http://www.archives.gov/exhibits/charters/declaration_transcript.html

Dee, Jonathan (1999), "The Reanimators: On the Art of Literary Graverobbing," *Harpers* 298(1789)(June): 76–84.

De Man, Paul (1979), *Allegories of Reading: Figural Language in Rousseau, Nietzsche, Rilke, and Proust*. New Haven and London: Yale University Press.

Diamant, Anita (1997), *The Red Tent: A Novel*. New York: Picador.

Diethe, Carol (2003), *Nietzsche's Sister and the Will to Power: A Biography of Elisabeth Förster-Nietzsche*. Urbana and Chicago: University of Illinois Press.

Doctorow, E. L. (1977), "False Documents," *American Review* 1(26): 215–32.

Douglas, Christopher (2009), *A Genealogy of Literary Multiculturalism*. Ithaca and London: Cornell University Press.

Duffy, Bruce (1987 [2010]), *The World As I Found It*. New York: New York Review Books.

Duffy, Bruce (2011), *Disaster Was My God: A Novel of the Outlaw Life of Arthur Rimbaud*. New York: Doubleday.

Duffy, Bruce (2014), "In the Fog of the Biographical Novel's History," in *Truthful Fictions: Conversations with American Biographical Novelists*. Editor and Interviewer Michael Lackey. New York and London: Bloomsbury, pp. 113–28.

Ebershoff, David (2000a [2001]), *The Danish Girl*. New York: Penguin Books.

Ebershoff, David (2000b [2001]), "A Conversation with David Ebershoff," in *The Danish Girl*. New York: Penguin Books, pp. 5–11.

Eckart, Dietrich (1928), "Das Judentum in und außer uns," in *Dietrich Eckart: Ein Vermächtnis*. Ed. Alfred Rosenberg. Munich: Franz Eher, pp. 193–230.

Eckart, Dietrich (1966 [1999]), *Bolshevism from Moses to Lenin: A Dialogue between Adolf Hitler and Me*. Hillsboro, WV: National Vanguard Books.

Eckart, Dietrich (1978), "Jewishness in and around Us: Fundamental Reflections," in *Nazi Ideology before 1933: A Documentation*.

Ed. Barbara Miller Lane and Leila J. Rupp. Austin and London:
University of Texas Press.

Egerton, Douglas R. (1993), *Gabriel's Rebellion: The Virginia Slave Conspiracies of 1800 & 1802*. Chapel Hill and London: The University of North Carolina Press.

Ehrlich, Leonard (1932), *God's Angry Man*. New York: Simon and Schuster.

Elbe, Lili (2004), *Man Into Woman: An Authentic Record of a Change of Sex*. Ed. Niels Hoyer. London: Blue Boat Books.

Ellison, Ralph (1952 [1995]), *Invisible Man*. New York: Vintage Books.

Ellison, Ralph (1969), "The Uses of History in Fiction," *Southern Literary Journal* 1(2)(Spring): 57–90.

Ellison, Ralph (1995), "What America Would Be Like without Blacks," in *Going to the Territory*. New York: Vintage Books, pp. 104–12.

Ellison, Ralph (2013), "Statement," in *The Haverford Discussions: A Black Integrationist Manifesto for Racial Justice*. Ed. Michael Lackey. Charlottesville and London: University of Virginia Press, pp. 111–14.

Endore, Guy (1934 [1991]), *Babouk*. New York: Monthly Review Press.

Endore, Guy (1991), "History, Fiction and the Slave Experience," in *Babouk*. David B. Gaspar and Michel-Rolph Trouillot. New York: Monthly Review Press, pp. 183–99.

Enright, Anne (2002 [2003]), *The Pleasure of Eliza Lynch*. London: Vintage Books.

Ernest, John (2004), *Liberation Historiography: African American Writers and the Challenge of History, 1794-1861*. Chapel Hill and London: The University of North Carolina Press.

Fanon, Frantz (1967), *Black Skin, White Masks*. Trans. Charles Lam Markmann. New York: Grove Weidenfeld.

Faulkner, William (1958), *Faulkner in the University: Class Conferences at the University of Virginia, 1957-1958*. Ed. Frederick L. Gwynn and Joseph L. Blotner. New York: Vintage Books.

Field, Geoffrey G. (1981), *Evangelist of Race: The Germanic Vision of Houston Stewart Chamberlain*. New York: Columbia University Press.

Fischer, Heinz-D. and Erika J. Fischer (2007), *Chronicle of the Pulitzer Prizes for Fiction: Discussions, Decisions and Documents*. München: K.G. Saur Verlag, Print.

Foley, Barbara (1986), *Telling the Truth: The Theory and Practice of Documentary Fiction*. Ithaca: Cornell University Press.

Förster, Bernhard (1881), *Das Verhältnis des modernen Judenthums zur deutschen Kunst*. Berlin: Verlag von M. Schulze.

Förster, Bernhard (1883), *Parsifal-Nachklänge: Allerhand Gedanken ueber Deutsche Cultur, Wissenschaft, Kunst, Gesellschaft*. Leipzig: In Commission bei Theodor Fritsch.

Förster, Bernhard (1991), "Antisemites' Petition," in *Antisemitism in the Modern World: An Anthology of Texts*. Ed. Richard S. Levy. Lexington, MA and Toronto: D.C. Heath and Company, pp. 125–7.

Förster-Nietzsche, Elisabeth (1894), "Aufruf," *Bayreuther Blätter* 17(4–6): 175–6.

Foucault, Michel (1970 [1994]), *The Order of Things: An Archaeology of the Human Sciences*. New York: Vintage Books.

Foucault, Michel (1972), *The Archaeology of Knowledge and the Discourse on Language*. Trans. A. M. Sheridan Smith. New York: Pantheon Books.

Foucault, Michel (1977), "A Preface to Transgression," in *Language, Counter-Memory, Practice*. Ed. Donald F. Bouchard. Ithaca: Cornell University Press, pp. 29–52.

Frank, Bruno (1935), *A Man Called Cervantes*. New York: Popular Library.

Frus, Phyllis (1994), *The Politics and Poetics of Journalistic Narrative: The Timely and the Timeless*. Cambridge: Cambridge University Press.

Garrett, George (1971), *The Death of the Fox*. New York: Doubleday & Company, Inc.

Gayle, Addison (1975), *The Way of the New World: The Black Novel in America*. Garden City, New York: Anchor Press.

Gilbert, Martin (2006), *Kristallnacht: Prelude to Destruction*. London: Harper Press.

Gilroy, Paul (2000), *Against Race: Imagining Political Culture Beyond the Color Line*. Cambridge, MA: Belknap Press of Harvard University Press.

Goebbels, Joseph (1962), *The Early Goebbels Diaries: 1925-1926*. Ed. Helmut Heiber. New York: Frederick A. Praeger.

Goebbels, Joseph (1987), *Michael*. Trans. Joachim Neugroschel. New York: Amok Press.

Gordon-Reed, Annette (2008), *The Hemingses of Monticello: An American Family*. New York and London: W.W. Norton & Company.

Graves, Robert (1962), *Wife to Mr. Milton: The Story of Marie Powell*. New York: The Noonday Press.

Gruening, Martha (1934), "Some Recent Fiction," *The New Republic*, 17 October.

Gruening, Martha (1936), Review of *Black Thunder*, *The New Republic* 86(1108): February 26, 1936.

Haller, Rudolf (1988), "What do Wittgenstein and Weininger have in Common?," in *Questions on Wittgenstein*. Lincoln: University of Nebraska Press, pp. 90–99.

Hernton, Calvin (1990), "The Sexual Mountain," in *Wild Women in the Whirlwind: Afra-American Culture and the Contemporary Literary Renaissance*. Ed. Joanne M. Braxton and Andrée Nicola McLaughlin. New Brunswick, New Jersey: Rutgers University Press.

Heschel, Susannah (2008), *The Aryan Jesus: Christian Theologians and the Bible in Nazi Germany*. Princeton and Oxford: Princeton University Press.

Higashida, Cheryl (2011), *Black Internationalist Feminism: Women Writers of the Black Left, 1945-1995*. Urbana, Chicago, and Springfield: University of Illinois Press.

Hilberg, Raul (1961), *The Destruction of the European Jews*. Chicago: Quadrangle Books.

Hitler, Adolf (1941), *My New Order*. Ed. Raoul de Roussy de Sales. New York: Reynal and Hitchcock.

Hitler, Adolf (1942), *The Speeches of Adolf Hitler: April 1922-August 1939*. Trans. and Ed. Norman H. Baynes. London, New York, and Toronto: Oxford University Press.

Hitler, Adolf (1971), *Mein Kampf*. Trans. Ralph Manheim. Boston: Houghton Mifflin.

Hitler, Adolf (1974), *Hitler's Letters and Notes*. Ed. Werner Maser, Trans. Arnold Pomerans. New York, Evanston, San Francisco, and London: Harper & Row.

Hochschild, Adam (1998), *King Leopold's Ghost: A Story of Greed, Terror, and Heroism in Colonial Africa*. New York: Mariner Books.

Hoess, Rudolf (1959), *Commandant of Auschwitz: The Autobiography of Rudolf Hoess*. Trans. Constantine FitzGibbon. Cleveland and New York: The World Publishing Company.

Hollowell, John (1977), *Fact & Fiction: The New Journalism and the Nonfiction Novel*. Chapel Hill: The University of North Carolina Press.

Holy Bible: The New American Bible (1971), Nashville, Camden, and New York: Thomas Nelson Publishers.

Hurston, Zora Neale (1939 [1991]), *Moses, Man of the Mountain*. New York: Harper Perennial.

Hurston, Zora Neale (1979a), "Crazy for this Democracy," in *I Love myself when I am laughing…And then again when I am looking mean and impressive: A Zora Neale Hurston Reader*. Ed. Alice Walker. New York: The Feminist Press at the City University of New York, pp. 165–8.

Hurston, Zora Neale (1979b), "What White Publishers Won't Print," in *I Love myself when I am laughing…And then again when I am looking mean and impressive: A Zora Neale Hurston Reader*. Ed. Alice Walker. New York: The Feminist Press at the City University of New York, pp. 169–73.

Hurston, Zora Neale (2003), *Zora Neale Hurston: A Life in Letters*. Ed. Carla Kaplan. New York: Anchor Books.

Hurston, Zora Neale (2006), *Dust Tracks on a Road*. New York, London, Toronto, and Sydney: HarperPerennial.

Hurston, Zora Neale (2011), "from HEROD THE GREAT," Edited by Michael Lackey. *Callaloo* 34(1)(Winter): 121–5.

Hussey, Mark (2012), "Woolf: After Lives," in *Virginia Woolf in Context*. Ed. Bryony Randall and Jane Goldman. Cambridge: Cambridge University Press.

Hutcheon, Linda (1988), *A Poetics of Postmodernism: History, Theory, Fiction*. New York: Routledge.

Iggers, George G. (1997), *Historiography in the Twentieth Century: From Scientific Objectivity to the Postmodern Challenge*. Hanover: Wesleyan University Press.

Irr, Caren (1998), *The Suburb of Dissent: Cultural Politics in the United States and Canada during the 1930s*. Durham and London: Duke University Press.

J.D. Review of *Black Thunder*. *The Saturday Review*. February 15, 1936.

Jefferson, Thomas (1955 [1785]), *Notes of the State of Virginia*. Ed. William Peden. Chapel Hill: The University of North Carolina Press.

Johnson, Barbara (1997), "Moses and Intertextuality: Sigmund Freud, Zora Neale Hurston, and the Bible," in *Poetics of the Americas*. Ed. Bainard Cowan and Jefferson Humphries. Baton Rouge and London: Louisiana State University Press.

Kanner, Rebecca (2013), *Sinners and the Sea: The Untold Story of Noah's Wife*. New York: Howard Books.

Kant, Immanuel (1949 [1993]), *Critique of Practical Reason*, Trans. Lewis White Beck. Upper Saddle River, New Jersey: Prentice Hall.

Kant, Immanuel (1960), *Religion within the Limits of Reason Alone*, Trans. Theodore M. Greene and Hoyt H. Hudson. New York: Harper Torchbooks.

Kaplan, Cora (2007), *Victoriana: Histories, Fictions, Criticism*. New York: Columbia University Press.

Kaufmann, Walter (1974), *Nietzsche: Philosopher, Psychologist, Antichrist*. Princeton: Princeton University Press.

Keener, John F. (2001), *Biography and the Postmodern Historical Novel*. Lewiston: The Edwin Mellen Press.

Kendall, Murray Paul (1965 [1967]), *The Art of Biography*. New York: W.W. Norton & Company.

Killens, John Oliver (1971), "The Black Writer vis-à-vis His Country," in *The Black Aesthetic*. Ed. Addison Gayle, Jr. Garden City, New York: Doubleday & Company, pp. 379–98.

Kohlke, Marie-Luise (2013), "New-Victorian Biofiction and the Special/Spectral Case of Barbara Chase-Riboud's *Hottentot Venus*." *Australasian Journal of Victorian Studies* 18(1): 4–21.

Kraus, Daniela (1999), "Bernhard und Elisabeth Försters Nueva Germania in Paraguay: eine antisemitische Utopie." Diss. University of Vienna.

Lackey, Michael (1999), "Killing God, Liberating the 'Subject': Nietzsche and Post-God Freedom." *Journal of the History of Ideas* 60(4) (October): 737–54.

Lackey, Michael (2006), "Modernist Anti-Philosophicalism and Virginia Woolf's Critique of Philosophy." *Journal of Modern Literature* 29(4) (Summer): 76–98.

Lackey, Michael (2012), *The Modernist God State: A Literary Study of the Nazis' Christian Reich*. London and New York: Continuum.

Lackey, Michael (2013), "Conceptualizing Christianity and Christian Nazis after the Nuremberg Trials." *Cultural Critique* 84(Spring): 101–33.

Lackey, Michael (2014a), "Introduction," in Jay Parini's *Conversations with Jay Parini*. Ed. Michael Lackey. Jackson: University Press of Mississippi.

Lackey, Michael (2014b), *Truthful Fictions: Conversations with American Biographical Novelists*. New York and London: Bloomsbury.

Lackey, Michael (2016), "The Scandal of Jewish Rage in William Styron's *Sophie's Choice*," *Journal of Modern Literature* (forthcoming).

Lang, Berel (2003), *Act and Idea in the Nazi Genocide*. Syracuse: Syracuse University Press.

Latham, Monica (2012), "'Serv[ing] under two masters': Virginia Woolf's Afterlives in Contemporary Biofictions." *a/b: Auto/Biography Studies* 27(2)(Winter): 354–73.

Lee, Harper (2015), *Go Set a Watchman*. New York: Harper.

Levecq, Christine (1999), "Philosophies of History in Arna Bontemps' *Black Thunder*," *Obsidian III* 1(2): 111–30.

Levi, Primo (1989), *The Drowned and the Saved*. Translated by Raymond Rosenthal. New York: Vintage International.

Levy, Richard S. (1991), "Antisemitism in Germany," in *Antisemitism in the Modern World: An Anthology of Texts*. Ed. Richard S. Levy. Lexington, MA and Toronto: D.C. Heath and Company, pp. 121–5.

Lodge, David (2004), *Author, Author*. New York: Viking.

Lodge, David (2006), *The Year of Henry James or, Timing is All: the Story of a Novel*. London: Harvill Secker.

Lukács, Georg (1937 [1983]), *The Historical Novel*. Lincoln: University of Nebraska Press.

Lukács, Georg (1992), "Realism in the Balance," in *Aesthetic and Politics*. Translation editor Ronald Taylor. London and New York: Verso, pp. 28–59.

Luther, Martin (1971), *On the Jews and Their Lies*, in *Luther's Works*, Vol. 47. Philadelphia: Fortress Press.

Lyotard, Jean-François (1979 [1984]), *The Postmodern Condition: A Report on Knowledge*. Minneapolis: University of Minnesota Press.

Mack, Michael (2003), *German Idealism and the Jew: The Inner Anti-Semitism of Philosophy and German Jewish Responses*. Chicago and London: The University of Chicago Press.

Mailer, Norman (1979 [1998]), *The Executioner's Song*. New York: Vintage Books.

Malcolm X (1965 [1993]), *The Autobiography of Malcolm X*. New York: Ballantine Books.

Malmgren, Carl Darryl (1985), *Fictional Space in the Modernist and Postmodernist American Novel*. Lewisburg: Bucknell University Press.

Malouf, David (1978), *An Imaginary Life: A Novel*. New York: George Braziller, Inc.

Mamet, David (1997), *The Old Religion*. New York: The Free Press.

Mann, Heinrich (1935 [1964]), *Die Jugend des Konigs, Henri Quatre*. Berlin: Aufbau-Verlag.

Mann, Thomas (1939 [1960]), *Lotte in Weimar: The Beloved Returns*. Oakland: University of California Press.

Mann, Thomas (1943 [2005]), *Joseph and His Brothers*. New York: Alfred A. Knopf.

Mantel, Hilary (2009 [2010]), *Wolf Hall*. London: Fourth Estate.

Mantel, Hilary (2012), *Bring up the Bodies*. New York: Henry Holt and Company.

Marx, Karl (1977), "Preface" to A Critique of Political Economy, in *Karl Marx: Selected Writings*. Ed. David McLellan. Oxford: Oxford University Press.

McGuinnes, Brian (1988), *Wittgenstein: A Life: Young Ludwig 1889-1921*. Berkeley, Los Angeles, and London: The University of California Press.

Melville, Herman (1854 [1982]), *Israel Potter: His Fifty Years of Exile*. Evanston and Chicago: Northwestern University Press.

Michael, Robert (2006), *Holy Hatred: Christianity, Antisemitism, and the Holocaust*. New York: Palgrave Macmillan.

Middeke, Martin and Werner Huber (1999), *Biofictions: The Rewriting of Romantic Lives in Contemporary Fiction and Drama*. Suffolk: Camden House.

Miller, James A. (2009), *Remembering Scottsboro: The Legacy of an Infamous Trial*. Princeton and Oxford: Princeton University Press.

Mills, Charles W. (1997), *The Racial Contract*. Ithaca: Cornell University Press.

Monk, Ray (1990), *Ludwig Wittgenstein: The Duty of Genius*. New York: The Free Press.

Monk, Ray (2001), "Philosophical Biography: The Very Idea," in *Wittgenstein: Biography and Philosophy*. Ed. James C. Klagge. Cambridge: Cambridge University Press, pp. 3–15.

Monk, Ray (2007), "The Fictitious Life: Virginia Woolf on Biography and Reality," *Philosophy and Literature* 31(1)(April):1–40.

Mujica, Barbara (2001 [2012]), *Frida*. New York: Overlook Press.

Mujica, Barbara (2016), "Going for the Subjective: One Way to Write Biographical Fiction." *a/b: Auto/Biography Studies*. (Forthcoming).

Neale, Hurston Z. (1991), "Foreword: Lines of Descent/Dissenting Lines," in *Moses, Man of the Mountain*. Intro. Deborah E. McDowell. New York: HarperPerennial.

"Negroes in Revolt," *The New York Times Book Review*. September 9, 1934.

Nietzsche, Friedrich (1968), *The Will to Power*. Trans. Walter Kaufmann. New York: Vintage Books.

Nietzsche, Friedrich (1989a), *Anti-Christ*. Trans. R. J. Hollingdale. New York: Random House.

Nietzsche, Friedrich (1989b), *On the Genealogy of Morals*. Trans. Walter Kaufmann and R. J. Hollingdale. New York: Random House.

Nietzsche, Friedrich (1989c), *Twilight of the Idols*. Trans. R. J. Hollingdale. New York: Random House.

Nietzsche, Friedrich (1990), *The Gay Science*. Trans. Walter Kaufmann. New York: Penguin.

Novak, Julia and Sandra Meyer (2014), "Disparate Images: Literary Heroism and the 'Work vs. Life' Topos in Contemporary Biofictions about Victorian Authors," *Neo-Victorian Studies* 7(1): 25–51.

The Nuremberg Transcripts. The Jewish Virtual Library. http://www.jewishvirtuallibrary.org/jsource/Holocaust/nurlawtoc.html

Oates, Joyce Carol (1992 [1993]), *Black Water*. New York: Plume.

Oates, Joyce Carol (2000 [2009]), *Blonde*. New York: Harper Collins.

Oates, Joyce Carol (2014), "Enhanced Symbolic Interiors in the Biographical Novel," in *Truthful Fictions: Conversations with American Biographical Novelists*. Editor and Interviewer Michael Lackey. New York and London: Bloomsbury, pp. 179–92.

O'Brien, Conor Cruise (1996), *The Long Affair: Thomas Jefferson and the French Revolution, 1785-1800*. Chicago and London: The University of Chicago Press.

Olsen, Lance (2006), *Nietzsche's Kisses*. Tallahassee: Fiction Collective Two.

Olsen, Lance (2014), "The Biographical Novel's Practice of Not-Knowing," in *Truthful Fictions: Conversations with American Biographical Novelists*. Editor and Interviewer Michael Lackey. New York and London: Bloomsbury, pp. 193–204.

Parini, Jay (1997a), *Benjamin's Crossing: A Novel*. New York: Henry Holt.

Parini, Jay (1997b), *Some Necessary Angels: Essays on Writing and Politics*. New York: Columbia University Press.

Parini, Jay (2009), *The Last Station: A Novel of Tolstoy's Final Year,* 1990. New York: Anchor Books.

Parini, Jay (2010 [2011]), *The Passages of H.M.: A Novel of Herman Melville*. New York: Anchor Books.

Parini, Jay (2014a), "Reflections on Biographical Fiction," in *Truthful Fictions: Conversations with American Biographical Novelists*. Editor and Interviewer Michael Lackey. New York and London: Bloomsbury, pp. 205–16.

Parini, Jay (2014b), "The Uses of History in the Biographical Novel: A Conversation with Jay Parini, Bruce Duffy, and Lance Olsen," in

Conversations with Jay Parini. Ed. Michael Lackey. Jackson: University Press of Mississippi, pp. 125–48.

Parini, Jay (2016), "Writing Biographical Fiction: Some Personal Reflections," *a/b: Autobiography Studies.* (Forthcoming).

Patterson, Orlando (1982), *Slavery and Social Death: A Comparative Study.* Cambridge and London: Harvard University Press.

Podach, Erich F. (1932), *Gestalten um Nietzsche.* Weimar: Erich Lichtenstein Verlag.

Rampersad, Arnold (2008), *Ralph Ellison: A Biography.* New York: Vintage Books.

Redding, J. Saunders (1942), *No Day of Triumph.* New York and London: Harper & Brothers Publishers.

Redding, J. Saunders (1962), *On Being Negro in America.* Indianapolis and New York: Charter Books.

Review of *Babouk, The Nation.* 139(3618)(November 1934).

Review of *Babouk, The Saturday Review of Literature.* September 29, 1934.

Review of *Black Thunder, The Literary Digest.* February 1, 1936.

Rorty, Richard (1979), *Philosophy and the Mirror of Nature.* Princeton: Princeton University Press.

Rorty, Richard (1989), *Contingency, Irony, and Solidarity.* Cambridge: Cambridge University Press.

Rosenberg, Alfred (1927), *Houston Stewart Chamberlain: als Verkünder und Begründer einer deutschen Zukunft.* München: Bruckman.

Rosenberg, Alfred (1993), *The Myth of the Twentieth Century: An Evaluation of the Spiritual-Intellectual Confrontations of Our Age.* Trans. V. Bird. Newport Beach, CA: The Noontide Press.

Ross, Daniel W. (2012), "William Styron, James Baldwin, and *The Confessions of Nat Turner*: The Dream of a Common History," *CEA Critic* 74(2–3): 88–99.

Rubenstein, Richard L. (1987 [1978]), *The Cunning of History: The Holocaust and the American Future.* New York: Harper & Row.

Russell, Paul (2011), *The Unreal Life of Sergey Nabokov.* Berkley: Cleis Press.

Ryan, Judith (2012), *The Novel after Theory.* New York: Columbia University Press.

Said, Edward W. (1993), *Culture and Imperialism.* New York: Vintage Books.

Santaniello, Weaver (1994), *Nietzsche, God, and the Jews: His Critique of Judeo-Christianity in Relation to the Nazi Myth.* Albany: SUNY Press.

Sartre, Jean-Paul (1948 [1995]), *Anti-Semite and Jew: An Exploration of the Etiology of Hate.* Trans. George J. Becker. New York: Schocken Books.

Savery, Pancho (1990), "'Git a Stool. Let Me Tell You Something': Call and Response in *No Day of Triumph*," *Black American Literature Forum* 24(2): 277–98.

Schabert, Ina (1982), "Fictional Biography, Factual Biography, and their Contamination," *Biography* 5(1)(Winter): 1–16.

Schabert, Ina (1990), *In Quest of the Other Person: Fiction as Biography*, Tubingen: Francke Verlag.

Scott, Joanna (1990), *Arrogance*. New York: Picador.

Scott, Joanna (2016), "On Hoaxes, Humbugs, and Fictional Portraiture." *a/b: Auto/Biography Studies* 31(1)(Winter): 27–32.

Seidman, Naomi (1996), "Elie Wiesel and the Scandal of Jewish Rage," *Jewish Social Studies* 3(1)(Autumn): 1–19

Shirer, William L. (1960), *The Rise and Fall of the Third Reich: A History of Nazi Germany*. New York: Simon and Schuster.

Silverman, Lisa (2009), "'Wiener Kreise': Jewishness, Politics, and Culture in Interwar Vienna," in *Interwar Vienna: Culture between Tradition and Modernity*. Ed. Deborah Holmes and Lisa Silverman. Rochester: Camden House, pp. 59–80.

Southgate, Beverley (2009), *History Meets Fiction*. Harlow: Longman/ Pearson Education Limited.

Stackelberg, Roderick (1981), *Idealism Debased: From Voelkisch Ideology to National Socialism*. Kent, OH: The Kent State University Press.

Stadler, Friedrich (1995), "The Vienna Circle and the University of Vienna," in *Vertreibung der Vernunft: The Cultural Exodus from Austria*. Ed. Peter Weibel and Friedrich Stadler. Wien and New York: Springer-Verlag, pp. 44–55.

Steigmann-Gall, Richard (2003), *The Holy Reich: Nazi Conceptions of Christianity, 1919-1945*. Cambridge: Cambridge University Press.

Stern, David (2001), "Was Wittgenstein a Jew?" in *Wittgenstein: Biography and Philosophy*. Ed. James C. Klagge. Cambridge: Cambridge University Press, pp. 237–72.

Stern, David G. and Bela Szabados (2004), *Wittgenstein Reads Weininger*. Cambridge: Cambridge University Press.

Stone, Irving (1957), "The Biographical Novel," in *Three Views of the Novel*. Washington: Library of Congress, pp. 1–16.

Styron, William (1967 [1993]), *The Confessions of Nat Turner*. New York: Vintage International.

Styron, William (1979 [1992]), *Sophie's Choice*. New York: Vintage International.

Styron, William (1992), "Nat Turner Revisited," *The Confessions of Nat Turner*. Vintage International, pp. 433–55.

Styron, William (1995), "Extracts from Conversations with William Styron," in Gavin Cologne-Brookes' *The Novels of William Styron: From Harmony to History*. Baton Rouge: Louisiana State University.

Sundquist, Eric J. (1992), *The Hammers of Creation: Folk Culture in Modern African-American Fiction*. Athens and London: The University of Georgia Press.

Szabados, Bela (1999), "Was Wittgenstein an Anti-Semite? The Significance for Wittgenstein's Philosophy," *Canadian Journal of Philosophy* 29(1)(March): 1–27.

Thompson, Mark Christian (2007), *Black Fascisms: African American Literature and Culture between the Wars*. Charlottesville and London: University of Virginia Press.

Tompkins, Lucy (1936), "Slaves' Rebellions: BLACK THUNDER," *New York Times*. February 2, 1936.

Troyanov, Iliya (2008), *The Collector of Worlds*. Trans. William Hobson. London: Faber and Faber.

Tuck, Lily (2004), *The News from Paraguay*. New York: HarperCollins.

Tusa, Ann and John (1986), *The Nuremberg Trial*. New York: Atheneum.

Vidal, Gore (1973 [1993]), *Burr: A Novel*. New York: Ballantine Books.

Vidal, Gore (1984 [2000]), *Lincoln: A Novel*. New York: Vintage International.

Washington, Booker T. (1901 [1996]), *Up from Slavery*. Ed. William L. Andrews. New York and London: W. W. Norton & Company.

Weininger, Otto (1906), *Sex and Character*. New York and Chicago: A.L. Burt Company.

West, James L. W. (1998), *William Styron, A Life*. New York: Random House.

West, James L. W. (2005), *The Perfect Hour: The Romance of F. Scott Fitzgerald and Ginevra King, His First Love*. New York: Random House.

West, M. Genevieve (2005), *Zora Neale Hurston & American Literary Culture*. Gainesville: University Press of Florida.

White, Edmund (2007 [2008]), *Hotel de Dream: A New York Novel*. New York: Harper Perennial.

White, Hayden (1973), *Metahistory: The Historical Imagination in Nineteenth-Century Europe*. Baltimore: Johns Hopkins University Press.

White, Hayden (1987 [1989]), *The Content of the Form: Narrative Discourse and Historical Representation*. Baltimore: Johns Hopkins University Press.

White, Hayden (1992), *Tropics of Discourse: Essays in Cultural Criticism*. Baltimore: Johns Hopkins University Press.

Wittgenstein, Ludwig (1922 [1988]), *Tractatus Logico-Philosophicus*. Trans. C. K. Ogden. London and New York: Routledge & Kegan Pau LTD.

Wittgenstein, Ludwig (1980 [1984]), *Culture and Value*. Trans. Peter Winch. Chicago: University of Chicago Press.

Wittgenstein, Ludwig (2008), *Wittgenstein in Cambridge: Letters and Documents 1911-1951*. Ed. Brian McGuinness. Oxford: Blackwell.

Wood, Gordon S. (1997), "Liberty's Wild Man," *The New York Review of Books* 44(3)(February): 23–26.

Wood, Gordon S. (2009), "Gordon S. Wood replies," *Callaloo* 32(3) (summer): 823–25.

Woolf, Virginia (1933), *Flush: A Biography*. New York: Harcourt, Brace, & World, Inc.

Woolf, Virginia (1942), "The Art of Biography," in *The Death of the Moth and Other Essays*. London: The Hogarth Press, pp. 119–26.

Wright, Richard (1936), "A Tale of Folk Courage," *The Partisan Review* 3(3)(April): 31.

Wright, Richard (1953 [2008]), *The Outsider*. New York and London: HarperPerenial.

Wright, Richard (1958 [2000]), *The Long Dream*. Northeastern University Press: Boston.

Yalom, Irvin D. (1992 [2005]), *When Nietzsche Wept: A Novel of Obsession*. New York: Perennial Classics.

Yalom, Irvin D. (2006), *The Schopenhauer Cure*. New York: HarperPerennial.

Yalom, Irvin D. (2012), *The Spinoza Problem*. New York: Basic Books.

Young, Julian (2010), *Friedrich Nietzsche: A Philosophical Biography*. Cambridge: Cambridge University Press.

Zavarzadeh, Mas'ud (1976), *The Mythopoeic Reality: The Postwar American Nonfiction Novel*. Urbana: University of Illinois Press.

INDEX